Friends and Comrades

How Quakers helped Russians to survive famine and epidemic

Sergei Nikitin

Translated by Suzanne Eade Roberts

Q

First Published in Great Britain in 2022 by
Quacks Books
7 Grape Lane, Petergate, York YO1 7HU
Tel: +44 (0)1904 635967
Email: Info@quacks.info
Website: QuacksBooks.info
Quacks Books is an Imprint of Radius Publishing Ltd

A CIP catalogue record for this book is
available from the British Library.

ISBN (Paperback): 978-1-912728-57-2
ISBN (eBook): 978-1-912728-60-2

Kak Kvakery Spacali Rossiyu
[When Quakers were saving Russia]
was originally published in Russian in 2020 by
"Novoe Literaturnoe Obozrenie" Journal Publishers Ltd
13a Tverskoi Bulvar, 123104 Moscow
Tel./Fax: (495) 229-91-03
E-mail: real@nlobooks.ru
Website: www.nlobooks.ru
ISBN 978-5-4448-1242-6

Set in twelve point Baskerville with a page size of 130mm x 200mm
printed by offset lithography on an eighty gsm book wove chosen
for its sustainability.

Acknowledgements

I would like to express my very great appreciation to the late Bill Chadkirk. Many years ago, he was the first person to tell me about the Quakers in Buzuluk. I would like to offer my special thanks to my friend David McFadden, an American historian, with whom I spent many hours in the archives and travelling around the Buzuluk area. Andrei Mitin and Nadezhda Fedotova, researchers of the local history of the Buzuluk district, gave me access to a huge number of interesting documents. Sergei Kolychev and Anna Melnikova, who live in Buzuluk, gave me advice and information. Dmitrii Shabelnikov, a Moscow-based historian, found some crucial data for me. Ros Batchelor, a British researcher of the history of Quaker families, gave me many useful pointers, and Meg Hill shared information about her relative who had worked in Buzuluk. Disley Quaker Meeting has always supported me and helped me to obtain vital books, while a grant from the Friends Historical Society, the Hodgett Grant, enabled me to work in the Quaker archive in the library at Friends House in London. Dr Luke Kelly, Research Associate at the Humanitarian Conflict Response Institute, shared numerous documents with me. Peter Jarman's memoirs were extremely helpful in my research. Vitali Ziusko, head of the Kompas Guide publishing house in Moscow, gave me invaluable advice. Sergei Grushko of Friends

House Moscow did a colossal amount of work for me in the State Archives of the Russian Federation (GARF). Mikhail Aleksandrovich Fedotov, the former head of the Russian Presidential Human Rights Council, kindly agreed to introduce me to Irina Dmitrievna Prokhorova, the head of NLO, the Moscow-based publishing house, and it was thanks to her that my book in Russian became accessible to hundreds of Russian citizens. The translation of the text from Russian to English has been done meticulously by Suzanne Eade Roberts, to whom I am very grateful for her professionalism and help. I also want to thank Patricia Stewart and Donald Davis for searching for relevant photographs in the AFSC archives. I am thankful to Daphne Sanders who first contacted Quacks Books to ask them whether they would be interested in publishing a translation of my book, and for her considerable help since then. The book has become a reality thanks to Quacks Books and generous funding by the Sessions Book Trust and the William A. Cadbury Charitable Trust.

Contents

Introduction to the English edition of the book Friends and Comrades

War cannot go on forever, give peace a chance

My grandma used the Soviet newspaper *Izvestia* to teach me to read when I was four. My horizons have been significantly broadened since then. When I was five, I came across a Russian book on Mr Khrushchev's visit to the USA called *To Live in Peace and Friendship*. One photograph from the book I remember to this day. The picture was taken near Des Moines, Iowa, which the Soviet leader was due to pass by. Local people made a huge welcome poster with a phrase coined by a Mrs Lokner who had won a competition for the best message. The message was written in broken Russian, and it read «Товарищ Хрущов, вместе должны стремлятся к мирному свету» (*Tovarishch Khrushchev, vmeste dolzhny stremlyatsya k mirnomu svetu*): 'Comrade Khrushchev, we should strive to peaceful light together'.

My childhood and my adolescent years fell during the long periods of hostility between the USSR and the West. Both sides accused each other: the Caribbean Crisis, the wars in Vietnam, in Afghanistan — the list was long. It was impossible back then to find any stories of positive cooperation between Soviet Russia, America and Britain, between Russians and foreigners. Even the stories about Lend Lease and the Military Alliance during the Second World War were not told to us at school. The story of foreign famine relief in the 1920s did not exist in Soviet books and magazines. It was erased from the history books.

I found it hard to live in a world full of mutual suspicion and hostility. I wanted to read something positive, I looked for stories with 'peaceful light'. Gorbachev's Perestroika brought new opportunities: the Iron Curtain was lifted, the borders were open, hidden information was revealed. I went to England when I was 34, and it was my first trip abroad, something I could never have imagined during my childhood years. A Quaker, Bill Chadkirk, whom I met in London, told me about Friends' cooperation with Russia in the 1920s. I decided to find out more about it. Research in Russian, British and American archives, meetings with eyewitnesses, the dozens of articles and books I read resulted in the book I called *Friends and Comrades*. It is a story of the peaceful light to which I have always been striving.

Preface

'You know, they even had a poster in Soviet Russia which said, "Learn to work like the Quakers do", because the Quakers were respected and valued so much'. Bill Chadkirk, who was then head of Quaker International Social Projects, once told me this at Friends House in London. He had come out of his office to have a quick chat with me while I was visiting London after taking part in a Quaker project in the town of Dudley in the summer of 1993. What Bill said really took me by surprise. Quakers in Bolshevik Russia? The Religious Society of Friends in the country of militant atheism? 'Yes, that's right', Bill confirmed, 'in the town of Buzuluk'. I had not even heard of Buzuluk back then, but it turned out that Bill knew exactly where and when the Quakers had been in Russia: in Samara province, during the famine in the Volga region. It was all thanks to Bill Chadkirk that I became interested in this episode in history.

That winter, Bill sent me his manuscript entitled *Famine and Relief*. I could not put it down! I realised how little we in Russia knew about the history of Quaker work in the Volga region, and that this was something for me to work on, something to research, a story to tell.

I had never been to an archive before. The internet was still a curiosity in our region in that era, so I had to go to the regional archives in St. Petersburg just to find out the address of the archives in Buzuluk. Then I sent a letter of inquiry to the Buzuluk archive, but they replied that there were no documents available from the period when Quakers worked there. Just a couple of weeks later, though, I was woken by the phone ringing. A kind archivist in Buzuluk told me she had found a folder of materials that might interest me. And with that, I was off!

At night, I slept in the cheap dormitory at Buzuluk railway station; each morning, I walked into the town. It was quite a distance from the station: in the nineteenth century, Russian railway lines were laid out in such a way that towns were sometimes a long way from their stations. After three days of copying out archival materials, I was stunned! The British Quakers who had come from so far away had saved my compatriots from starvation. They had not taken any money for it – and in any case, the peasants who were dying of hunger did not have any money. The Quakers had collected money in their country to buy food and have it delivered to a town far away from London. I wandered the dusty streets of Buzuluk, and in the market I went up to old people who were selling vegetables from their vegetable patches.

'Tell me, do you happen to remember the famine of 1921?' I asked one old lady. 'How could I forget! You can't forget something like that. It was foreigners who saved me and many others. I don't know whether they were American or English, but they definitely weren't Russian. We were only little children, and they gave us food - they were such good people'.

The subject of Quakers in Russia had now got me hooked. After the Buzuluk archives, I went on to do research in the archives in Samara, St. Petersburg, Philadelphia, London and Moscow. I flicked through hand-typed reports that Quakers had prepared about their work in Russia, reports which had gone yellow over time. I held in my hands diaries filled with spindly handwriting, full of fascinating details of the life of an American lady in the steppes of Buzuluk district. I examined the faces on old photographs. My work in the archives gave me unexpected joy and kept leading to new discoveries. I read books of memoirs by British and American Quakers who worked in my country and saved my fellow countrymen during the awful years of famine.

I went to an old people's home for elderly Quakers in New Jersey in the USA, where I met Rebecca Timbres-Clark, aged 100, who had worked with her husband in Sorochinskoye, in Samara province, in 1923. I corresponded with Helen Hughes from New Zealand, the daughter of Theodore Rigg who had headed the Quaker mission in 1916.

Rebecca Timbres in 1930s

©The archives of the American Friends Service Committee

I then became friends with American historian David McFadden. He was doing research into the Quakers' work in Russia, and we spent hours happily discussing the details of Nancy Babb's exploits in Totskoye, or the success of Parry Paul's Tractor School in Sorochinskoye. I went with David several times to Buzuluk, where the British Quakers had worked, and to Sorochinskoye, where the American Friends had their centre. We talked with eyewitnesses to the famine years who were still alive at that time. We gave presentations to school pupils in Mogutovo and talked to journalists in Totskoye and Buzuluk.

David wrote an excellent book, *Constructive Spirit: Quakers in Revolutionary Russia*[1], for which he invited me to write the foreword, and so I did. Meanwhile, my own materials were still in my bottom drawer, waiting for the right time.

I did not have any chance to think about the documents I had collected during the almost 15 years I spent working at Amnesty International in Moscow. I kept adding to my store of materials, though, as additional information about the Quakers in Russia came to light on the internet. My retirement gave me the chance to finally get started on the task I had been drawn to for so long: the amazing history of the Quakers in Soviet Russia, which had in fact begun earlier, in Tsarist Russia...

---

[1] David McFadden, Claire Gorfinkel and Sergei Nikitin, *Constructive Spirit: Quakers in Revolutionary Russia*. Pasadena, CA: Intentional Productions. 2004.

Chapter 1. *The prehistory: Quaker contacts with Russia before the 20th century. The First World War and refugees in the Russian Empire: British Quaker concerns. The Quaker mission's arrival in Petrograd in April 1916. Three Quakers visit Moscow, Samara and Buzuluk. Contact with Tsarist officials and the Tatiana committee for war victim relief. The decision to help refugees in Buzuluk district in Samara province. The opening of hospitals, workshops for refugees and an orphanage across four villages in Buzuluk district. Revolutionary news from the capital...*

The Religious Society of Friends (Quakers) arose as a Protestant, pacifist church in England in the middle of the 17th century. Contacts between the Society of Friends and Russia began soon after. Notably, there was the letter that George Fox[2] sent to Tsar Alexei in 1654; Peter the Great's meeting with Quakers in England in the 17th century; and Alexander I's meeting with Quakers, also in England, in the 19th century. Later that century, an English Quaker, Daniel Wheeler, lived with his family in Shushary near St. Petersburg. His job was draining the swamps near the city, the capital of the Russian Empire. British Quakers made a few trips to Russia, particularly during the 1890s, in an attempt to prevent hunger in the Russian Empire at that time.

---

[2] George Fox (July 1624 – 13 January 1691) was an English religious dissident, mystic and founder of the Religious Society of Friends, or Quakers.

It was in 1916 that real cooperation began, however. It was prompted by the horrors of the First World War and the flood of refugees streaming into Central Russia from the western borders of the empire. Poles, Lithuanians and Belarusians had left their towns and villages to head to Petrograd[3], Moscow and further eastwards.

As Quakers are pacifists, they did not take part in hostilities. Instead, they helped the victims of wars. Conscientious objection never pleases the authorities of any country, of course, but Britain allowed pacifists to avoid taking up arms.[4] British Quakers had the chance to go to the front as part of the Friends Ambulance Unit, as it was called, and work as doctors, nurses and technical personnel in field hospitals and ordinary hospitals. The Quakers also tried to find ways to alleviate the suffering of the civilian population, the main victims of the war. The Society of Friends took part in refugee assistance programmes and reconstruction work in places where war had destroyed everything. Indeed, the Quakers helped the civilian population of any countries that were participating in the war, regardless of whether these countries were allies of Britain or not.

[3] St. Petersburg was renamed Petrograd in 1914.

[4] A typical article of that time which described pacifists in a negative way was entitled 'The English Tolstoyans', in the Russian newspaper *Zemshchina* (issue of 5 June 1916). It said that the *Daily Telegraph* had reported that a military court in North Wales had had to try the first case of principled opponents of military service. Seven pacifists who were enrolled in non-strategic units refused to obey the orders of the senior officer. The court sentenced them to two years' hard labour each.

British Quakers worked in many countries in Europe, such as France, Montenegro and Austria. British Quakers found out about the refugee crisis in Russia in early 1916. According to one version, Sergei Sazonov, the then Minister of Foreign Affairs, wrote a letter to London requesting assistance. In another version, the Friends War Victims Relief Committee (FWVRC)[5] in London found out that the refugees who had streamed into the central and eastern areas of the European part of Russia were starving, had nowhere to live, and had no jobs or means of subsistence in places where the local population was not exactly pleased to see the new arrivals.

Whatever the background, British Quakers decided in 1916 to help the refugees. Their top priority was to work out what kind of assistance from Britain would make a difference to the lives of these civilians in Russia.

Representatives of the FWVRC had negotiations with the London Embassy of the Russian Empire. Russian diplomats wanted to be sure that the planned mission would not contradict the policy of the British government. The First Secretary of the Imperial Russian Embassy, Evgeny Vasilyevich

---

[5] The FWVRC was the official body of British Quakers created during the First World War to relieve the suffering of the civilian population in practical ways. It had first been founded in 1870, after the outbreak of the Franco-Prussian War, and been revived twice more (in Bulgaria in 1876 and in the Balkans in 1912), after which it was officially restored during World War I. It was then revived for a fifth and final time in 1940, before its name was changed to Friends Relief Service in 1941.

Sablin, replied[6] to the Friends' request in the most gracious manner:

Imperial Embassy of Russia   *London*

                                       28th March 1916

To Mrs Fry

Dear Madam,

I beg to acknowledge your letter of 27th instant while thoroughly appreciating your most excellent proposal to send a party to Russia to give assistance to Polish and other Refugees, we would be glad to receive a recommendation from the British Foreign Office in support of your Scheme, and also a similar document of the kind from the joint Committee of the British Red Cross Society and the Order of St John of Jerusalem.

When we have had the certified agreement of these authorities approving of your plans we shall then be glad to render you all the assistance necessary for facilitating your expedition.

I am, Dear Madam,

Yours faithfully,

---

[6] Friends House London archives. *YM/MfS/FEWVRC/ MISSIONS/7/2/1.*

Sabline

The First Secretary of the Imperial Russian Embassy.[7]

Ruth Fry replied to Sablin the very next day:

... I have communicated with the Foreign Office by telephone and they have assured me that they will communicate directly with you recommending our party for your kind help.

I hold certificates from the British Red Cross and the Order of St John of Jerusalem for the gentlemen concerned, which they will submit to you when you are so kind as to grant the interview which I hope may be on Friday morning as proposed.

Ruth Fry.[8]

As we can see, both sides were very actively involved in organising the trip, and in April 1916 the four Quakers arrived in Petrograd, the capital of the Russian Empire.

Quakers William Cadbury, Joseph Burtt and Robert Tatlock arrived in Russia in the middle of the month, joined a week later by Theodore

---

[7] Ruth Fry (full name Anna Ruth Fry) was General Secretary of the Friends War Victims Relief Committee (FWVRC).
[8] Friends House London archives. *YM/MfS/FEWVRC/ MISSIONS/7/2/1.*

Rigg. The four of them were entrusted with thinking up a project to help refugees from the Western Front. Numerous meetings were held for this purpose, with the British Ambassador and with important Russian officials. Rigg wrote in his diary: 'We found all the Russians helpful. William Cadbury, who has taken a leading part in these interviews, has been given letters of introduction to Prince Lvov[9] and other Russian officials connected with the Zemstvo Union and the Red Cross at Moscow'.[10] One of these letters, signed by the Minister of Foreign Affairs, Sergei Sazonov, addressed to a comrade of the Minister of Internal Affairs, Vladimir Volkonsky[11], is shown below:

Foreign Office. Petrograd

Dear Count,

The bearer of this, Mr Cadbury, is an Englishman who has been recommended to me by the British Embassy. He has come to Russia with three friends, their object being to try to find a use for funds at their disposal in the relief of the distressed in Russia.

---

[9] Prince Georgy Yevgenyevich Lvov (2 November [O.S. 21 October] 1861 – 7/8 March 1925) was a Russian aristocrat and statesman.
[10] *Chronicles of a Quaker worker in Russia.* 1916–1918. Theodore Rigg. Archives of Friends House, London YM.
[11] Prince Vladimir Mikhailovich Volkonsky (September 17 [29], 1868- March 23, 1953) - Russian public and political figure.

These gentlemen are Quakers, whose trustiness is beyond question. Perhaps you remember how helpful this Society was to our people during the famine. If you will be good enough to help and protect then I shall be grateful.

Yours most truthfully,

Sazonoff.[12]

The Russian police seem to have had a traditional wariness of foreigners, seen both back in those days and nowadays. This is evidenced by a document informing the head of the Police Department of the Russian Empire, Evgeny Klimovich[13], of the arrival of the British Quakers in Petrograd:

On the subject of the arrival in Petrograd of representatives of the English Quaker sect to provide material assistance to refugees affected by the war.

Begun on 27 April 1916

Top secret

---

[12] Friends House London archives. YM/MfS/FEWVRC/MISSIONS/7/2/1.
[13] Evgeny Konstantinovich Klimovich (January 24, 1871 - 1930)- Russian statesman and administrative figure, head of the Police Department of the Russian Empire.

To His Excellency, Evgeny Konstantinovich Klimovich.

My dear sir, Evgeny Konstantinovich

Representatives of the English Quaker sect have arrived in Petrograd, reportedly to provide material assistance to refugees affected by the war.

I therefore consider it my duty to inform Your Excellency of the following information available to my office in the Department about the afore-mentioned sect, regarding its attitude to the internal affairs of our Fatherland.

The Quaker sect, or as they call themselves 'The Religious Society of Brothers', arose in England in the seventeenth century and was initially severely harassed by the English Government.

This sect has been considered a recognised confession since 1690, and currently it adheres to religious doctrines identical to those of our Tambov Molokans[14]. There is a severe discipline in the internal structure of the sect, and concerning the attitude of this sect towards the state, the negative attitude towards the war and prohibition on its members to enter military service deserves special attention according to the conditions of the wartime circumstances we experience.

At the head of this sect, [F.W.] Fox, who died in 1915, was at the same time the chairman of a society in London called the Anglo-German Friendship Society, and there were some indications in the foreign press

---

[14] [Translators Note: The Molokans, or 'dairy eaters', were a pacifist Christian sect. The Tambov Molokans lived in the province of Tambov.]

in the early days of the present European war that the British Quakers had not shown enough sympathy.

The Quaker sect is known for its strenuous efforts to promote sectarian ideas and, according to the General Secretary of a London-based Baptist organisation called the Russian Society for Evangelisation, Russian sectarianism has 'generous helpers' in the form of Quakers. The Department of Spiritual Affairs has not established what form Quakers' assistance to Russian sectarians takes and which of its representatives are in contact with them, but the Quakers' interest in Russian sectarianism is also confirmed by the Minister of Foreign Affairs' letter of 11 March 1914, no. 19, to the Minister of Internal Affairs, stating that V. Fetler, the former mentor at the Petrograd Baptist congregation who was expelled from Petrograd by order of the Council of Ministers, was a sympathiser, and Fetler's arrest and prosecution made such an unfavourable impression on the Quakers that, according to the Imperial Ambassador in London, this could lead to a loss of sympathy for us among English Quakers and, in general, have a very unfavourable effect on English society's attitude towards us.

In view of all the above, I have the honour to ask you, sir, whether it would be appropriate to order the special observation and surveillance of the foreigners in question, as well as those with whom they will have particularly close relations, and to keep me informed.

Your humble servant,

Georgy Petkevich[15].[16]

However, it appears that the Quaker delegation's arrival did not concern the head of the Police Department too much: the British held meetings at a fairly high level, and the Russian authorities took them wherever they wanted to go.

The travellers were detained in Petrograd when Cadbury and Burtt went down with a sudden bout of flu, and since they had arrived at Orthodox Easter, everywhere was closed. They ended up not setting off for Moscow until early May, as the head of the delegation, W. Cadbury, reported in a letter to Ruth Fry, sent by diplomatic mail from the British Embassy in Petrograd:

Petrograd April 19 – May 2 1916

Dear Miss Fry,

By the kindness of the Embassy we are sending you a report in their bag.

---

[15] Georgy Boleslavovich Petkevich (September 8, 1873 - October 6, 1937), Director of the Foreign Confessions Religious Affairs Department of the Ministry of Internal Affairs (1915-1916).
[16] Russian State Historical Archive, St. Petersburg, fonds 821, series 133, file 318.

… We have been here for a long time… Burtt and I were on our backs with influenza and a temperature, and then the long Easter holiday came — the longest in the year…

The Minister of the Interior has provided us with full statistics of refugees and letters to Governors in various provinces along the Volga. It is here that the greatest congestion seems to be, so it is proposed to take a journey to some of these centres, Simbirsk, Kazan, Samara and perhaps Orenburg. Tatlock and I hope to go to Moscow tonight, as we want to catch Lvoff and understand he shortly leaves there. Burtt and Rigg follow tomorrow. We expect to stay a week or 10 days in Moscow.

The climate is trying and for reasons I can explain better on return I have decided not to go on past Moscow. The other three are <u>quite enough</u>, and I need to say quite capable. Beyond Moscow I think they'll have to have an interpreter.

W.A. Cadbury.[17]

The first meetings with refugees took place at train stations where people were waiting for ways to travel further into the country. The Quakers also managed to find out during their stay in Moscow the conditions in which displaced people were living. Theodore Rigg wrote in his diary:

We arrived in Moscow yesterday. Here everything is green and summer has come. Moscow is most picturesque

[17] Friends House London archives. YM/MfS/FEWVRC/ MISSIONS/7/2/1.

with its many churches with their coloured domes and gilded crosses. The beautiful walls of the Kremlin and the boulevards with trees in full leaf make a charming picture.

We find the Russian officials very friendly and anxious to show us as much as possible of the relief activities for refugees located in the town. We were amazed at the size and scope of the Moscow work. At one centre, on the outskirts of the town, some 3200 were housed. They were of mixed nationalities including Poles, Lithuanians and Russians. Almost every aspect of life was catered for at this centre. The accommodation was good; food and clothing were supplied; schools had been built for the education of children and separate churches for Roman Catholic Poles and the Greek Orthodox Russians were maintained.

We have been advised that many refugees from the Western Russian Front are located in the Volga districts and that the condition of the refugees, particularly in the villages, is far from satisfactory.[18]

The statistics for several different cities were as follows, as described in William Cadbury's report:

Total refugees confirmed by ministry of the Interior (April 1916) is 2,768,395 (2,562,000 in European Russia)

---

[18] *Experiences of a Relief Worker of the Society of Friends during the First World War.* Theodore Rigg. Published by Christchurch Monthly Meeting. 1976.

City	Refugees	% of the normal population
Samara	*38,000*	*26.6%*
Petrograd	*62,000*	*2.9%*
Moscow	*53,000*	*3.3%*

The cost to the Government in cash of the 25 kop[19] / per day grant works out as £25,261,650 per year.

A huge map of Russia showed the various agencies working around each centre.

> 1) *The National Committee (called Tatiana after the Princess)*
> 2) *'Sobej'*
> 3) *Agencies of special races — Polish, Jews, […] Purely local or private agencies.[20]*

Interestingly, in their messages to London, the Quakers noted: 'English almost useless, of many officials we have called upon, none have spoken English enough for conversation, thanks Tatlock's good French needed no interpreter (yet), German is now "*verboten*"'.

While Cadbury went from Moscow to Petrograd, before going back to London, the three remaining Quakers headed to Samara, further to the east.

---

[19] 'Kop' stands for kopeck. There were a hundred kopecks in a rouble.

[20] To the Friends War Victims Relief Committee from Moscow, 25 April (old style) 1916. Friends House London archives. YM/MfS/FEWVRC/MISSIONS/7/2/4.

The train journey took 36 hours. The travellers had letters of recommendation with them to the governor of Samara, to the local council (*zemstvo*) and to the Red Cross Society. The local authorities gave the Quakers a very warm welcome. Governor Andrei Afanasevich Stankevich, genuinely hoping to see the Quakers come to work in his province, told them that there were 170,000 refugees living in the territory he governed, many of whom had travelled from the west during the harsh, cold winter. He said that thousands of refugees had died of typhus or general hardship. He highlighted the fact that there were many orphaned children among the refugees who needed more care than it had been possible to give them so far. Numerous officials who met the three Quakers in Samara advised them to travel to Buzuluk, a rural town located in the east of Samara province. Refugees there were said to be living in the worst conditions of all.

The British visitors were first shown several centres for refugees in Samara. They went to Vladimirovka, located 60 km from Samara, and to Ekaterinovka. Refugees were living in both villages. According to Rigg[21], the refugees were housed in three large buildings which were completely at their disposal, with about fifty people living in each. It turned out that Poles were housed separately from Russians because of their different religious denomination

---

[21] *Experiences of a Relief Worker of the Society of Friends during the First World War.* Theodore Rigg. Published by Christchurch Monthly Meeting. 1976.

and, as officials explained to Quakers, because of differences in their food.

The refugees said that the authorities provided them with housing, firewood and kerosene, but that they had to live on a daily living allowance set at forty kopecks a day per person. They expressed their dissatisfaction with the fact that the food allowance was delayed and that no clothes were provided at all, even though they should have been.

Rigg and his colleagues listened to the advice to travel to Buzuluk and went there as soon as they had obtained letters of recommendation from Samara. The governor's representative and the staff of the local council in this provincial town received the British Quakers very warmly. In the spirit of traditional Russian suspicion, however, some Buzuluk residents could not understand why the three foreigners would want to help refugees. They wondered whether the proposed work with refugees was actually part of some secret plan for allied diplomacy in Russia. Nevertheless, the hospitable local council officials organised a meal in honour of the guests and a trip to villages which had already housed refugees. The subject of medical care in rural areas was discussed: it turned out that the local authorities had had to close hospitals and outpatient clinics due to a shortage of medical personnel, caused by the war.

In 1913, Buzuluk district in Samara province

had had six *stans* and 51 *volosts*[22], with villages and hamlets. Before the war, one health centre had served several volosts, so there were several health centres for the district as a whole. Each health centre had a hospital and a district doctor, and each of these doctors served a large territory, equivalent in size to the English counties of Surrey or Sussex. By the time the Quaker delegation arrived in the district, though, there was no one left to provide medical care: hospitals had closed in many areas, as doctors and their assistants had been called up to serve in the army and been sent to the front.

1912 map of Buzuluk District (Ooezd).

©*Quickprint Partnership, A.A. Levenson, Samara, 1912*

---

[22] *Volosts* and *stans* were traditional administrative subdivisions in Russia. The Buzuluk *ooyezd* had the volosts and stans that were subordinated to the ooyezd city of Buzuluk. Buzuluk was the 'capital' of its ooyezd which was an administrative part of the Samara *gubernia*, or governorate. A gubernia was a major administrative subdivision of the Russian Empire.

The Quakers began to survey the district. Their very first trip was to the village of Mogutovo in the northern part of Buzuluk district, accompanied by the secretary of the local council and a translator, Miss L. Munier. The Quakers were told that there was a big building in this village which was uninhabited. It had once belonged to a Moscow tobacco merchant called Vasilii Nikolayevich Bostanzhoglo, but the local council now owned the empty building. The Quakers decided on the spot – on their very first journey into the Russian hinterland – that this building, which they were yet to see, could be turned into a children's home for refugee children. Theodore Rigg describes[23] all the details of his first trip: the hospitality of the local squires, each of whom insisted on meeting the British visitors and giving them food and drink. They also made the acquaintance of local Buzuluk nobility: the former Marshal of the Nobility, Andrei Pavlovich Zhdanov, and the Stobeus family.

After Mogutovo, the group headed to the nearby village of Derzhavino, where there was a small hospital and outpatient clinic. This hospital had served peasants in the whole northern part of Buzuluk district during peacetime. Now both the outpatient clinic and hospital were closed, due to the lack of medical personnel. The next stop was Pleshanovo, where the Quakers viewed

---

[23]*Experiences of a Relief Worker of the Society of Friends during the First World War.* Theodore Rigg. Published by Christchurch Monthly Meeting. 1976.

an outpatient clinic and hospital. They were pleasantly surprised by the working conditions and staff. From Pleshanovo they went on to Grachevka, where there was a hospital which served the volosts of Talli, Kliuchi and Kuzminovka. About 700 people from the Russian part of Poland had found refuge in Grachevka. The Quakers were told that the hospitals in Lyubimovka and Andreevka had closed. The British travellers, who were quite tired by now, moved on again, and spent a day in both villages. The Quakers were shocked by the conditions in which both refugees and local peasants were living in this area. The standard of living was appalling: the refugees had hardly anything. The closure of hospitals in Andreevka and Lyubimovka made life very difficult for both the local population and the refugees in the southern part of Buzuluk district, as well as in the adjacent territory, the Urals district. Unsurprisingly, volost officials were very interested in the prospect of reopening hospitals in these two villages and promised to assist the British.

Rigg and his two colleagues thanked the town authorities for organising their trip in a report[24] they presented to them on their return to Buzuluk on 23 May (5 June) 1916. In particular, they mentioned that 'The 6-day expedition so kindly arranged by the Marshal of the Nobility, has been of great help and interest [...] We desire to thank

[24] Friends House London archives. YM/MfS/FEWVRC/ MISSIONS/7/1/2/4.

our guide, Mr Nicholas Dimitrieff, and everyone we met'.

The Quakers then met the local council again, to make sure officials understood their idea for Quaker work in Buzuluk district. They presented them with their proposals:

1. Opening a hospital and outpatient clinic in Lyubimovka and providing personnel.

2. Opening a children's home in the tobacco merchant's home in Mogutovo, and opening an outpatient clinic there too, which could partially compensate for the closure of the hospital in Derzhavino.

3. Opening centres to give work to refugees in Lyubimovka and other villages, as soon as the necessary staff could be found.

4. Distributing clothes and food rations to refugees in the villages in the vicinity of the medical centres.

This programme was approved by the local council, and the British relief workers were promised every possible support for carrying out their work.

At the same time, a report with proposals for work in Buzuluk County was ready for submitting to the Friends War Victims Relief Committee in London. As Joseph Burtt had gone back to England, he kindly agreed to present the report in person for the committee's consideration.

This is what Rigg wrote in an accompanying letter:

June 8, 1916

Dear Ruth Fry,

… Now at last we feel we have hit upon a district in which conditions are extremely favourable for our work and where undoubtedly great need exists for medical work and material assistance in clothing. There are about 35,000 refugees in the Buzuluk Department and another 10,000 are expected from Tashkent and Turkestan. They are mainly scattered out in villages, in fact there are only 1500 refugees in Buzuluk itself. We have completed a tour of representative parts of the Buzuluk Department which gave us a fairly good idea of refugee condition and the life of the local peasants in these parts. […]

I am quite certain if our women could only speak Russian that a small army of them could be employed to great advantage in distributing clothes and in organizing workrooms etc right throughout the Buzuluk Dept.

Just yesterday the Chairman of the Tatiana Committee [for war victim relief] expressed his hope that we would be able to help them in distributing the clothing which they now have in hand for refugees. When our workers gain a little knowledge of Russian more women, I feel sure, could be brought out to personal work among refugees. As far as men are concerned we cannot see how they could be usefully employed. As the work grows undoubtedly a few will be required but for the moment we cannot advise you to send any out.[25]

---

[25] Friends House London archives. YM/MfS/FEWVRC/ MISSIONS/7/1/2/1.

After Joseph Burtt's departure, Theodore Rigg and Robert Tatlock got on with making an accurate assessment of their recruitment requirements and compiling a list of what would be needed for carrying out the planned work. The first step was to rent a building which would serve both as the Quakers' office and somewhere for them to live. Rigg went to Lyubimovka and Mogutovo again to clarify what kind of renovation and repairs would be required in the two buildings which would become the new centres. He needed to think through all sorts of details: furniture, bedding, food and firewood.

The first group of medical staff and aid workers travelled from Britain to Russia via Norway and Sweden, arriving in Buzuluk in June. The second British group came by the same route and reached their destination at the end of August 1916. There were some extraordinary people among them. The chief medic was Dr. J. Tylor Fox, and some of the aid workers were already known for their work in France and Serbia: Florence Barrow, Dorothy White, Mary Pattison and Eleanor Lindsay.

Their next task was to work out a detailed work plan and make arrangements for the Quaker staff in Lyubimovka and Mogutovo. The shortage of interpreters was a serious problem, which might prevent the Quaker staff members being distributed more widely. Miss Munier was in the group from the very start. She had provided a crucial service as an interpreter at the early stage of negotiations with the local authorities. Fortunately, two others, Miss Webster and Miss K. Zhukova, the latter of whom had travelled from Rostov, joined the team a little later.

The Quakers decided that their main task was to open a hospital in Lyubimovka. They also needed to do a survey among refugee families in order to find which children would benefit from coming to live in the children's home. Dr. J. Tylor Fox, Elsie Fox, Dorothy White and the necessary nursing staff went to Lyubimovka to open the hospital and also to prepare job opportunities for refugees. Florence Barrow, aided by other workers, surveyed refugee families in the vicinity of Lyubimovka and Andreevka.

Sometime later, in the autumn, a second group of aid workers arrived from England. Their arrival allowed the Quakers to complete the staffing of the children's home in Mogutovo, and to open centres for refugees in Bogdanovka and Efimovka.

Workers of the British Mission in Russia, September 1916.

Florence M. Barrow	*Buzuluk, head of the relief section*
Dr. J. Tylor Fox	*Buzuluk, head of the medical section*

Elsie L. Fox	*Buzuluk, head of the nursing section*
Theodore Rigg	*Buzuluk, treasurer*
Robert R. Tatlock	*Buzuluk, secretary*
Ellen Butt, Charles Colles, Dora Fox, Bertha Graveson, C. Gordon Lewis, Wilfrid R. Little, Dr Herbert C. Manning, Elizabeth Morgan, Mary B. Pattison, Dr George H. Pearson, Dr John Rickman, Margaret Webster, Anne Wells, Theodora Williams.	*Buzuluk, staff of the British mission*
E. St. John Catchpool and Thomas D. Heald.	*Moscow*

One of the first meetings of the Quaker committee took place in Lyubimovka on 26 August 1916:

Present: Dr Tylor Fox, Mrs Fox, Florence Barrow, Theodore Rigg, R.R. Tatlock

1 [...] Wilfrid Little to be treasurer to the Committee

2 Theodore Rigg [...] it was agreed to appoint him to

be in charge of Buzuluk centre, where much of his time is spent [...] one of his duties should be to look after the maintenance of the party [...]

4 Dr Fox emphasised the danger of keeping a large number of children in Mogutovo house with no medical assistance within reach. It was agreed that a doctor or a nurse should be stationed there.

6 Dr Fox was asked and accepted chairmanship of the Committee

7 Some uneasiness was felt by the secretary on account of repeated failure to obtain interpreters. He gave an account of the search which had been made for interpreters. The position of Hanna Bellows was brought forward.

8 [...] a conviction was expressed that large sums of money would be required for Russia, it was agreed to ask the London Committee for a further allowance of £2,000.[26]

Judging by the Quakers' diaries and letters, the local authorities were on very good terms with the British mission. The local population, which had not really accepted the refugees, welcomed the British visitors, since they helped both refugees

[26] Minutes of the Meeting held at Lyubimovka on 26 August (English date) 1916. Friends House London archives. YM/MfS/ FEWVRC/MISSIONS/7/1/1.

and local people. That autumn, an article entitled 'English people in the countryside' was published in the Samara newspaper *The Volga Day* (Volzhsky den), which mentioned that they helped everyone: 'Some representatives of the English society "Friends" ("Friends of Humanity") have spent some time in Buzuluk, giving aid to those who have suffered as a result of military action'.[27] The newspaper stated that Buzuluk local council (*zemstvo*) had provided them with two hospitals in the district, in Lyubimovka and Andreevka, and a building on the estate of Mr Bostanzhoglo, in the village of Mogutovo, which now belonged to the council. At the same time, a condition was imposed on the British visitors: that medical care in medical institutions would not only be provided to refugees, but also to the local population. The journalist wrote that the Quakers received all essential medicines directly from England and underlined the fact that 'The population is fully receptive to their help, and the doctors themselves do their work very conscientiously'.

The Quakers organised the transfer of several refugee families, as well as orphans, from the southern part of the district, into the renovated, former Bostanzhoglo building in Mogutovo in October 1916. The fathers had either died or were absent in several refugee families. The transfer proved harder than expected. By mid-October, though, all the refugee families had been transferred to the house in Mogutovo, and

---

[27] *Volzhsky den*, issue no.194, 7 September 1916.

everyone rejoiced. The Quakers realised that the transfer would have been much more difficult still if they had not managed to finish it before the first snow. At the end of November, due to an increase in the number of people being looked after and other difficulties in Mogutovo, the Quakers appointed one of their workers, Miss Webster, to be in charge of the house there. Miss Graveson and Miss Lindsay worked in the same small village. Wilfrid Little was appointed to work in Mogutovo as the Committee's representative.

Now the routine work began, carried out over the vast territory of Buzuluk County, across six centres created in large villages. This was mainly medical care for locals and refugees who lived close to the Quaker medical centres. In addition to the clinic and hospital in Mogutovo, the Quakers also opened workshops there to keep the refugees occupied and give them ways to earn a living.

The main office, which was the centre of the Quaker relief mission and the meeting place for all the British relief workers, was at 27 Orenburg Ulitsa (Street) in Buzuluk. Its official title was 'The English Mission. The Society of Friends providing war victim relief'. Theodore Rigg wrote: 'At present, I am in Buzuluk which I regard as my hometown. Here, three of the men have their headquarters. It is seldom that we are all here together for we all do some travelling, although I am away the most. I am always glad to see the domes and crosses of the Buzuluk

churches appearing on the horizon when I am
on my homeward journey. These tell me that my
journey will soon be ended'.[28]

Of course, not everything went smoothly, and
some mistakes were made. Sometimes things
were not coordinated properly, so time and effort
was wasted on inessential matters. A common
mistake, both then and in the years that followed,
was that the Quakers tried do everything as
if they were in England, following a familiar
pattern. For example, they tried to organise
nursing care according to the standards in British
hospitals. The Quaker committee in London,
in turn, made a series of mistakes in its choice
of staff for what was a challenging mission, and
these miscalculations often led to difficulties and
mutual misunderstandings between Buzuluk and
London, as well as friction within the Quaker
team working in Russia. Unfortunately, not one
of the workers who came to Buzuluk was a good
administrator. Everything had to be learned on
the job, which is never satisfactory.

In their defence, it is important to remember
that most of the relief workers who came to
Russia were very young, and even those who were
somewhat older were still middle-class people,
travelling to Russia from a sheltered lifestyle in
comfortable houses in Britain. Many of them had
never encountered the realities of life for destitute

[28] Theodore Rigg, *Experiences of a Relief Worker of the Society of Friends
during the First World War.* Published by Christchurch Monthly
Meeting. 1976.

people or the horrors of epidemics. None of them knew what it was to lose your house, your farm, your place in life, give up everything, and travel hundreds and thousands of miles away from home. Even those who had studied to become social workers in England found themselves in medieval conditions in Russia. The reality around them was nothing like what they had been taught in their homeland and not what they were used to. Reading the reports and letters people sent home, we can see their confusion and loneliness.

It is easy to see the failures and mistakes from the outside: they are always glaringly obvious to a superficial, critical eye. However, we cannot fail to be impressed by the courage and perseverance with which the members of this motley team approached the challenges they faced. It might have seemed as though all their attempts to help and comfort impoverished people were doomed to failure from the start. Yes, the Quakers only touched the tip of the iceberg of the problems they encountered. Their efforts might seem negligible when you look at them, knowing how big a problem the Quakers were trying to solve in a particular area. But they did what they could, what they were capable of, and they devoted themselves completely to their work. Through their sincerity and honesty, they unknowingly paved the way for the next Quaker mission in these parts, which would begin in 1921, in the terrible years of famine.

The Quakers successfully responded to the refugees' most pressing demand: for an occupation. Refugees desperately wanted to escape the monotony of their daily lives, to get rid of the apathy, boredom and despair that engulfed every displaced person. Having had an active life in their own homes, these people suddenly found themselves with nothing to do. Overnight, they found themselves paupers, dependent on the mercy of others. When they met the Quakers, they gave them a clear message: refugees need a job, not soup kitchens or other forms of charity, if they are to regain their lost self-esteem. It was this kind of constructive assistance from the Quaker mission that would be welcomed, they said. The Quakers urgently needed to create working conditions for refugees which would let them earn a living, as well as keep them busy. They had to find premises for workshops, and any necessary materials had to be brought in from Buzuluk, which was at least eight to ten hours away by horse-drawn cart: all the Quaker centres were that far away from the town. The other challenge was to find types of activity that any refugee could do, which was not easy. The Quakers' limited funds meant they needed to look for products which would be in high demand so that the outlay for materials and wages would be reimbursed as soon as possible. At the same time, the product itself had to be something which could be sold to make a profit for the Quaker mission, thus ensuring the mission's future and sustainability.

After several experiments, it was decided that the best solution was to produce wool. Warm clothes, such as socks, stockings and undergarments for the winter, could be knitted from the wool. It was also possible to make house linen with simple embroidery. Older women were able to spin yarn which the younger women would knit, and a small group of refugee women were specialists in embroidery. Others learned how to sew undergarments, and so on. People began to receive a salary in line with the level of earnings in the region and based on the market price of the products manufactured. While the Quaker mission's limited means could not perform miracles, a minimum of one person from each refugee family had work for at least three or four days per week.

Workshops opened in Bogdanovka, Lyubimovka, Andreevka and Mogutovo by November 1916, although many of them were crammed into small premises. Each workshop was run by a Quaker from the British mission. In Preobrazhenskoe, the refugees were initially given wool to spin and knit at home, until another workshop opened in February 1917. Theodore Rigg wrote in his diary: 'We are opening a new relief centre at the village of Efimovka. I have been busy making certain alterations to the rooms which we will use for relief work. Another job has been the purchasing of supplies and materials required for this new centre. This is a slow business as some of the goods must be purchased in Samara and then arrangements made for their transport to Buzuluk by train and thence to Efimovka by peasants' sledges'.[29]

As a result, 730 women and girls were employed over the winter, providing financial support to a total of 2,800 refugees. Over time, it became clear that the most profitable activity was weaving fabric: the price of production was rising everywhere, and the quality of production was falling. Fabric production was first trialled in Andreevka. When it worked well, the Quakers decided to move into weaving at all the Quaker centres. The looms were made by refugees who were old enough to have sufficient experience and knowledge. The knitters had to retrain as weavers, and the refugees' weaving business became the biggest in the local handicrafts industry. They started to make excellent clothes. Such things were in such short supply in the town that when the goods reached shops or markets, buyers had to pay good money to buy these products, which were made by refugees.

Theodore Rigg and his colleagues met up with Alexander Buligin, the former Marshal of the Nobility of Buzuluk district, in Samara in February 1917. The head of the Quaker mission wrote to London: 'We interviewed Mr Buligin at the Grand Hotel, Samara [...]. We explained that after consultation with our London Cmt and in view of the increasing possibility of an earlier peace,

---

[29] Ibid.

we had decided to inquire into the conditions of Refugee needs in the devastated governments of Russia and Poland'. Prince Lvov, whom the Quakers had met back in February, advised them to be sure to contact Alexei Borisovich Neidgardt, the then head of the Tatiana Committee, in Petrograd.

The Tatiana Committee was the central body responsible relief work for refugees in the Russian Empire. It ran many children's homes, similar to the one the Quakers had organised in Mogutovo, and one of their orphanages was in Minsk. When they met Lvov, the Quakers mentioned their intention to meet Countess Olga Tolstaya. Lvov said that Countess Tolstaya had told him about the Quakers just the previous day, and he hoped that she would introduce the British to one of his relatives who happened to be running an orphanage for refugee children in Minsk.

However, although Friends considered plans for expanding their work into other areas in the Russian Empire, they ended up staying in Buzuluk district. The regular meeting of the Quaker Committee, held in Lyubimovka in February 1917, decided that £1,000 per month would be enough to cover all the British mission's expenses. At the April meeting, held in the same village, Dr Fox gave an account of his trip with Tatlock to Samara, Moscow and Petrograd. They had had many useful meetings, both with officials and with political opponents of the Tsarist regime

who had been released. They had even witnessed
the February Revolution in the capital, Petrograd.

Dr Fox said that he had been pleased to meet
Countess Tolstaya and her friends in Moscow.
He suggested sending her an invitation to visit
Buzuluk and see for herself what the Quakers
were doing in the district. Interestingly, at this
same meeting, the secretary was requested to ask
the London Committee to send information to
Buzuluk about historical Quaker ties with Russia.
We can assume that an idea was developing at
that time about the prospect of stable relations
between Quakers and Russia, and the Russian
people. The revolutionary events in the country
produced so much hope and expectation! Perhaps
this was when Theodore Rigg first had the idea of
a Quaker embassy, an idea which he promoted in
his conversations with colleagues in both Russia
and London. Nor is it out of the question that the
meeting with Olga Tolstaya in Moscow could have
been one of the impulses behind his idea.

But who was Olga Tolstaya? She was the daughter-
in-law of the author Lev Tolstoy; the mother-in-
law of the poet Sergei Esenin; the sister of the
subject of a famous painting, 'Kursistka', by the
artist Nikolai Yaroshenko; as well as the sister
 of Alexander Kolchak's[30] Chief of Staff, Mikhail

[30] Alexander Vasilyevich Kolchak, the 'Supreme Leader and
Commander-in-Chief of All Russian Land and Sea Forces', was
the anti-Bolshevik military leader during the Russian Civil War
(1918-1920). [Translator's note: the conventional English spelling
'Alexander' has been used throughout. An exact transliteration
would be 'Aleksandr'.]

Diterikhs. Countess Olga Konstantinovna Tolstaya, née Diterikhs, was an interesting character. Later on, she would even become the first Russian to join the Religious Society of Friends.

Olga was beautiful, clever, educated and already attracted to Tolstoy's ideas. Her sister Anna was married to a prominent Tolstoyan, Vladimir Chertkov, who was Tolstoy's assistant. When Olga was 27, she met Andrei Tolstoy, the writer's son, who was a gregarious bon vivant. They soon got married, in Tula, and went on to have two children: Sonya (born in 1900) and Ilya (born in 1903). But in 1904, after five years of family life, Andrei fell in love with Anna Tolmacheva, the daughter of General Sobolev. When Olga found out about their liaison, she left Russia with her children to join her sister in England. Anna was living there with her husband, who had had to leave Russia seven years earlier. He had been exiled by the authorities for helping the Russian Doukhobors, a Christian sect. It was in England that Olga Tolstaya encountered Quakers: they were very interested in Tolstoy's ideas and in Chertkov. In fact, Olga had much in common with Quaker ideals: she was wise, religious, strove to help people in need and was an advocate of non-violence.

Olga, Tolstoy's daughter-in-law, had a similar outlook to the great Russian writer himself, and indeed he loved Olga and his grandchildren – the children of his frivolous son, Andrei. Andrei

Tolstoy, who had already separated from Anna Tolmacheva, now became involved with the wife of the Governor of Tula, Artsimovich. This time he was serious enough that he even went to England to ask his first wife for a divorce. He married Ekaterina Artsimovich in 1908. Olga never remarried, however. She continued to look after her two children, and returned to Moscow.

Village school

©The archives of the American Friends Service Committee

The meeting with English Quakers had made her name known to the British Society of Friends, and they kept in touch with Olga even once she returned to her homeland. Two British Quakers, Fox and Tatlock, met up with Olga Tolstaya in Moscow in spring 1917 and tried to spark her interest in their activities in Buzuluk. They asked her, for example, whether she could help them find a permanent teacher for the orphanage in Mogutovo, because 'the teacher who was sent to the village by the local council cannot be considered satisfactory'. Although the Quakers tried everything to get Olga Tolstaya to come to Buzuluk, she never left Moscow.

Meanwhile, it was announced at the May meeting of the Quaker committee in Buzuluk that Friends were due to arrive from the USA. The Quakers in Russia had approved London's decision that four relief workers could be sent from America to help refugees. It was suggested that three of those workers should be delegated to work in the southern part of the district and that the fourth would work in Mogutovo.

The tumultuous events in the country did not bypass the Quaker mission. Theodore Rigg wrote about the Russian revolution in his diary in April 1917: 'Great things are happening in Russia: the Revolution was accepted by the people of Buzuluk with little demonstration; there was a procession with flags — some cheering and a few speeches but no disturbances whatsoever. The whole of this part of Russia seems to be in agreement with the Revolution: it was a great day for Russia; the possibilities ahead are staggering; it may be dawn of a new era. Two of our members, Dr. J. T. Fox and R. R. Tatlock, are investigating the possibility of commencing reconstruction work for refugees in the Vilna and Grodno districts. Personally, I do not think much can be done in this direction at the present time as several of our workers are returning to England'.[31]

Several members of the mission did indeed go home that spring and summer. The Quakers lost three highly qualified nurses within just one month. It was a serious blow, as there had not been a full complement of medical staff as it was. At the same time, there was an outbreak of typhus in Lyubimovka. Margaret Barber, about whom it was said that 'she knows everyone, and all the peasants know her', succeeded in recognising the danger at an early stage. She identified those who were sick and convinced them to go into hospital in time. Fortuitously, Dr Neville Bradley, a member of the British medical mission in China and a specialist in rare diseases typical of the Far East, arrived in Buzuluk. He had decided to spend his six-month leave in Russia and been sent to Andreevka. His experience was invaluable. Many of the mission workers who had stayed in Russia caught typhus themselves, which made it more complicated to allocate workers to the different centres: the team had to be shuffled around, moving people from one place to another. Another reason for concern was that the crop failure in 1917 threatened a shortage of food the following spring. It was becoming increasingly difficult to plan work, bearing in mind the unclear political situation and economic outlook in the country. The displaced people were getting increasingly anxious, and the

[31] Theodore Rigg, *Experiences of a Relief Worker of the Society of Friends during the First World War*. Published by Christchurch Monthly Meeting. 1976.

British mission staff was shrinking. Spring 1917 was a period of confusion and uncertainty.

Chapter 2. *Six Quaker women from the USA travel to Buzuluk in August 1917. Work in the Quaker hospitals, children's homes and workshops continues. The Bolsheviks arrive in Buzuluk. 'The Bolsheviks demonstrate their complete respect for the Quaker mission'. A Quaker wedding and the registration of the marriage between the Englishman and the American woman at Buzuluk's Soviet council. The monastery house was an orphanage for refugee children in Spaso-Preobrazhenskii monastery. The idea of a Quaker embassy in Buzuluk district. Hopes and plans in spring 1918.*

Late one evening in August 1917, a train came into Buzuluk station. Six young women stepped down from a carriage, but only one of them could understand and speak Russian. Her name was Amelia Fabirzhevskaya. She was from the kingdom of Poland and had once been a Russian citizen. After emigrating to the United States, she had managed to obtain citizenship of her new country just before leaving for Russia. The remaining five women were called Nancy Babb, Emilie Bradbury, Anna Haines, Lydia Lewis and Esther M. White.

There were already quite a number of workers from England in Buzuluk and the area at that time:

Workers of the British Mission in Russia, August 1917.

Charles Colles, C. Gordon Lewis, Dr John Rickman and E. Theodora Williams	*Andreevka*
Edith Boughton-Leigh	*Efimovka*
Richard R. Ball	*Preobrazhenskoe*
S. Kate Anderson, Hinman J. Baker, sister Louisa Ball, Margaret Barber, Ellen Butt, Ethel Cox, Elsie L. Tylor Fox, Dr J. Tylor Fox, Sister Kerr, and Dr George H. Pearson	*Lyubimovka*
Eleanor T. Lindsay and Mary B. Pattison	*Bogdanovka*
Frank Keddie (in charge of warehouses), Theodore Rigg and Robert R. Tatlock, the clerk	*Buzuluk*
Florence M. Barrow, Phyllis M. Ball, K. Zhukova (interpreter), Elizabeth A. Little, Wilfred R. Little (treasurer), Margaret A. Webster, Gregory Welch, Anne Wells, Dorothy White	*Mogutovo*

Emilie Bradbury, an American Quaker, wrote in her diary:

August 26, 1917, SUNDAY. Took a train (from Kinel) and landed in Buzuluk about 10 hours – no one to meet us and no one at the station seemed to know of English Mission nor anyone in it. Officials telephoned around for someone who could speak English or French. Finally succeeded in getting a gentleman who was awful nice after saying he would go and get Mr. Rigg. He brought his wife who insisted on our coming to their house until Mr. Rigg arrived. [...] bed about 2.

August 27, 1917. MONDAY. Mr. Rigg came for us to take us to the office for breakfast – office about 16 minutes walk from hotel – house was about three rooms and kitchen etc where servants live – all the servants for mission are refugees – mostly Germans.[32]

And so the Quaker team in Buzuluk became international. The British Quakers were surprised by the way the American women spoke, as Rigg noted in his diary: 'I did not realize that the "Quaker" form of speech was retained by American Friends, for the young generation of English Friends do not use "thee" and "thou". It is quaint to hear them address one another. Their conversation in typical American style is refreshing to say the least. At present they are somewhat of a curiosity to the English members

---

[32] American Friends Service Committee (AFSC) archives, Philadelphia. FSR (Foreign Service Russia).

of our Unit. I happened to be the only senior member of our party in Buzuluk when they arrived and their allotment to different centres became my problem. However, with the help of Anna Haines, I got them sorted out and allocated to centres where I thought they would be best suited. They have all settled into their new homes extremely well and will soon take an active part in our work'.[33]

The American women were distributed as follows:

Miss L. Lewis	*House in Mogutovo*
Miss N. Babb	*Mogutovo, hospital*
Miss Bradbury	*Efimovka*
Miss Haines	*Lyubimovka*
Miss Fabirzhevskaya	*Lyubimovka, polyclinic*
Miss White	*Bogdanovka - assistant to Miss Lindsay*

Anna Haines was nominated on 15 September to represent the American contingent on the Quaker committee in Buzuluk. She was also responsible for liaising between her compatriots in Russia and the American Friends Service Committee (AFSC) in Philadelphia.

---

[33] Theodore Rigg, *Experiences of a Relief Worker of the Society of Friends during the First World War.* Published by Christchurch Monthly Meeting. 1976.

The American visitors got to work cheerfully and enthusiastically. Little could they imagine that in just two months there would be another revolution, one which would cause as much suffering as the war had. For the time being, though, in September 1917, the arrival of their transatlantic sisters in the faith felt like a breath of fresh air for the British Quakers working in Buzuluk district.

This was the first time that American and British Quakers had worked together, and some differences made themselves felt. The American women found their English colleagues' working methods amateurish, often leading to an ineffective use of human resources. The Americans' approach to problem-solving was more impersonal, even though they were just as involved in the project. They wanted to do everything on a large scale and act strategically with very limited resources. The American Quakers wanted to go and distribute as much as possible, based on their understanding of justice and equality in the situation in which they found themselves.

Work progressed in the workshops at the Quaker centres for refugees. In their correspondence with London, the British Quakers asked for wool to be bought in England and delivered to Buzuluk, where the refugees were already working with yarn. The refugees made woollen stockings which were sent to the Tatiana Committee in Samara, and the Tatiana Committee either sold the goods or swapped them for other items of clothing.

The children's home in Mogutovo filled up with new children. There was a constant shortage of interpreters and an urgent need for a teacher at the 'Mogutovo house', as the Quakers called the children's home in their correspondence. They knocked on every possible door in their search for a teacher, even, as we saw earlier, contacting Princess Olga Tolstaya, who was by then living in Moscow.

The medical side of the project in Mogutovo developed too, with the establishment of a small hospital there for the first time – it had not existed prior to the Quakers' arrival. When English doctor John Rickman began working there in August 1917, he was at last able to draw up a schedule of work, something he had long dreamed of. He realised that the Quakers at this hospital had the same policy of maintaining 'British hospital standards' as at the other two Quaker hospitals in Buzuluk district, but he knew that it was a pipe dream to think of implementing such high standards.

As we saw above, trying to organise everything as if they were in England was one of the mistakes the foreigners made. When he took an inventory of the equipment available, John Rickman realised just how little there was: a few surgical instruments, a fish-kettle which did duty as a steriliser, barely enough bandages, and some stocks of medicine. However, there was no sanitation or running water. There was no boiler, no baths and no means of disinfection. They had to use a primus and a wood stove even to boil water. Dr Rickman bravely decided to change policy and make Mogutovo hospital into a centre where the patient's relatives could learn how to look after the patient in conditions very similar to those in their huts. His ideas were a radical break from tradition, as we can see in the reduction in the use of disinfectant (except for wounds, of course). Surprisingly, though, while several cases of typhoid and meningitis were reported in the district at the time, these diseases did not break out in Mogutovo.

Amelia Fabirzhevskaya was sent to Mogutovo and appointed head of the hospital. She began teaching two peasant girls the basics of nursing in domestic settings. This combined Russian-foreign approach brought results: the local population appreciated the fact that the Quakers did not keep themselves to themselves or impose their own rules, and could adjust easily to local conditions.

The strategic goal began to be achieved: it was crucial to teach the locals, so that when the Quaker mission went home, local people could continue the work. The Quakers were hardly likely to be around for a century. The local girls who had been trained up in the hospital would themselves become medical instructors, transmitting their knowledge and experience to their friends and relatives. Many of the skills needed were very basic: how to make a bed, how to make a good stew, how to calm people's nerves and help people to get to sleep. John Rickman recalled that they tried to instil a desire for order and cleanliness, to show the Russians how to fight against diseases in the future when caring for the sick at home. Household hygiene was one key aspect.

Buzuluk was still relatively calm in autumn 1917, despite the turbulent revolutionary events in Petrograd. The minutes[34] of the monthly meetings of the Quaker committee paint a picture of the problems of everyday life: 'It was agreed to encourage the Mogutovo workers to pay occasional visits to Buzuluk during the coming winter; the isolated position of Mogutovo and the indoor life necessary there had been found last winter to be a considerable strain on the workers'. The Quakers also realised that the term 'Secretary' was not of sufficient weight when used in meetings with prominent officials of outside organisations. The Executive therefore agreed with the suggestion that the name 'Head' should be adopted. Another minute was 'to telegraph London for a young man with practical knowledge of dairying, curing meat and gardening, for educational purpose at Mogutovo'. It was decided to print and circulate 2000 copies of two short pamphlets in Russian on the 'Feeding of children' and 'Diet'. A recommendation from Mogutovo workers was

---

[34] Minutes of the Meetings. Friends House London archives. YM/MfS/FEWVRC/MISSIONS/7/1/1

considered, who said that Quaker work should be made more widely known to Russians. It was felt that this was particularly desirable at the present time. The Secretary was asked to write to Countess Tolstoy or Mr Chertkov regarding this matter.

A Russian girl balancing on a rail near Buzuluk station

©The archives of the American Friends Service Committee

However, this quiet way of life gradually changed for the worse. Echoes of the far-off revolution even reached the area. The American Quaker Emilie Bradbury wrote in her diary:

November 5, 1917 MONDAY. Michael, a boy of 15, said to Miss Leigh today – 'They talk about svoboda [freedom], but it isn't anything but every man looking out for himself and doing only for himself' — which is a fairly good commentary on the attitude of the natives here.

November 7, 1917 Quite a lot of excitement — soldiers arrived and are forcing natives to give grain to the refugees. There seems to be quite a lot of feeling against us, so it must seem rather queer to them to have the soldiers suddenly appear.[35]

In December 1917, the Quakers considered whether to buy flour in Siberia. They planned to spend £30,000 on food, and sent requests for additional funding to London and Philadelphia. Frank Keddie was asked to focus all his efforts on obtaining flour. The shortage of foodstuffs was very worrying for the Quaker mission, and so Anna Haines of the American group was asked to contact the head of the American Red Cross, Raymond Robbins, to inform him of the situation and ask for help. The Quaker meeting in December 1917 decided to cancel their plan to expand the shoemaking workshop in Andreevka. Richard Reynolds Ball had asked for 4000 roubles to create the workshop, but the meeting decided to only spend money on food instead.

In December 1917, Soviet forces arrived in the area, and the Quakers wrote in their report to the London Committee:

To the clerk of the FWVRC London

---

[35]AFSC archives. FSR.

English Mission
Society of Friends
Buzuluk

18 December 1917

Dear Ruth Fry,

[...] a detachment of some 2000 Bolshevik soldiers have arrived in Buzuluk with the idea of using Buzuluk as a base against the Cossack forces of the Orenburg Govt [...]

So far the presence of the Bolshevik forces has made no difference to our work [...] So, at the present time we, The Angliskaya Missia[36], remain among the few representatives of the intelligentsia class living in the district.

[...] At the time when the peasants will to a large extent be served by the entire intelligentsia class who alone possess the necessary skilled knowledge to administer to their ailments, we the Mission of the Society of Friends will be alone left to aid them.

[...] I therefore have no hesitation in saying that now is the time to help. By helping now we will do something towards bridging the gap between the various parties in Russia. We'll help in rebuilding the republic.

[...] We will make the name of the Society of Friends blessed by thousands and the name of English and the Americans to be remembered for years to come with gratitude and love.

---

[36] 'English mission' in Russian.

The Quakers wrote in their reports to London and Philadelphia on 8 February 1918 that 'We are treated with the utmost respect by the Bolshevik representatives here', and a little later (on 21 February): 'During the last two weeks the Bolshevik Commissioners have carried out some drastic measures against the capitalistic and property-owning class of Buzuluk [...] The position of the refugees at the present moment is exceedingly bad for the peasants are refusing to supply them with but scantiest ration'.[37]

Fears of hunger were still strong, so the Quakers discussed Keddie and Little's trip to Samara and Uralsk to replenish food supplies so that relief work could continue. A hundred poods[38] of flour were purchased in the Urals region. In Samara, the two Quakers met the head of the Food Committee of the Samara government, who promised to supply the mission with the flour needed to maintain hospitals and the Mogutovo House.

Also in February, it was decided that Miss Haines should visit Petrograd to speak directly to the American Red Cross (ARC) about the possibility of receiving financial assistance from them to solve the problems of hunger in Buzuluk district. Anna Haines set off for Petrograd where she met Raymond Robbins, the head of the ARC mission,

---

[37] Friends House London archives. YM/MfS/FEWVRC/ MISSIONS/7/1/2

[38] A *pood* is a unit of mass equal to 40 funt (a funt was a Russian pound). Since 1899 it has been set to approximately 16.38 kilograms (36.11 pounds).

and in March she reported back on her trip to the capital. She said that officials from the American Red Cross in Petrograd had already received a telegram from Washington, D.C., asking about the feasibility of a grant for the work in Buzuluk and the surrounding district in the fight against hunger. Since Miss Haines was there at such an opportune moment, she managed to persuade the Red Cross to send a representative to acquaint themselves with the Quakers' work. However, the German army's surprise attack made the trip impossible. The American Red Cross Commission therefore decided to send a telegraph to America immediately, instructing the ARC office in Washington to send $25,000 to the AFSC. The ARC Petrograd Mission also recommended that the ARC supply the Quakers with the full amount for any purpose related to their work, except for grain purchase if the peasants were to pay for the grain. Representatives of the ARC also offered the Quaker representatives a large stock of medicines and medical instruments, but due to the sudden advance of the German army and the confusion that ensued in the city, it proved impossible to deliver these supplies from Petrograd to Buzuluk.

In happier news, the English Quaker doctor John Rickman got married to the American Quaker Lydia Lewis in March 1918, and they registered their marriage in Buzuluk. Even today, at Buzuluk registry office, you can find the entry in the register of Buzuluk's Soviet (district council) of Peasant, Worker and Soldier Deputies for 1918, on page 23. Interestingly, the foreigners' names were russified: the records state that Ivan Richardovich Rickman and Lydia Ivanovna Lewis were declared husband and wife. The witnesses to this important event were recorded as 'English citizen' Frank Keddie and 'British citizen' Theodore Rigg.

This was the first wedding in Buzuluk to be registered by the new Bolshevik authorities of the town, and it just so happened that the bride was American and the bridegroom was English.

John Rickman, a young conscientious objector, a British Quaker, who had received his medical education in Cambridge and gained excellent practical training at St Thomas's Hospital in London, had refused to serve in the army for religious reasons and had ended up in Buzuluk. He had organised work at the hospital in Andreevka, before being transferred to the hospital in Mogutovo.

John Rickman's towel, a gift from Russian peasants of Andreevka. 1917.

©*Daniel Green and Sarah Vitali*

It was there that he met Lydia Lewis, one of the six American Quakers who arrived in the area in August 1917. It is typical that as well as having a Quaker marriage ceremony, the bride and groom decided to register their status at the local Bolshevik council. In this way, the Quakers wanted to demonstrate their recognition of the new authorities and so gain their support, which was crucial for working with the local population and with refugees.

At the museum in Dorking[39], John Rickman's hometown, this document, confirming his trust in the Bolshevik authorities, is still on display. Alongside it there is a yellowing card, dated May 1918, urging 'all government and public institutions and officials to be pleased to provide appropriate assistance to Ivan Rickman'.

This authorisation, together with the other documents which the Buzuluk authorities issued to Rickman, saved the English doctor's life.

The Quakers closed Mogutovo hospital on 29 March 1918. A month later, in April, the Quakers decided to close the children's home in the village too. The children at the home were resettled with pupils' relatives or acquaintances across Buzuluk district. Those who could not be placed were transferred to the children's home in Buzuluk.

It was a difficult time for the Quakers while the hospitals were being prepared for transfer

---

[39] A town in Surrey in the south of England.

to Russian medical personnel, the children from Mogutovo house were being resettled, the workshops were being tidied up, and the rest of the provisions were being distributed to the local population. The local authorities gave advice and assistance.

A Buzuluk newspaper entitled *News from Buzuluk District's Executive Committee of the Soviet of Workers' and Peasants' Deputies* wrote in April 1918: 'At the meeting of delegates of Buzuluk District Council of Refugees. On 8 March 1918, Chairman Shirmulevich reported that he heard that the English mission serving the needs of refugees in this county might liquidate its activities, and therefore suggested to the meeting whether it wished to enter into communication with the mission about the transfer of its equipped medical facilities, etc., to the district refugee council. The meeting decided to ask the English mission to transfer all the medical facilities, children's homes, workshops and other facilities it had set up for refugees in the event of their liquidation to the district council of refugees free of charge and to express its deep gratitude on behalf of the meeting for the care the English mission had rendered to the refugees'.[40]

Almost all the Quaker mission's workers had left the local villages by the end of May 1918. There were a couple of exceptions: Eleanor Lindsay stayed behind in the village of Labazi, and

[40] *News from Buzuluk District's Executive Committee of the Soviet of Workers' and Peasants' Deputies*, issue no.56, 10 April 1918.

Hinman Baker stayed in Andreevka to supervise the ploughing of 13 acres of land and the planting of potatoes there, on behalf of the local peasants. With the closure of the hospitals in the district and the children's home in Mogutovo, the Quakers concentrated all their work on the town of Buzuluk and its immediate vicinity.

After the children's home in Mogutovo had closed, the Quakers decided to take over responsibility for a children's home which some refugees themselves had set up. It was located on the land of the Buzuluk Spaso-Preobrazhensky monastery, on the hills above the city, near a river which wound its way between mighty trees. The Quaker mission promised 10,000 roubles of funding for the children's home, on condition that the local authorities would give them complete freedom to run the home. The Bolsheviks agreed readily to this request.

This came about after the secretary reported at the Executive Committee Meeting held at Buzuluk on 27 April 1918 that, at the urgent request of the President of the Council of Refugees, he had promised assistance in terms of personnel and money to continue the maintenance of the refugee children's home at the Monastery in Buzuluk. The Quakers called it the priot.[41] Several members of the Unit visited the home and all were agreed that much could be done to improve the conditions of

---

[41] The Quakers often used Russian words in their correspondence: *priot* is the way they spelled the Russian word *priyut*, meaning orphanage.

life for the children there, many of whom were orphans.

Charles Colles read a report on the findings of the small Quaker commission which had been established to investigate the conditions in the 'Buzuluk Refugee Priot'. The report made it clear that aid, training and education for the children was urgently needed; the children were also short of clothing and footwear. The Commission's proposals were as follows:

A woman and male representative to live at the priot. The woman representative to be responsible for instructional and educative work for the girls and oversight of the household arrangements of the Priot. The male representative to be responsible for the practical work for the organisation of instruction for the boys and oversight of the cultivation of the ground attached to the Priot.

E. White consented to act as woman representative and C. Colles and G. Welch conjointly as male representatives. Just a few weeks later, the children's home was unrecognisable, thanks to Esther White and Charles Colles' competence, patience and hard work. Unhelpful former orphanage staff were fired, the buildings were repaired and cleaned, and the children's clothes were mended and washed. At the end of May, Esther White wrote: 'We think in time it will be nearly as good an orphanage as Mogutovo was'.

A few months later, the Quakers counted up the changes for the better which had taken place in the Monastery house:

The total number of inmates now is 122, all being either feeble or under 14 years. We now have a staff of 7 persons, including a young doctor who is a Magyar prisoner. In addition there are 13 female servants, washerwomen etc., and two farm and garden hands, and three skilled tradesmen teaching in the new industrial workshops.

The buildings, consisting of four wooden houses, are cramped and inconvenient for so large a number of people, but the number of critical urgent cases is very large even in this Government of comparative plenty.

We are lucky in having a pretty situation for the House and several small acres of arable land which has been laid out in potatoes and other vegetables and proved a very useful and healthy form of instruction for the children. They have worked under the charge of a young Polish agricultural student from Warsaw, taking alternate weeks on the garden and in the workshops. The diet has been altered and augmented. Twenty-two of the children under six years of age receive special care. In the place of sad and dirty little waifs who seemed to belong to know one [sic], one is now met by a cheerful little gang of 'everybody's babies' who are clean and healthy and certainly very greatly changed in two months.

With the aid of remnants of English clothes from Mogutovo, a not unwelcome variety has been introduced into the dresses of the girls and babies. An unrelieved sea of cheap grey cotton print such as is distributed wholesale by what was the Tatihana [sic] Committee must be as uninspiring to the wearer as it is depressing to the visitor.

In the prosperous times the Russian Committee had provided all the children with boots, but by now they were in rags: and walking barefoot on a farm which grows an exceptional lot of mosquitoes is not by any means a pleasant job.

Now all are properly booted. The tailoring shop has been very busy and has practically clothed the Home. The carpenters have had their hands full with the urgent repairs to the premises and have also constructed a new form of beehive, new in these parts. We have two beehives and the children get practical demonstrations and instructions in bee keeping.

When the English Mission took over this Home the children were undoubtedly in moral and physical distress.

The diet had become poor and the children had been made sour and suspicious by a well-grounded distrust of the intentions of the administration. They did not want to work, and what was worse they did not want to play either. No chance visitor could fail to notice this saddest symptom of all, that, although the weather would be most inviting, and the grounds around the House attractive, yet scarcely a child is playing a game. The little ones grub about in the dust unheeded, and the older boys are sitting in groups like old men.

It is not easy to estimate the change in the spirit of these children, but games and laughter are certainly the rule now. An open smile is quickly replacing that old bow that used to send a shiver down the back of anyone who loves children.

Punishments are becoming rare, and these young victims

*of the war are becoming less like the proverbial 'orphan'
and more like children with the hope of life before them.*[42]

Gregory Welch supervised work in the joinery
workshops in both the children's home and in
Buzuluk. Boys also travelled from Mogutovo and
Andreevka to the boys' workshops in Buzuluk.

In May 1918, the Quakers decided to ask the
Buzuluk Soviet for identity papers for every
member of the Quaker mission. The Council
issued certificates which stated that 'The Society of
Friends has worked and is working to help refugees
and the population affected by undernourishment
and hunger' and that 'all government and public
institutions and officials will be pleased to provide
appropriate assistance'. They were received by
everyone in the Quaker mission on 24 May 1918,
and one of them, as we saw above, is still kept at
the museum in the English town of Dorking.[43]

On the eve of the civil war, the Quakers in Russia
were very optimistic and full of plans. For example,
at the May meeting[44] of the mission workers,
American Quaker Anna Haines was asked to take
over the role of the head of all Quaker work to help
refugees in Buzuluk and its district. Miss Zhukova
(the interpreter) was asked to go on short break
to the dacha (yes, the Quakers actually rented a

---

[42]AFSC archives.
[43]<https://www.dorkingmuseum.org.uk/dorking-friends-in-action/
john-rickmans-russian-certificate-of-identity-dorking-quakers/>
[44]Meeting of Workers in Buzuluk, May 20, 1918. Friends House
London archives. YM/MfS/FEWVRC/MISSIONS/7/1/2/

summer house near Buzuluk!) and then to find out about the living conditions of the refugee children from the Mogutovo home who had been transferred to live in villages. The meeting asked Theodore Rigg to go to Petrograd in order to receive £3250 (this is equivalent to £180,000 in today's money – a huge amount!) which had been sent from London to the British consulate so that diplomats could transfer the money. Once again, the Quakers tried to get the first Russian Quaker interested in their work: it was decided to ask Theodore Rigg and Dr Pearson to talk to Olga Tolstaya in Moscow, to see if she wanted to get involved with the Quakers' work to relocate refugees. Dr Rickman suggested asking the London Quaker Committee to send a small group of people to Buzuluk district who would be willing to settle in a few of the villages where the Quakers had worked over the last two years. The idea was that the new settlers could help community life in the villages. A firm belief was expressed that the Quaker mission's work had prepared the ground for the arrival of such a group of people, who could be considered as Quaker Embassy staff in this part of Russia.

The Buzuluk paper reports that at the general meeting of delegates of the District Council of Refugees on 9 April 1918 there was talk of opening workshops for refugees in Buzuluk, and that the Quakers were ready to help: 'There are almost no costs for the workshops, as the carpenter's and shoemaker's workshops are given free of charge and with all equipment, and initially the English mission is providing the materials too, as well as the equipment. The meeting only has to decide whether to permit these workshops to open or not'.[45] An advert was posted: 'The English committee "Society of Friends" hopes to buy several good bicycles for men and women. Please contact the secretary at 27 Orenburgskaya Ulitsa, Buzuluk". The Quakers clearly intended to stay in Buzuluk district for a long time, and ultimately to set up a Quaker embassy. Spring 1918 was a spring of hope and plans.

[45] *News from Buzuluk District's Executive Committee of the Soviet of Workers' and Peasants' deputies*, issue no.85, 26 April 1918.

Chapter 3. *Problems receiving funding from abroad due to instability in Russia. Soldiers of the Czechoslovak Legion enter Buzuluk. The head of the Quaker mission travels to Petrograd to get money. A journey through the frontline with a bag of money. The Quaker mission splits in two: two workers go to Moscow to work in children's residential centres (colonies) in the provinces, while the remaining workers of the Anglo-American mission leave Buzuluk and head eastwards.*

In mid-May 1918, the head of the Quaker mission in Buzuluk, Theodore Rigg, set off for Moscow, which had already become the capital of Soviet Russia by that time. His diary contains numerous details of trips and reads like an adventure novel: 'At a recent meeting of the executive of our Unit, it was decided to send me to Moscow to obtain a large sum in Russian currency. The banks are not functioning in a normal way and apparently it is not possible for the Committee in London to transfer sterling to Russia. It is imperative that we obtain a considerable sum of roubles to meet the costs of the Buzuluk work and to provide every member of our party with a reserve fund so that in case of our evacuation of Buzuluk, each member would be able to pay travel expenses across Siberia to Vladivostok and thence to the USA. I was pleased to obtain a change from Buzuluk as I have been tied rather closely to my secretarial duties ever since Robert Tatlock left Buzuluk over six months ago'.[46]

Rigg did not travel alone from Buzuluk: Dr
Pearson, Richard Ball and Margaret Barber
went with him to Moscow. Dr Pearson intended
to inspect the living conditions of refugees in
Orsha district[47], and then go to England. The two
others wanted to join the staff of the American
Committee for the Independence of Armenia
(ACIA), subsequently renamed the Armenian
National Committee of America. Rigg, who had
stayed in Moscow, received funds in pounds,
and converted them into 250,000 roubles with
the help of the British consulate. It was quite a
brave decision to convert hard currency into
local money in those days of general uncertainty!
Rigg wrote that half the sum was in the form of
a cheque from a well-known bank in Omsk, and
the rest was handed over to him in cash in various
denominations, from 10-rouble to 1000-rouble
banknotes. While he was still in Moscow, Rigg
found out about the revolt of the Czechoslovak
Legion, and shortly later about the capture of
Samara by Czechoslovaks and Cossacks. The
railway connection with Samara was suspended,
but the team in Buzuluk was waiting for Theodore
Rigg and the delivery of money.

---

[46] Theodore Rigg, *Experiences of a Relief Worker of the Society of Friends*
during the First World War. Published by Christchurch Monthly
Meeting. 1976.

[47] Orshansky Ooezd was one of the districts of the Mogilev
Governorate of the Russian Empire. It was situated in the northern
part of the governorate, and its administrative centre was Orsha.

Rigg recalled, 'I decided to go anyway. I obtained certificates from the British Consulate for use in Czech-held territory and another certificate from the Russian Minister of External Affairs for use in Soviet territory. Naturally I did not mention to anyone that I proposed to carry £5,000 worth of bank drafts and Russian currency with me'.[48]

Theodore Rigg describes in detail his journey through the frontline with an enormous sum of money in his book *Experiences of a Relief Worker of the Society of Friends during the First World War.* A tall foreigner with hesitant Russian must have stood out like a sore thumb in provincial Russia and been a magnet for bandits, of whom there was no shortage at the time. He himself described his adventures in an understated way: 'We all spent an uncomfortable two or three hours while passengers were examined and luggage inspected for concealed papers and money. Some passengers were recognised as counter-revolutionaries and were taken off the barge and in one or two cases shot out-of-hand. I was lucky. My certificate from G. Chicherin[49] held good and my baggage received only superficial examination'. Fate spared Theodore Rigg: he reached Buzuluk safe and sound, with all the money tucked inside his

---

[48] Theodore Rigg, *Experiences of a Relief Worker of the Society of Friends during the First World War.* Published by Christchurch Monthly Meeting. 1976.
[49] Georgy Vasilyevich Chicherin (24 November 1872 – 7 July 1936), a Soviet politician who served as the first People's Commissar for Foreign Affairs in the Soviet government from March 1918 to July 1930.

coat. He wrote: 'It was a great relief to me to find that all the members of the Buzuluk party were safe and that no member of the party had been injured during the shelling of the town and its occupation by Czech and Cossack soldiers'.[50]

On 1 July 1918 Theodore Rigg recounted his trip to Moscow and back at a meeting of the Quaker workers. It is interesting to note that apart from Rigg's report and the other workers' presentations on their work in Vorontsovka, Andreevka and Buzuluk, the minutes of the meeting record the following: 'It was decided to ask the London Committee to forward to Russia at the first opportunity 250 yards of a suitable brown cloth for making uniform for the members of the Unit'.[51]

John and Lydia Rickman, who had got married in Buzuluk in March that year, left the town on 7 July 1918 and headed eastwards, intending to travel to England via the United States. Theodore Rigg wrote[52] to Ruth Fry in London on 8 July 1918 of his belief that the majority of Quaker workers would be willing to stay in Buzuluk for one more winter, if absolutely necessary. However, they were not in a position at that time to delegate workers to travel to Siberia, in deepest Russia, to see the refugee situation with their own eyes. Furthermore, wrote Theodore Rigg, American

---

[50] The Czechoslovaks took Buzuluk on 26 June 1918.
[51] Meeting of Workers in Buzuluk, July 1, 1918. Friends House London archives. YM/MfS/FEWVRC/MISSIONS/7/1/2/
[52] Ibid.

worker Esther White and he were both leaving for Moscow. The Buzuluk Quakers had released them when he told them about the probability of famine in the residential centres for the Moscow children who had previously been sent to the provinces of Tambov and Voronezh, as we will see below.

During his trip to Moscow over May and June 1918, Theodore Rigg had realised that the coming winter looked very bleak for the residents of Moscow, the new Russian capital. There were shortages of everything: food, fuel and clothing. Theodore Rigg had met members of the Pirogov Society, one of the groups close to the Tolstoyans. Through them, he found out about four summer colonies where around three hundred children were living. Since there was such a lack of food in cities, people tried to send their children away to the countryside, to be nearer to agricultural production. In those years, this sort of settlement was called a 'colony', a residential centre. Members of the Pirogov Society, the 'Pirogovtsy', had organised centres like this with the help of the Voronezh and Tambov provincial authorities, but then the Pirogovtsy ran into financial problems. However, they knew that it was unwise to send the children back to Moscow as a harsh winter approached. The Pirogov Society had therefore contacted the Quakers to ask them to take on the burden of running the residential centres for the next six months.

All the Quaker workers in Buzuluk supported the

idea of helping the children in residential centres. Two of the various options considered were working with the State Committee for Helping Hungry Children, or transferring the Moscovite children to Samara province. Theodore Rigg informed Ruth Fry about this in the letter[53] which he sent to London with the Rickmans. It was decided that, as a first step for working on this project, it would be sensible to send two members of the Quaker mission to 'reccy' the situation in Moscow and in the four residential centres. The mission decided that two people should be sent on the reconnaissance trip: one who was a good organiser and one with experience of working in a children's home. The two people chosen were Theodore Rigg, who had just returned from a trip to Moscow and still had valid papers from the Soviet authorities with whom he had had quite recent contact in Moscow, and Esther White.

They set off from Buzuluk for Samara on 14 July 1918. The Quaker mission's financial situation was good at this point, following Rigg's delivery of funds. He himself suggested that soon, within four months, the situation in the country would change for the better, and then it would become possible to bring the Moscovite children to Buzuluk district. On his departure – so Theodore Rigg wrote to Ruth Fry in London – he advised his colleagues to take the opportunity to relax, so that they would have renewed energy for working in the children's homes if the starving Moscovite children ended up being

[53] Rigg's correspondence with Fry. Friends House London archives. YM/MfS/FEWVRC/MISSIONS/7/1/2.

brought to Buzuluk district. These plans were not destined to come to pass. The civil war flared up and battles were fought over vast swathes of land. Rigg and White became cut off from Buzuluk and never managed to get back there. It dawned on the Buzuluk staff that it was time to leave. For them, the way out was in only one direction: to the east.

For the time being, however, the whole staff of the Quaker mission stayed in Buzuluk. They were now organising daily meals at the soup kitchens for around 500 of the refugees living in the town. Later on, the Quakers wrote in their report: 'The soup is prepared by four refugee women assisted by a boy who carries water, attends to fires etc. this kitchen staff, except the cook, is changed every week in order to give more women a chance of earning a little money. We are feeding only people over 50 years of age or under 14. Five times a week soup is made from potatoes, millet and buckwheat. Twice a week milk soup is made from milk given, coinciding with the fast days. This soup is much appreciated and already the people seem better for having one certain meal a day. The old people are particularly pleased and many of them enjoy coming themselves to take it away. Our soup kitchen is now supplying 412 people, shortly to be increased to about 500 from the poorer town refugees, unless the re-opening of the railway to Samara makes it unnecessary. Actual cost per meal – 19 kopecks'.[54]

---

[54] AFSC archives.

Gradually, similar soup kitchens were opened in the villages along the railway line, and the Quakers opened a job centre – a Labour Bureau for Refugees – to find them employment. Interestingly, the report[55] on the job centre, entitled 'Forest Work', states: "Our workers who have been running the soup kitchens so successfully for the last two months in Buzuluk and outlying villages have constantly been struck by the claim on the part of the refugees that they have no work and cannot get it. Considering the abundant hay-crop there has been this summer and the splendid harvest in process of being reaped just now one is surprised to hear that the able-bodied men and women cannot find work, more especially when farmers cry everywhere is that the labour is scarce. It was with the object of finding suitable work for unemployed refugees that our Labour Bureau was started; so far our work for men has been almost exclusively forest work of one kind or another". There were not enough people to do logging in the nearby forests. Working parties were formed with the Labour Bureau's help. The labourers would reach the woods by train and be led by one of the Quaker mission staff. However, the same report explains that the complaints about unemployment were spurious, as there were far fewer responses to the job advert than there were vacancies. For example, when there was a request to send 23 labourers to work in Koltubanka, only 17 of the refugees turned up. Only eight people

---

[55] Report on the Labour Bureau for refugees. Forest Work. AFSC archives.

turned up to work in Rogozhinskoe forest rather than the ten who had been requested. By 10 August 1918, the Quakers had managed to get only 40 people to work, i.e., 25% of those who had promised to turn up. This was even though the Quakers were paying wages: 15 roubles a day for carpenters and 10-12 roubles a day for labourers, according to the report.

By the end of the summer, the Quakers who had stayed in Buzuluk, which was now occupied by the Czechoslovaks, began to feel shut off from the world. The money which Rigg had brought from Moscow no longer looked to be enough for future work. The Quakers sent Hinman Baker to Samara, where the Komuch[56] (Committee of Members of the Constituent Assembly) authorities had their capital, to find out what was going on in the world outside Buzuluk. He managed to talk to American consulate staff there who were rushing to pack their bags to leave. Nonetheless, American consul in Samara, Willoughby Smith, transferred $20,000 to Baker. Smith would later report in America that 'the [Quaker] workers were all well'.[57]

The American diplomats kept advising Hinman Baker to tell the Quakers to leave too. It was no

[56] The Committee of Members of the Constituent Assembly (Komuch) was an anti-Bolshevik government that operated in Samara, Russia, during the Russian Civil War of 1917-1922. It was formed on June 8, 1918, after the Czechoslovak Legion had occupied the city.
[57] Report by the AFSC Russian Committee, signed by Henry Cadbury on 21 November 1918. AFSC archives.

secret that the Czechoslovak Legion had no desire to hold the line of defence along the Volga river. The consulate staff believed that nothing good would come out of meeting with the Bolsheviks due to the Bolsheviks' animosity towards the Americans and British. After long, earnest discussions, the Quakers reached the decision that they should go. They disliked the very thought of leaving the town which had come to feel like home, the district where they had spent two years. They left a group at a time.

The last group of Quakers to leave Buzuluk on 4 October 1918 consisted of Anna Haines, Emily Bradbury, Hinman Baker and Jack Catchpool. They took the last train heading east as the Bolsheviks got closer and closer to Buzuluk.

The Quakers were in no hurry to leave Russia. Even as they travelled eastwards, they were willing to stop on the way to strive to improve the lives of refugees they encountered.

For instance, Gregory Welch and Charles Colles helped around 400 children from Petrograd who had been stranded away from home by the civil war. The two Englishmen looked after these children at a colony in Turgoyak[58] and then took them all the way to Vladivostok. The Russian children then completed their trip around the world, getting back to their hometown of Petrograd in 1920, and would never forget their English caregivers. One of the young people from

[58] A village in the South Urals.

Petrograd, Pyotr Alexandrov, wrote in his diary: 'Because of the poor-quality food and constant malnutrition, my body was covered with ulcers and boils which wouldn't heal. Gregory Welch noticed my suffering. He took me by the hand and led me to the infirmary. Even now, many years later, I remember my relief and joy when my 22 wounds were treated with zinc ointment and wrapped in clean bandages. God bless the memory of these people!'[59]

Anna Haines, Nancy Babb, Emily Bradbury and Hinman Baker stayed in Omsk to work with refugees. However, their work also came to an end. Almost all the members of the Quaker mission had gone home, safe and sound, having survived adventures and overcome difficulties, by the end of 1918.

---

[59] <http://colonia.spb.ru/archivs.htm>

Chapter 4. *Theodore Rigg from England and Esther White from America doing Quaker work in Bolshevik Moscow. Cooperating with the Pirogov Society. Cooperating with Soviet officials: 'At a time when many British and French officials had been sent to prison, these two foreigners were able to move around completely freely, whether in the city or in the countryside'. 60 A work trip to Tambov and Voronezh provinces. Working with children in four colonies (residential centres). Quaker mission staff leave Soviet Russia via Vladivostok.*

Theodore Rigg and Esther White were due to set off from Buzuluk to Moscow on 14 July 1918. Earlier the same day, Howard Hadley, the former American consul in Tbilisi, arrived in Buzuluk, passing through on his journey from Orenburg. He wanted to see the American staff of the Quaker mission on his way to Samara. As Hadley was a high-ranking official, a private carriage awaited him at Buzuluk railway station, provided by the ataman of the Cossacks, Alexander Dutov. Hadley invited Rigg and White to travel to Samara in his private carriage.

The Quakers who were staying behind in Buzuluk saw them off. They were all quite sure that they would see Rigg and White again around six weeks later. In the event, though, they would never see them again.

As soon as they arrived in Samara, Howard Hadley

---

[60] Richenda Scott, *Quakers in Russia*, p. 210.

gave White and Rigg certificates which, he believed, would protect them as they crossed the frontline. At the time, the frontline was to the south of Simbirsk[61]. These papers were only valid, though, on territory where there were no Reds. Fortunately, Rigg realised it was vital to make sure no Bolshevik commissars spotted the certificates.

Rigg and White met the American consul in Samara, Mr Williams; the representative of the American YMCA, Mr Christie; and the Czechoslovak commander of the city. They all thought the two Quakers were crazy: just as the Allies (the British and French) were leaving Moscow, these two were trying to reach Moscow! Their extreme adventures would appeal to any author – crossing the frontline and travelling to Moscow despite being foreigners with poor Russian. They spent sleepless nights on board a barge, then on overcrowded steamboats to Kazan and on to Nizhny Novgorod. Once there, the two Quakers got on the train to Moscow.

In the new capital of Soviet Russia, they settled at the house of Lev Tolstoy's son Sergei, at 15 Bolshoi Levshinskii Pereulok (Lane). This was a stroke of luck: the Tolstoy family was not subjected to countless searches. The Quakers explained this exception by the great respect that all Russians felt for Sergei's father, Lev Tolstoy. Whatever the reason, Rigg and White were spared searches by the secret police, the Cheka, while they were resident at the Tolstoys' home.

[61] [Translator's note: Simbirsk would be renamed Ulyanovsk in 1924. It was Lenin's birthplace.]

Given the general turmoil and the fact that Western countries were intervening, the two foreigners might have expected to encounter great suspicion on the part of the Soviet commissars. However, that was not their experience. The Russian People's Commissar for Foreign Affairs, G. Chicherin, willingly gave them documents encouraging the military and civil authorities to give them with every assistance in their work with starving children. The Soviet People's Commissar for Social Security was delighted to agree to help the foreigners and handed over the running of the four children's colonies to them. As Richenda Scott put it in her book *Quakers in Russia*, 'At a time when many British and French officials had been sent to prison, these two foreigners were able to move around completely freely, whether in the city or in the countryside'.

The two Quakers therefore decided to take up the cause of the children living in the four colonies the Pirogovtsy had told them about. They needed to visit the centres and see what was going on there, what resources were available on the ground and what options there were for helping, in order to work out what they would be able to do. Rigg and White set off for the centre in Anna (Voronezh province), and then went to Znamenka, Vorontsovka and Bezobrazovo, in Tambov province. Late autumn in the depth of Russia made an unforgettable impression on the two foreigners, Esther White from America and Theodore Rigg, a Yorkshire man originally from

New Zealand. Once back home, Esther White would later recount her journeys in 1918 in a booklet entitled *Mission to Moscow: The Experiences of Two Relief Workers in the First World War.*[62] It recounts many details of everyday life and how they managed to help 400 children from two Russian provinces safely get through the winter amid the devastation and horror of 1918.

Once they had got back to Moscow from the trip to inspect the colonies, Theodore Rigg and Esther White produced a report about what they had seen and sent it to the Commissariat for Social Security. Now that many members of the Pirogov Society were in prison or on the run, the Pirogovtsy were not in a position to give any support at all. The Soviet authorities, meanwhile, had neither the money nor staff for continuing work in the children's residential centres. For this reason, they were very keen for the Society of Friends to take on all the trouble of looking after the four colonies, at least until 31 March 1919. The two Quaker representatives therefore signed an agreement with the Department of Social Security, according to which the department promised to provide sheets, blankets, towels and winter clothing to three colonies so that children could stay there over the winter. The most important articles of the agreement were the following:

---

[62] *Mission to Moscow: the Experiences of Two Relief Workers in the First World War.* Published by Walter S. Metcalf for Christchurch Monthly Meeting of the Society of Friends, New Zealand. 1976

1) The Soviet Department of Social Security will transfer the organisation and administration of three colonies located at Voronsofka, Znamenka and Bezobrazova to the representatives of the Society of Friends until the 31st March, 1919. The fourth colony, situated at Anna, will be brought back to Moscow and the children distributed to different orphanages where room was available.

2) The Soviet Department will provide linen, blankets, towels, and winter clothing for all children in the colonies and will pay the sum of 100,000 roubles for repairs and reconstruction of buildings in the three colonies to be continued during the winter, and in addition pay a basic charge of 70 roubles per head per month for the children and staff at the colonies.

3) The representatives of the Society of Friends will undertake the organisation of the colonies for the winter; the reconstruction of sanitary and washing facilities; the purchase of foodstuffs; the establishment of school classes and handicraft work for the children, and the administration of the colonies until March 31st, 1919.

4) The representatives of the Society of Friends agree to make available statements of all expenditure in connection with the work of the colonies; to pay out of their own funds the salaries of all members of the staff at the three colonies, and in addition to pay all expenditure in excess of the amounts mentioned in paragraph 2.[63]

The two Quakers took upon themselves the tasks of supervising the work, arranging classes for the children, paying money from the Quaker

---

[63] Ibid, pp. 32-33.

mission's funds for the salaries of the Russian staff at the colonies, and covering other expenses if they exceeded the 70 roubles per person which the Soviet authorities had already paid out.

A race against time began, as it was crucial to do everything essential and buy everything necessary before winter set in. The Quakers opened the office of the Society of Friends, as they were called in negotiations with the Soviets, at the following address in Moscow: Bolshaya Nikitskaya Ulitsa (Street), Bryusovsky Pereulok (Lane), building 1, flat 5. Mikhail Khorosh, the former secretary of the Pirogov Society, was appointed to run the office. He was responsible for continuing negotiations with the Department of Social Security, and for receiving and transferring the materials the Department provided. Esther White wrote in a letter on 2 October 1918 addressed to Doctor Pearson, her colleague in Buzuluk: 'We have an office here in Moscow now on Brusovsky Street off the Bolshoy Nikitskaya St. [sic] and I come here every day from 10 to 2.30 to interview would-be teachers and bosspitatelnitsas [sic: caregivers] and to try to keep an eye on Horresh. Mr Rigg has already left for the colonies to begin repairs on buildings and the buying up of winter stores. I shall follow within two or three weeks'.[64] White was responsible for selecting new staff to add to those already in post. She also supervised the distribution of clothing and bedlinen among the three residential centres. Theodore Rigg

---

[64] AFSC archives.

made several trips to the colonies to check that the repairs and reconstruction work were going to plan. In addition, he arranged for grocery deliveries to the colonies, firewood and kerosene for the whole winter.

Theodore Rigg and Esther White left Moscow for one of the colonies at the end of November 1918, when it was already bitterly cold. They spent the next two months – December 1918 and January 1919 – on the Zagryazhskie-Stroganovy estate on the outskirts of the village of Znamenka, where one of the colonies was located.

In January 1919, Rigg and White began to discuss the possibility of going home. A trip to Moscow in the middle of winter seemed a risky undertaking to the foreigners in their current state of health, vitamin deficiency and lack of strength. Nonetheless, they decided to attempt it at the end of the month. Esther White wrote: 'We, ourselves, were in a weakened physical condition as a result of the privations and anxiety which we had experienced during the past six months. We knew that if either of us got seriously ill, there would be little hope of recovery under the conditions then prevailing in Russia. There was a great dearth of essential medicines and soap was a rarity'.[65] With the bare minimum of luggage and enough food for three days, they said goodbye to the children and set off for Moscow. To their

[65] *Mission to Moscow: the Experiences of Two Relief Workers in the First World War.* Published by Walter S. Metcalf for Christchurch Monthly Meeting of the Society of Friends, New Zealand. 1976.

surprise, the journey from the colony to Moscow took them 40 hours but was without incident. When they reached Moscow, the two foreigners again enjoyed the Tolstoys' hospitality. Indeed, they would stay with the Tolstoy family right up until they left Russia.

They had a lot to do while in the capital.

Firstly, they needed to work out how to leave Russia. They went to the Swedish consulate, which kept their money for them. The consul told the Quakers about the state of play at the fronts and told them about Finland's declaration of independence. He also said that French citizens were authorised to leave Russia on a special train which went to Beloostrov, formerly a suburb of Petrograd and now a border town – on the border between Soviet Russia and the recently formed country of Finland. When they found out about this, the two Quakers went to meet the French officials who were responsible for organising the evacuation by train, saying they would like to join them as soon as they had received the necessary permits from the Soviet authorities. Rigg and White now had to obtain these papers. The Commissar for Foreign Affairs had no objection, and the Quakers gave him their passports, along with the forms they had filled out for getting their exit visas.

Secondly, Rigg and White went to the Commissar for Social Security to hand over all their responsibilities formally to their Russian secretary, Mr Khorosh, for the remaining period that had been agreed to, until 31 March 1919. The Commissar did not object either. He expressed his grateful thanks to the two foreigners for their work and his regret that they had decided to leave. Mikhail Khorosh participated fully in all these administrative matters – he was an experienced person, who could overcome all obstacles in his way. At the same time, his own interest in the work with the children's colonies gave the Quakers the confidence that he would succeed. Reading Rigg and White's memoirs, it is evident that they wanted to justify somehow their desire to leave Russia a few months before the agreement with the Soviet authorities expired. We can quite understand, though, and they probably made the right decision: you could hardly call life in Russia calm in 1919, even in Moscow. Esther White wrote: 'At last all our business was completed. We had made the necessary financial arrangements for the continuance of the colonies under the administration of the Society of Friends until the 31st March and had appointed M. Horosh as our agent. We had obtained our passport visas and were ready to leave Moscow'.[66]

It took two days for the train to reach Beloostrov from Moscow. All the passengers on this unusual means of transport were foreigners, including

[66] *Mission to Moscow: the Experiences of Two Relief Workers in the First World War.* Published by Walter S. Metcalf for Christchurch Monthly Meeting of the Society of Friends, New Zealand. 1976.

Theodore Rigg, the British man from New Zealand, and Esther White, who was American. After leaving Moscow on 10 February, the train reached the border on 12 February. At that point, all the passengers left their seats and walked onto the bridge across the river Sestra. The most dramatic episode of the two Quakers' journey is described in Esther's diary: 'At last all was ready for our transference to Finnish territory. The Soviet Commissar with his guards stood at the Russian end of a bridge over the small river at Belo-Ostrov. At the other end of the bridge was the Finnish Commandant with a small detachment of soldiers. A list had been prepared setting out in alphabetical order the names of the party. One by one our names were called; our passports were handed to us and we walked across the bridge into Finnish territory. Although there may have been inward rejoicing there was complete silence until the last traveller was passed across the bridge. Fortunately for E.M.W. and T.R., their names followed fairly closely one another but for both of them, particularly for T.R. who was called first, it was a period of great suspense until E.M.W. was passed across the bridge. With the last member of our party safely on Finnish soil, there was general rejoicing – smiles, congratulations and jokes were the order of the day. We were free at last of the misery and privations of life in Soviet Russia and could look forward to happy days in the future.

'Of course, we all underwent examination by the Finnish administration of this frontier town. For most of us the inspection was superficial – we were only in transit through Finland. Very soon we were ushered into two railway carriages standing on the Finnish side of the frontier and shortly commenced our somewhat round-about journey to Abo – a Finnish port with summer connections to Stockholm'.[67]

And so the work of the Quaker mission, begun in 1916, came to an end in 1919. The Quakers had been through a great deal: they had shared all the hardships of the Russian people themselves. They had looked after refugees, children and starving Russians as if they were their own family. They were driven by love for their neighbour, the Christian understanding of kindness, and the faith and practice of the Religious Society of Friends, for whom religion is not ceremonies and objects of worship, but how you live your life and how you help your neighbour. For them, faith meant love and peace.

The first Quaker mission in Russia is not just interesting for historical reasons – it also has lessons for us today. The country the Friends arrived in and the country they left were totally different. We can see how the honesty and sincerity of their intentions and their tireless work for suffering people led both Tsarist officials and Bolshevik comrades to treat them with respect and courtesy. I believe these Quakers demonstrated one of the Quaker truths: that openness, integrity and

---

[67] Ibid.

love for one's neighbour can open all doors and circumvent all obstacles. The short-lived English mission in Buzuluk and the surrounding villages left behind warm memories, and the same warm feelings were felt by the mission's staff towards the Russian people whom they had helped during such hard years.

No wonder that once his mission was over, Theodore Rigg would discuss the possibility of opening a 'Quaker embassy' in Russia – but not the sort of embassy where diplomats work. What he had in mind was a small Quaker unit whose workers would come alongside Russian peasants to help them to develop their agriculture and improve public health. And the place that Rigg suggested for this 'embassy' was Buzuluk and the local district. In May 1918, he wrote to Ruth Fry: 'The Buzuluk district seems to be a particular[ly] favourable place for the establishment of a Quaker Embassy for in several of the southern volosts we have groups of Russian peasants who call themselves the name of Quakers and others who are Tolstoyans. The Patrovka volost in particular has groups of peasants who go by the name of Quakers and Tolstoyans. One intelligent Friend established in any of the southern villages could do incalculable good in raising the ideals and the standard of life of these Russian peasants. However, such work could not be done unless the group of people who were desirous of undertaking service in Russia were prepared to spend several years here.

'The villages of Loobimofka, Andriefka or Mogutovo will be long remembered in the hearts of the peasants with gratitude and love for the work of the English mission. A group of English or American Friends imbued with the right spirit of service and variously trained in handicrafts such as farming, carpentry, mechanical engineering, hygiene or nursing could all contribute immensely to the communal life of these Russian villages. Their work would follow naturally that of a more temporary nature which the present Unit has just completed'.[68]

In 1919, the Friends' War Victims' Relief Committee in London published a booklet entitled *Where and how we have helped*.[69] It presented a succinct account, over a few pages, of what the Quakers had done in Buzuluk district over the last two years:

'Our centres and the different ways in which the refugees and the peasants have been helped at each of them at one time or another are shown below. In addition, individual members have made expeditions for special work, to Moscow, Siberia and the German frontier districts.

---

[68] Rigg's correspondence with Fry, May 1918. Friends House London archives. YM/MfS/FEWVRC/MISSIONS/7/1/2
[69] *Where and how we have helped*, FWVRC, Headley Bros, 1919.
[Translator's note: Village names spelt as in the booklet.]

Buzuluk.

Agricultural town of 20,000 inhabitants. Centre of the Department; at the junction of the river Samara and the river Buzuluk. Main railway line station a mile and a half away.

Office and headquarters of the Mission.

Central stores depot.

Monastery refugee home and orphanage.

Large central workrooms.

Home employment given to the surrounding villages.

Mogutovo.

A village near the forest surrounded by other small villages. A disused country house here lent by the Zemstvo was the starting point of all the work. It is as far to the North-west of Buzuluk as Andreyefka is to the South (forty miles), but for travelling purposes as far from it

Home for 150 refugees from all centres.

Out-patient department, dispensary, and hospital with ten beds.

Relief and clothing distributed here and in surrounding villages.

Boys trained in carpentry and gardening.

as Aberdeen from London.

Home employment extended to surrounding villages.

School with four graded classes.

Evening classes for older girls.

Andreyefka.

Forty miles south of Buzuluk, along the River Buzuluk. Centre of a population of 60,000 with a weekly market. Beyond the hospital buildings at the end of the village the steppe stretches away covered with a grey-green growth. There is a compound on one side of which is the hospital, on another the living quarters of workers, and on another the block in which relief

Russian hospital re-opened.

Out-patient department (100 clients a day).

Two in-patient wards (twenty beds).

Urgent calls for doctors often answered from places up to forty miles distant.

Residence for workers on famine relief.

Potato fields cultivated.

Classes for children.

Carpentry and

work was done. A small house was taken, for famine workers to call at, and for a worker [to] live in while rebuilding the relief work, which had been burnt down.

shoemaking classes for boys.

Circulating library.

Stocking knitting, home spinning, wool cleaning and embroidery.

Disused house used as a weaving-room.

Efimofka.

A village eight miles further south of Andreyefka, further up the River Buzuluk. Rooms in peasant houses had to be used both for dispensary and workroom. Two women workers were here alone throughout one winter.

District nursing centre with trained nurse.

Dispensary open daily, and weekly visit from doctor.

Relief workrooms, weaving and spinning.

Carpet-weaving and knitting.

Clothing and relief distribution.

Lyubimofka.

A straggling wind-swept town of 4,000 inhabitants among low undulating hills, treeless and fenceless. Twenty-five miles south-east of Andreyefka, across the angle made by the river where it turns to the East. First and most complete medical centre. The hospital is just outside the village and the relief workers had two houses in the village.

Russian hospital re-opened.

Out-patient department and dispensary.

Weaving and spinning in room formerly used as village tea-room.

Home knitting.

Wool-picking.

Circulating library.

Clothing and felt boots distributed to outlying villages.

Bogdanofka.

A low straggling village between low-lying hills, twelve miles further east than Lyubimofka, on a northern tributary of the river Buzuluk. Much disease among refugees.

District nursing centre with trained nurses.

Dispensary open daily.

Weekly visits from Lyubimofka doctor.

Weaving and spinning rooms in peasant's home and old volost buildings.

String and rope-making, stocking and glove-making and embroidery.

Clothing and felt boots distributed in outlying villages.

Circulating library.

Preobrazhenka.

Near Bogdanofka, and like it, an outpost of Lyubimofka.

Workroom for fifty people.

Lobazi.

A small village half-way between Buzuluk and Andreyefka. A woman relief worker spent five winter months in a peasant's hut here.

Three large relief workrooms.

Weaving and spinning.

Distribution of clothing in surrounding villages.

Circulating library.

On the last page of the booklet, a letter of thanks from the residents of the village of Bogdanovka was published, translated into English. It read: 'Fathers and Mothers do not take care of us as do the English doctors and sisters. They are so tender and delicate. Your kind manners with all us Russians who are used only to rough ways […] make us love you at once and regard you as our real friends. Our people in Bogdanofka as well as the refugees who are banished from their own homes will remember you always. We Russian people give you our hearty Russian thanks'.

As it turned out, the Quakers would come back to Russia the following year.

Part II

1919 — 1931

*

Chapter 5. *The Quakers attempt to return to the Russian Soviet Federative Socialist Republic.[70] Quaker humanitarian relief work to Moscow. Two Quakers in the capital city. The idea of a 'Quaker embassy'. What would it be for? A Communist Quaker relief worker. Welch and Watts: English Quakers with contrasting points of view. Meetings with the Tolstoyans. Anna Haines, an American Quaker, came to replace Welch. Meetings with Chicherin and Lunacharsky; Lenin's speech to the Congress. Attempts to increase the number of Quaker workers in Russia.*

The Russian Revolution and the Russian Civil War changed many aspects of people's lives and caused deep trauma. Many people perished; there was a change of the form of government; violence and cruelty became commonplace. Along with the destruction of people's usual way of life, there were related disasters: famine and disease. People suffered, as the innocent civilian population – children, elderly people and women – always does.

The end of the First World War and the Bolshevik revolution in Russia fixed the global plans of Allied

---

[70] [Translator's note: The Russian Soviet Federative Socialist Republic (RSFSR) was the official name of Soviet Russia from 1918 to 1922, when it became part of the Union of Soviet Socialist Republics. For convenience, Soviet Russia is the translation used in this book.]

countries for the post-war world order and how the world and the countries which had won – Russia's former allies – would decide their policies towards the new regime which had seized power in Russia. Henry Cadbury[71] wrote: 'Its [Russia's – S.N.] present lack of disinterested friends is notorious; and it is probable that in the future its material resources for reconstruction will be smallest and its need the greatest. […] From the late belligerents of one side or the other Belgium, France, Poland, Serbia, Syria, etc., will all receive material aid either as indemnity, charity, or loan. But Russia cannot even borrow money or buy relief".[72] The American authorities ceased to trade with Soviet Russia at the end of 1917, and Britain and France did the same in 1918. In October 1919 the governing body of the Anglo-French Entente Cordiale announced a total ban on any economic contact and links with Communists. However, the two Entente governments ended up lifting their trade blockade in January 1920, and that July, the US State Department loosened restrictions on trade with Moscow. New opportunities opened up.

The Quakers, who had looked with great hope at the first 'state of workers and peasants' in the world, sincerely believed that Russia was building a future society whose aims were entirely in tune with Quaker ideals. Besides, Friends of all eras have felt a close

---

[71] Henry Joel Cadbury (1 December 1883 - 7 October 1974) was an American theologian, Quaker historian, author and specialist in management in the non-profit sector.

[72] Report of the AFSC Russian Committee, 21 November 1918. AFSC FSR.

connection with the pain and suffering of innocent people. When American Quakers found out that the bans had been lifted, they applied immediately for a permit to send a cargo of humanitarian aid to Russia, along with a few people who would check on the distribution of aid. The US State Department said that it 'would not place obstacles in the way of a shipment of humanitarian aid to Soviet Russia'.[73] Nonetheless, the American authorities emphasised the following: 'The representatives who are going to be sent [to Russia] ...must understand that they go at their own risk and cannot count on our government's protection while on Soviet territory'

Quaker bails with humanitarian aid at a warehouse

©The archives of the American Friends Service Committee

British Quaker representatives were the first members of the Society of Friends to go to Soviet

---

[73] David McFadden et al, *Constructive Spirit*, p.40.

Russia after the lifting of the trade blockade. The Friends War Victims Relief Committee, together with two other British charities, the Russian Babies' Fund and the Save the Children Fund, collected money and bought dry milk, fish oil, soap, rice, oats and medicine to send to Russia.

Richenda Scott, president of the Quaker Historical Society, wrote in her wonderful book *Quakers in Russia*[74] that Hinman Baker and Frank Shaw of the Society of Friends were sent to accompany the cargo of aid on its voyage across the seas, along with Mrs Haden Guest and Anatole Saxe from the Save the Children Fund. In Copenhagen they met up with Maxim Litvinov, a member of Soviet Russia's Collegium of the People's Commissariat for Foreign Affairs, and talked about their work to give aid to undernourished children. Litvinov said that many aid organisations were trying to come to Russia, each of them with their own staff, and so he recommended setting up a joint commission to coordinate their actions. Nevertheless, the two Quakers set off for Helsinki at their own risk, still hoping to get permission to enter Russia. In the end, they did indeed get permission, helped by Litvinov. Hinman Baker and Frank Shaw crossed the Finnish-Soviet border on 17 March 1920. They loaded their aid cargo – food and medicines – into freight cars at the border.

The first large city in which the Quakers arrived with their aid was Petrograd, Russia's former capital.

---

[74] Richenda Scott, *Quakers in Russia*. London, 1964, p.227.

They spent a few days there, meeting Bolshevik officials from the People's Commissariat for Labour, which was responsible for work with children. As a result of the negotiations, it was decided that the aid cargo would be distributed in children's hospitals and sanitoria (recuperation centres). Hinman Baker visited the institutions where the Quaker aid was being distributed, both in Petrograd and in the surrounding area, and found the conditions in these institutions to be entirely satisfactory. He later recalled that 'Everything I wished to see was shown to me, the better with the worse, and no preparation was made for my coming, for, in the main, the authorities had no previous notice of my visit till I was actually there'.[75]

Richenda Scott reports that Frank Shaw carried out a similar inspection of children's hospitals in Moscow, before returning to Petrograd to meet up with Hinman Baker. Numerous excursions were arranged for the foreigners to both medical and scientific establishments. They were shown around the Radiography and Radiology Institute (*Rentgenologicheskii i radiologicheskii institut*) by its founder and president, A. F. Ioffe, who had trained in Germany under Wilhelm Röntgen, the inventor of x-rays. This guided tour of such a leading scientific institution made a strong impression on the two Quakers. The medical staff who received food for starving children in Petrograd, told the Quaker volunteers: 'Come again, we want you and

---

[75] Ibid.

we want missionaries from you Friends'.[76]

In Moscow, Baker and Shaw met the People's Commissar for Public Health, Nikolai Alexandrovich Semashko, who suggested they discuss a scheme for distributing the goods brought over from Britain. The British Quakers also met some Tolstoyans, Vladimir Chertkov and Alexander Sergeenko. Chertkov arranged for Hinman Baker to meet Lenin's secretary, Vladimir Dmitrievich Bonch-Bruevich, who asked Baker to bring from England, or have sent over, information about the Quakers' role in the resettlement of the Doukhobors in Cyprus and Canada[77]. Bonch-Bruevich, a specialist on sects, asked Hinman Baker to send him any books on this topic. Baker also managed to attend a meeting of the United Council of Religious Communities and Groups[78], held at Chertkov's house.

Interestingly, in 1922, *Izvestiia* newspaper would print an article on 'The activities of the Society of Friends (Quakers) in Russia' which would report positively on the Quaker mission: 'In May 1920 the English Society of Friends sent food supplies

---

[76] Ibid, p.228 [verbatim]

[77] For more on the Doukhobors and the Quakers, see Richenda Scott, Quakers in Russia, p.137 ff. [Translator's note: The Doukhobors, meaning Spirit Wrestlers, were a pacifist Christian sect.]

[78] The United Council of Religious Communities and Groups (*Obedinennyi sovyet religioznykh obshchin i grupp, or OSROG*) was a representative body of minority religious movements within Soviet Russia. It was created in 1918 by Vladimir Chertkov. Starting from January 1919, the United Council had an official role for a time, considering the validity of conscientious objection for the Council of People's Commissars.

costing 15,000 pounds sterling to children's hospitals, children's homes and nurseries in Moscow and Petrograd. Representatives of the Society of Friends, Misters Hindman, Naiker and Franz Shaw [sic] entered into an agreement with the Soviet government about the proper distribution of the supplies received. In July 1920 the next batch of supplies were sent, costing 25,000 pounds sterling, accompanied by Mr Arthur Watts, who stayed in Russia to observe the distribution of the food. The distribution was carried out by the People's Commissariat for Health (*Narkomzdrav*) and the People's Commissariat for Education (*Narkompros*)'.[79] The Soviet journalists managed to make two people out of Hinman Baker (Mister Hindman and Naiker); Shaw was more fortunate as only his first name was slightly distorted in print.

On his return to London from Russia, Hinman Baker wrote a report about his trip in which he described enthusiastically how the Russians were trying to construct a system of medical care and education despite the shortages of fuel, medicine, soap and milk. He said he was glad to know that a few thousand Russian children, at any rate, were being fed eggs, milk, fats, and other foods for a few months. His colleague on the first Quaker mission to Russia, Gregory Welch, described Baker's trip as follows: 'He was satisfied with their method of distribution and felt more confidence in the present officials than those he would have met under the old regime. It is difficult to describe Russian

---

[79] *Izvestiia* newspaper, issue no. 16, 22 January 1922.

appreciation. When Hinman Baker left Petrograd he was hugged and kissed by some of the officials. One can better imagine the significance of that'.[80]

Later in his letter, Welch refers to Baker's impressions: '[Hinman] found the Communist party as enthusiastic as ever (they compose about 1% of the population). Fully confident that given transport and free trade they can demonstrate to Russia, and to the rest of the world, the ideal society. There are indications that Shop Committees are being abolished and industry, where there is any, controlled from the top. In Petrograd and Moscow there is almost no industry owing to the shortage of fuel and raw material. Under communal law all surplus stock, crops and goods must be rendered to the state, which gives in exchange nominal sums of worthless paper money. The peasantry are opposed to this, and so long as the Government cannot exchange for their produce clothing, machinery and a thousand other things they need, the majority of Russia will be opposed to Bolshevism'.[81]

Welch, who was quite critical of the Soviet authorities and spoke Russian well, expressed his hope that a just society would be created in the country, while understanding that things were not that easy: 'Arthur Watts, Hinman Baker and I hope to be in Petrograd again, distributing another 100 tons of children's relief. This is, of course, temporary work.

---

[80] Letter from Gregory Welch with an account of Hinman Baker's trip to Moscow, 26 July 1920. Friends House London archives. FEWVRC-MISSIONS-7-3-9-1_REPORTS-ACCOUNTS_1920
[81] Ibid.

Our aim is to try and do something to help Russia as Quaker ambassadors. We hope that the way will open for a resumption of Friends' relief work in Russia, and that we shall see the opportunity for the establishment of work of a more permanent nature than we have so far been able to accomplish'.[82]

Gregory Welch himself was keen to get back to Russia, but the Bolsheviks were wary of him. Once Baker and Shaw had returned to Britain, it was English Quaker Arthur Watts who received a visa and entry permit to Russia.

Arthur Watts was born in Manchester in 1888 and went to a Quaker school, Ackworth, in Yorkshire. After leaving school he worked for a while with his father, Challacombe Watts: both were excellent carpenters and joiners. The family was large and close. All the children were brought up in the Quaker spirit, which affected Arthur's life and the lives of his brothers and sisters. Arthur was opposed to war and was a conscientious objector. During the First World War he refused to serve in the army in the Non-Combatant Corps and, when he was then transferred to work in a non-military 'Home Office Scheme' instead, again refused to serve. For this he was sentenced to hard labour. Later he was sent to jail for distributing leaflets opposed to weapons. Once released, he went to France as a member of the Friends War Victims Relief Committee. After France, Arthur Watts went to Moscow. He would go on to work in Russia from January 1920 to the

---

[82] Ibid.

start of 1923. He returned to the USSR in 1931, this time for good, right up until his death in 1958.

Let us get back to 1920. In July, Ruth Fry sent a telegram to Litvinov, who was by then the Soviet ambassador to Estonia: 'Friends' Relief Committee will much appreciate permission to enter Russia for Welch and Baker waiting Reval. In addition, distribution Relief Committee hope Welch assist return Petrograd children amongst whom he worked for many months near Vladivostok'.[83]

In the same month, Arthur Watts, who was by now in Moscow, also wrote of the difficulty obtaining an entry permit for Gregory Welch, noting that the Russians seemed not to want to let Baker in again and stating the explanation they gave: 'Permission for Hinman Baker is still withheld on the principle that he has no special and separate mission to perform. The authorities are very rigid in this matter as will be gathered from the fact that Nansen[84] was not allowed to bring his secretary in with him'.[85]

Welch did eventually receive an entry permit, but only for a very short stay. All attempts to extend his stay proved to be in vain, and the Soviet authorities even began to expel him from Soviet Russia the day

[83] Ruth Fry to M. Litvinoff on 13 July 1920. AFSC Archives, FSR.
[84] [Translator's note: Fridtjof Nansen had been a Norwegian explorer and was a representative of the League of Nations, the first worldwide non-governmental organisation.]
[85] Letter from Arthur Watts to the Friends War Victim Relief Committee, 21 July 1920. Friends House London archives. FEWVRC-MISSIONS-7-3-9-1_REPORTS-ACCOUNTS_1920

after he arrived. Gregory Welch reported: 'At the termination of a comfortable journey to Moscow, I was informed, by the Foreign Office[86], that I must leave Russia immediately. The same evening I was given a permit to stay in Moscow a week. Later I learned that the day I arrived in Moscow Krasin[87] was refused entrance to England. Three days later I had an interview with Lunacharsky[88] Cabinet Minister for Education, regarding the Petrograd Children's Colony. He gave a document stating I was in the service of the Department of Education and urgently needed re. these children. I presented this to the Foreign Office and within three minutes was told to hand in all my papers and books for censorship that evening and was to leave the country next day'.[89] He was constantly threatened with expulsion during the month he spent in Moscow, and wittily compared his experience to a game of chess: 'We were made very welcome wherever we went, but you see the Foreign Office has to play a sort of Chess with the rest of the world. Myself and the other few foreigners in there are all the chessmen the Soviet Government have left in their camp'.[90] Welch brought 160 tonnes of

---

[86] Gregory Welch apparently uses the term 'Foreign Office' for the Russian People's Commissariat of Foreign Affairs (NKID).

[87] Leonid Borisovich Krasin (1870–1926) was People's Commissar of Foreign Trade from 1920 to 1924.

[88] Anatoly Vasilyevich Lunacharsky (1875 –1933) was a Russian Marxist revolutionary and the first Bolshevik Soviet People's Commissar for Education.

[89] Letter from Gregory Welch to Ruth Fry, 2 September 1920. Tallinn, Estonia. Friends House London archives. FEWVRC-MISSIONS-7-3-9-1_REPORTS-ACCOUNTS_1920

[90] Ibid.

humanitarian aid for children to Moscow, where he had to help Watts inspect the distribution of food. He also had to decide where the Quakers could be the most helpful to the country's suffering civilian population, considering the London Quaker Committee's capacity. Working together, they managed to get a great deal done in a month. It would have been much harder for Watts by himself.

Welch wrote in his report that the humanitarian aid – the food supplies for children – had arrived in Moscow via Tallinn (previously called Reval until Estonian independence in 1918) and that all the goods were transferred successfully. Incidentally, this method of delivering goods, initiated in 1920, was used from then on. Goods would be shipped from Britain and received in Tallinn by an Estonian company, 'Johan Pitka and Sons'[91]. Pitka would transfer the cargo to Gukovsky[92], the new Soviet plenipotentiary (ambassador) in Tallinn. However, Welch continued, 'Gukovsky refuses to accept any responsibility for the goods handed over to him, but simply promises to direct them to Arthur Watts'.

Gregory Welch, who had taken part in accompanying children from Petrograd[93] from Turgoyak to

[91] Johan Pitka was an Estonian politician who led the Estonian Defence League from 1920 to 1924. He campaigned against red tape and corruption, and was also editor of a newspaper and journal.
[92] Isidor Emmanuilovich Gukovsky (1871–1921) was the former People's Commissar of Finance. From 1920 he was Soviet Russia's plenipotentiary and trade representative in Estonia.
[93] A remarkable book, *The Children's Ark* by Vladimir Lipovetsky, describes (in Russian) how hundreds of children from Petrograd ended up circumnavigating the world between 1918 and 1920:

Vladivostok in 1918 and had got to know many children, was hoping to meet up with them again. (After their odyssey around the world, these 400 or so children from Petrograd were now back to their homeland.) However, the Soviet authorities made it quite clear that they did not need his help, so Gregory Welch realised he had to give up trying to see the children he had looked after.

Watts and Welch had many meetings with Soviet officials from the Ministries of Health and Education (*Narkomzdrav* and *Narkompros*). They cycled around Moscow on bikes: they must have covered more than 350 miles as they travelled about the city from one meeting to the next. Welch deplored the complicated Soviet system of accountability and checks, which were sometimes impossible to understand. For example, had dried milk been delivered to a certain address or not? Whenever the Quakers tried to offer any assistance other than delivering humanitarian aid, they met with a sharp rebuttal. Welch recounted his attempts to make contact with other People's Commissariats: 'Whilst in Moscow I submitted offers to work with both Education Department and Textile Department and negotiations were almost concluded with the Peasant Industries Department of the latter when a very zealous Communist doubted the advisability of the presence of an unknown Englishman, which rapidly concluded our conversation. In the Education Dept, they courteously informed me they would be pleased to see me later on when the

Kovcheg detei, ili Neveroyatnaya odisseya. St Petersburg. 2005.

clouds rolled by, and a representative of Chicherin's thanked me for all my attempts to help them but thought I could be very much more useful carrying on propaganda in England'.[94]

As well as meeting Soviet officials, Welch found time to meet some Tolstoyans and representatives of other religious groups, as he reported on his return from Moscow. He mentioned in his letters the 'League of True Freedom' which, he said, consisted of groups 'in search after a way of life unhampered by the customs and traditions and institutions that are human and fallible'.[95] It seemed to the Englishman that 'the Tolstoyan movement of which the League of True Freedom is the centre, is rapidly becoming a national movement'[96]. Welch visited children's homes being run by the Tolstoyan Society and attended a general meeting of its members, at which he answered questions and spoke in front of 300 people about Quakers and their principles. The Tolstoyans asked Gregory Welch to help them reissue a booklet by Tolstoy called *Daily Reading*, containing extracts of the author's works. When he got home, Welch raised money for the booklet to be printed. The British Quaker was full of hope for the success of this enterprise – he believed it was crucial to print the book because 'this volume would be of immense value to the continually

[94] Letter from Gregory Welch to Ruth Fry from Tallinn, Estonia, 2 Sep 1920. Friends House London archives. FEWVRC-MISSIONS-7-3-9-1_REPORTS-ACCOUNTS_1920.

[95] Letter from Gregory Welch to Paul Furnas of the AFSC, 5 October 1920. Friends House London archives. FEWVRC-MISSIONS-7-3-9-1_REPORTS-ACCOUNTS_1920

[96] Ibid.

increasing number of groups and will prove a sound starting point and guide towards the end they attain to'. Gregory Welch was a person who had not fallen under the influence of Communist propaganda and had no misconceptions about the regime in power in Soviet Russia. Nonetheless, he could not help seeing opportunities for Quaker participation in the building of a beautiful Russia of the future: 'This is a unique opportunity of helping the real foundation of Russia without allying to any particular political party or outside organisation, as this is a deeply spiritual movement and in no sense political'.[97] This was quite a widely held belief among Quakers: we're not a political force, we're far from politics, we're concerned about spirituality. This Western approach was founded in common sense, which has always been in short supply in Russia, especially under Communist rule.

The Englishman's meetings did not go unnoticed, of course: Gregory Welch was never again given permission to enter Soviet Russia.

Another reason for the Soviets' refusal to let Welch return to Russia could be Welch's involvement in saving children from Petrograd in 1919, as we mentioned earlier. The children were being looked after by the American Red Cross, and at that time Welch was working closely with the Americans, something which aroused the Bolsheviks' suspicion. He helped a large group of Russian children, who came to love him. Even many decades later, those

---

[97] Ibid.

who had participated in this odyssey remembered Gregory Welch with kind words, and one of the girls, Valentina Rogova, kept a Christmas card[98] from him for her whole life. He had signed it in Russian: 'Your older brother Grigorii Welch'. He hoped that in future Quakers would find many like-minded people among the children from Petrograd. However, the Soviet authorities told Welch that they could do without him, thank you very much, and that the children would undergo a course of Sovietisation once they got back, in case they had turned into Quakers!

As a result, by autumn 1920 there was only one Quaker left in Russia, Arthur Watts from Manchester. As there was a lot of work to do, he asked for assistance. The Americans tried to send a representative from the American Friends Service Committee (AFSC). In October 1920, an American Quaker, David Robert Yarnall, who was in Germany on a Quaker mission, met Alexander Vladimirovich Eiduk[99] in Berlin, with Paul Anderson of the YMCA acting as intermediary. Paul Anderson had worked with Russian prisoners of war with Eiduk, who was an important Soviet dignitary: he was the former chair of the NKVD (Interior Ministry) Central Committee, chair of the NKVD's Central Council for Evacuation (responsible for refugees), and in charge of the Department for Local

[98] The birthday card can be seen online here: <http://colonia.spb. ru/rogova.htm>

[99] Alexander Vladimirovich Eiduk (1886–1938), was of Latvian origin. Besides having responsibility for refugees, he was a member of the Soviet secret police, the Cheka.

Foreign Agencies in the People's Commissariat for External Trade. Another American Quaker, Alfred G. Scattergood, was present at Yarnall's meeting with Eiduk. After the meeting, Yarnall sent Eiduk a letter[100] in which he summed up the key points from their conversation the day before. The letter shows that Eiduk responded positively to the offer of help from the American Quakers and expressed his hope that all the humanitarian assistance would be sent to large cities, to Petrograd and Moscow. Eiduk stressed that Russia needed milk and food for children, as well as warm underwear. At the end of his letter, Yarnall said he was willing 'to convey to our committee in Philadelphia such additional information as you feel inclined to give at this time which would help us reach a right conclusion as to our responsibilities towards the Russian people'. Yarnall even advised Alexander Eiduk to write a letter giving further information, and promised to consider any such letter as confidential, stressing that he would give the letter personally to the members of the AFSC in Philadelphia no later than 1 November.

The fact that a high-up member of the Interior Ministry, the NKVD, met with American Quaker representatives indicates how keen Soviet Russia was to receive even a minimal supply of food for children. This meeting is also evidence of the Bolsheviks' desire to break through the trade blockade with Western countries and establish any

[100] Letter from David Robert Yarnall to Wilbur Thomas about his meeting with A. V. Eiduk in Berlin regarding humanitarian aid to Russia, 6 October 1920. AFSC FSR.

sort of relations with American representatives, in the hope that the USA would recognise the country of Soviet Russia. Understanding that the Society of Friends had limited means, Eiduk – who would later become the Soviet representative for the American Relief Administration (ARA) and to all foreign famine relief organisations – only mentioned the option of sending aid to Petrograd and Moscow.

At that time, Lucy Biddle Lewis, an American Quaker, was in London. She was the mother of Lydia Lewis who had married John Rickman in Buzuluk in 1918. Lucy Biddle Lewis wrote a letter[101] to Wilbur Thomas, the executive secretary of the American Friends Service Committee, about her meetings with the Friends War Victims Relief Committee (FWVRC) in London. In particular, she mentioned Gregory Welch's critical assessment of the idea of helping the Russians, and the fact that he had only just returned from Russia. Lucy Biddle Lewis noted the obvious antagonism between Welch and Arthur Watts, who had stayed in Moscow. Gregory Welch claimed that Arthur Watts saw everything through rose-tinted spectacles and was a Communist himself, and that his presence in Soviet Russia as a representative of the Society of Friends would cause all the Quakers' efforts to be interpreted by the Soviets as an expression of their sympathy for the Bolsheviks' methods. Gregory Welch stressed that Arthur Watts did not know Russian, and so believed everything that

---

[101] Letter from Lucy Biddle Lewis to Wilbur Thomas about the meetings in London, 29 September 1920. AFSC FSR.

he was told, not realising that the Bolsheviks had strayed far from their original ideals. Welch stated that the Quakers could not support the methods of violent coercion which the Soviets used to retain power. All Quaker deliveries were only distributed by the authorities, who did not want any outside involvement or help, so that, Welch argued, the Quakers had practically no chance of getting their message to ordinary people. The Quakers in Russia would only be able to keep track of the transfer of aid cargo, but even that was so complicated that it was impossible to do in practice. Welch was sure that the Bolsheviks would not allow him to stay in Soviet Russia because he was not a Communist. He also realised that there was such colossal need in Russia that Quaker aid was only a drop in the ocean, and that if the authorities began to suspect Friends of doing propaganda, they would throw them out straightaway. Welch warned that if the Quakers maintained contact with people in Russia who were sympathetic to them, it would look like propaganda to the Bolsheviks, since the people in question were themselves under suspicion.

Gregory Welch's speech seems to have been the first critical comment among Quakers regarding the very idea of Friends working together with 'comrades'. The Quakers, who were always full of compassion, told the truth directly and expected truthfulness from others, were unaware of the quirks of the Bolshevik mentality and saw what they wanted to see in the new Soviet authorities. Not knowing the language did not help, of course.

Gregory Welch, who spoke Russian fluently and had spent two years in Russia during the Revolution and the Civil War, knew the danger of taking everything at face value. He rightly feared that the trusting Quakers could easily fall into a trap: the Bolsheviks would smile nicely and take the gifts, while refusing to let the Friends distribute the humanitarian aid independently and refusing to let them make contact with the Tolstoyans and other sects who were close to them spiritually. Most importantly of all, they would refuse to let the Quakers 'share their message of goodwill and brotherly love'.

It is hardly surprising that when they heard Gregory Welch's speech the British Quakers took a decision which, to them, seemed logical enough: since what we do stems from our Christian principles and we are striving to construct a worldwide kingdom of justice, love and brotherhood on earth, we must hold out our hand to the Russian people in their hour of need. Therefore, the British Quakers said, let us pass a 'Statement of Aims' to the Soviet government via Watts, including our spiritual aims, and see whether the Bolsheviks continue to want us in the country. If we do that, no one will be able to accuse us of misleading the Communist authorities.

Lucy Biddle Lewis was reticent about this idea, and as the text needed to be approved by the American Quakers too, she suggested to the meeting that she would contact Wilbur Thomas at the AFSC in Philadelphia about her cautious attitude towards the British Quakers' plan.

The London committee drafted a letter which began by complimenting the Kremlin[102]: 'We view with real appreciation the work we hear you are developing for the social uplift of your people, the Child Welfare, the Maternity work, the Social Maintenance the Popular Education, etc., with which we would gladly co-operate'. However, the Quakers went on to lay out their principles and talk about their aims: 'We are upon an active campaign to overcome the barriers of race and class and thus to make of all humanity a "Society of Friends"'. The letter's authors were frank about the historical examples of Quakers' dissidence due to their basic principles: 'This has led us to follow a course, on some occasions, different from that of fellow citizens; even to act contrary to the law of our country when our legislators bid us violate our principles, particularly when called upon to take human life in warfare'. In closing, the Quakers asked the Bolsheviks openly: 'Hence we seek to know your attitude towards us, and our concern to unite in fellowship with Russian people. With that in view we desire to ask if you will allow representatives of the Society of Friends to come to Russia for the purpose of establishing independent work for the administration of physical relief and to give expression to our international and spiritual ideals and principles of life'.

Despite the reservations of the Quakers in

---

[102] Letter from the (British and American) Society of Friends to members of the Soviet government, October 1920. Friends House London archives. FEWVRC-MISSIONS-7-3-9-1_REPORTS-ACCOUNTS_1920

Philadelphia, this letter was sent to Arthur Watts in Moscow, to ask for his opinion. Watts' reaction in his letter of reply[103] was emotional. He called the draft 'A mild lecture and an explanation of our "chief concerns"'. Reasonably enough, he criticised the part of the text where the Quakers talked about social class: 'It will be difficult for me to convince the recipients of the Activeness of your "campaign to overcome the barriers [...] of class"'. On this point, Watts was right to reproach the authors of the letter of hypocrisy, reminding them that British Quakers still withheld control in industry from their workers, and that their British employees did not have control of anything. He wrote: 'I have a strong objection to pretending to be better than we are'.

Arthur Watts also condemned the London committee's apparent caution and concern that Quaker help would be interpreted as an expression of sympathy for Bolshevik methods. He wrote that he could not believe that Quakers might abstain from helping Russian children out of fear of being misunderstood. He added: 'This is really most unworthy of you. Did you demand a statement from the Tsarist Government that our help was not to be taken as indicating approval of their aims and methods?' He drew parallels with the parables in the Bible, asking, 'I wonder if Christ thought of issuing a Statement of Aims before raising the Centurion's daughter', and made the sarcastic comment that if

[103] Letter from Arthur Watts to the Friends War Victims Relief Committee, 21 October 1920, no.126. Savoy Hotel, Moscow. Friends House London archives. FEWVRC-MISSIONS-7-3-9-1_REPORTS-ACCOUNTS_1920

the Good Samaritan had drawn up a careful minute, 'we might have admired his "Quaker Caution" but it would have spoilt the point of the parable'.

At the end of his letter Watts called for humanity: 'There are thousands of children who will suffer hunger and cold in Russia this winter. You can only help a few. Are you going to let these few shiver whilst you satisfy yourselves that you are not misunderstood?'

In fact, American Quakers too spoke out strongly against the text of the 'Statement of Aims'. In their opinion, the document would only make an already difficult situation even more complicated: they worried that the letter could make them lose all their contacts and slam shut a door which was only just ajar. The point was, though, that many lives could be saved. The Americans also said, justifiably, that the Russians would judge the Quakers by their actions. Later, when the grateful Russian people wanted to find out who Quakers were, that would be the time to answer any questions that arose and talk about the Society of Friends.

One of the important points in the 'Statement of Aims' was the Quakers' hope of opening a 'Quaker embassy' in Russia. The idea of such an 'embassy', we recall, was put forward by the workers in the first Quaker mission: in 1919, the head of the mission, Theodore Rigg, shared his vision of how and where an embassy could be opened, if the Bolshevik authorities agreed. The British Quakers, including Gregory Welch, supported the idea of the embassy.

In autumn 1920 he wrote: 'I feel the best way I can further a Quaker Embassy in Russia is to enter a civil occupation there to share the common life and its problems. The cultivation of a circle of Friends concerned with the search after the way of true life and with a mutual desire to find God will be a sound foundation for a Quaker Embassy to work upon for its establishment'.[104] However, as is even clear from this quote, Welch was discussing how to promote the idea of the embassy, not how to go about asking the Bolsheviks for permission to open an embassy. The suggestion is that, by their actions, Friends would manage to convince the authorities of their goodwill, and then it would be possible to start negotiations about the embassy or Quaker centre in Soviet Russia.

In November 1920, Watts took a more nuanced view of the real state of affairs when he laid out his vision of the prospects for opening a Quaker embassy in Russia:

Regarding the Quaker Embassy side of the work:

1)   I think that the best message that can be given to Russian people at the present time is that there are Christians that are sufficiently inspired with a spirit of love to be able to give disinterested physical relief to a suffering people.

2)   That physical relief ought not to be used as a means of securing permission to spread our views or to

---

[104] Gregory Welch's comments concerning future work in Russia, November 1920. Friends House London archives. FEWVRC-MISSIONS-7-3-9-1_REPORTS-ACCOUNTS_1920

create a favourable atmosphere but should be the simple expression of the same love which prompts us to desire religious fellowship with others.

3) I believe at the present time any request to be allowed to establish a Quaker Embassy would be met by a refusal, but there is nothing to hinder our workers meeting with Tolstoians and others similar groups or to have free conversation with recipients of our supplies and with others. [105]

Appropriately enough, Watts was showing a talent for diplomacy. He evidently understood the essence of the Bolshevik regime and knew how to work in Russia skilfully.

At this time, the US State Department finally agreed to let the Quakers ship aid cargo to Russia on the condition that the aid was distributed privately, not by the Soviet state. An American Quaker was found who was willing to go to Moscow: Anna Haines, who had worked in Buzuluk in 1917–1918 as a member of the Quaker mission. After leaving the USA for Europe, she was able to take part in the meeting of the Friends War Victim Relief Committee on 10 November 1920. Haines confirmed to the British Friends that the general opinion of the American Friends Service Committee in Philadelphia was critical of the text of the 'Statement of Aims'. In her confidential letter, sent to Wilbur Thomas from

---

[105] Arthur Watts' comments about the prospects of work in Russia to the Friends War Victims Relief Committee (London) and the American Friends Service Committee. Friends House London archives. FEWVRC-MISSIONS-7-3-9-1_REPORTS-ACCOUNTS_1920

London on 10 November, Anna Haines confirmed that Welch and Watts had contrasting characters and temperaments. She paid tribute to Gregory Welch: 'Welch does have a good knowledge of Russian conditions, and a real love for Russian people; his mind just does not work along political lines'.[106]

Gregory Welch was present at this meeting and insisted that the 'Statement of Aims' should be sent to the Russian authorities. After a long discussion, the participants in the meeting came to agreement that the text would be sent in a letter to Arthur Watts, who could do with it as he saw fit. Although, as we recall, Watts was opposed to giving the 'Statement' to the Bolsheviks, in practice he had already stated the essence of the document, in his own words, more than once to the Moscow authorities. As a person with a talent for negotiating, Arthur Watts knew when, how and to whom it was wise to talk about Quaker principles and ideals.

As a result, by the end of 1920, there were two points of view and two contrasting approaches to the work to be done in Russia. Anna Haines sums them up concisely in her letter to Wilbur Thomas: 'Gregory Welch feels that Russia's greatest need was for personal work along spiritual lines with the emphasis on a Quaker form of religion, and that the material relief which we might bring in should be used not exactly as a lever but as a point of contact for the more important other side of our mission. Arthur Watts felt that material relief was what could

[106] Confidential letter from Anna Haines to Wilbur Thomas, 10 November 1920, Kingsley Hotel, London. AFSC FSR.

best be understood by the great majority of suffering Russian people, and that it should be administered at present as an expression of disinterested Christian love. Later when [the] country is not in such an abnormal political and economic state he felt that the Quaker Embassy type of work would be possible without being misunderstood, as it is certain to be at present. All of us including Gregory Welch felt the strength of this statement and it has been made the basis of our common entrance into Russia'.[107]

Anna Haines rightly suggested that the essence of the 'Statement' was probably no secret to the Bolsheviks: 'I expect that [Watt's letter] was intercepted in transit and is already reposing on Chicherin's desk, [as] all mail bags are opened'. As we mentioned above, Arthur Watts, even though he had rejected the 'Statement', was already quoting the text in support in a letter to a Soviet official.

The official in question, Santeri Nuorteva[108] of the Department for the Entente (Britain and France) and Scandinavia, was sympathetic towards the Quakers. Watts wrote the following letter to Nuorteva: 'I believe that my Committee is always anxious to give material help wherever it is needed without attaching any condition as to their being allowed to spread the religious views held by the Society of Friends. They feel, however, that honesty

---

[107] Letter from Anna Haines to Wilbur Thomas, 25 November 1920. Tallinn, Estonia. AFSC FSR.
[108] Santeri Nuorteva (1881–1929) was a Finnish-born Soviet official in the People's Commissariat for Foreign Affairs.

demands that you should know of our desire to come into religious fellowship with people in Russia who share views similar to our own'.[109] The fact that the text of the 'Statement of Aims" had long since been intercepted by the Cheka, the secret police, may explain why these words about religious brotherhood did not come as a shock to Nuorteva: he did not send any reaction at all.

Anna Haines, who knew about mail interception in Soviet Russia, wrote to Wilbur Thomas about the first Russian Quaker: 'Countess Olga Tolstoi has been received into membership by London Yearly Meeting as a result of a request on her part verbally transmitted through Gregory Welch. Yesterday it seemed improbable that he would return to Moscow and therefore I was asked to take a verbal notification of admission to her as it was felt a written notice of membership in an English Society might work a hardship upon her at the present time'.[110]

Anna Haines received permission to enter Russia again on 24 November 1920. She headed from the Estonian capital, Tallinn, to Moscow via Petrograd on 27 November. From the very first day, she got on with many urgent tasks. Foodstuffs, medicines and other goods were being sent from Britain and the USA by sea to Tallinn. There they were loaded onto railway carriages and sent on to Moscow. In Moscow the goods were transferred to the Quaker

---

[109] Letter from Arthur Watts to Santeri Nuorteva, 18 October 1920. Moscow. AFSC FSR.
[110] Confidential letter from Anna Haines to Wilbur Thomas, 10 November 1920. Kingsley Hotel, London. AFSC FSR.

warehouse. Only a month after Anna Haines'
arrival, the *Tsentrosoyuz*, the Soviet organisation
for all trade in consumer goods, provided the two
Quakers with warehouse no.5 in the Moscow district
of Perevedenovka, right next to the railway tracks.
Once the goods had been sorted in the warehouse,
foodstuffs and medicines were distributed to
numerous organisations which Arthur Watts had
contacted: so-called 'forest schools', children's
hospitals, maternity hospitals and milk distribution
points for infants. Watts and Haines did not only
handle goods from Quakers: they also distributed
goods on behalf of the Save the Children Fund and
the American Relief Administration. Initially they
worked in an office inside the warehouse building,
but after a while the office was moved into the centre
of town to the premises of the People's Commissariat
for Food (*Narkomprod*), in a building now known as
GUM department store, in apartment 201 on the
third floor. Arthur and Anna recruited Russian staff
to work in the warehouse to unpack and pack up
the goods and do administrative tasks.

The Russian authorities paid a salary to the Russian
stall, but the Quakers realised that 'cold and hungry
people cannot handle our food stuffs and clothing
without a distinct loss to us', as Anna Haines
delicately put it. A decision was therefore taken 'to
allot to them some food and clothes apart from our
consignments to Russia generally, but no monetary
salary would be allowed, or desired probably'.

The People's Commissariat for Food signed an

agreement with the Quakers, granting themselves the right to keep and distribute the food and medicines sent to Moscow from the United States and Britain. While the goods were distributed by Soviet bodies, the Quakers had the right to inspect and check deliveries whenever they wished.

Anna Haines and Arthur Watts stayed at the Savoy Hotel, which was used at that time as a boarding house by the People's Commissariat for Foreign Affairs. The hotel was at the intersection of Rozhdestvenka Ulitsa and Sofiika Ulitsa. Watts cycled to work while Anna walked, as it was not far. Transport was a problem in Moscow in 1920: there were hardly any cars, taking a taxi was incredibly expensive, and the tram was extremely unreliable. Anna Haines therefore gave future workers some practical advice: 'Every new worker coming out should be accompanied by some means of locomotion, bicycle, motorcycle or Ford. Gasoline could be free for our use. Cab-hire now is at about 2000 rubles per mile'.[111]

The Eighth Congress of Soviets Workers, Peasants, Red Army and Cossack Deputies of Soviet Russia began on 22 December 1920. Arthur Watts went along to hear Lenin's speech to open the event. Watts reported that Lenin said that the Bolsheviks should make their programme intelligible to and popular with the peasants. Anna Haines went to the congress too and later recalled a speech on garden cities as the industrial ideal for living and working

[111] Letter from Anna Haines to Wilbur Thomas, 25 November 1920. Tallinn, Estonia. AFSC FSR.

conditions.

A small Anglo-American diaspora in Moscow, along with a few staff of the People's Commissariat for Foreign Affairs, organised a Christmas dinner in December 1920. One of the Soviet officials invited was Mr. Nuorteva, the assistant Foreign Secretary, as guest of honour. The Quakers had had most of their dealings with him. He complimented Friends, saying that they were the only relief organisation against which Soviet Russia had no grievance or fear that they were misusing their mission.

Quaker warehouse in Moscow 1920

©*The archives of the American Friends Service Committee*

Now that Quakers had their own office, a warehouse and a team of staff, it was time to think about the nature of the official representative office and – most importantly – what they should be called in Russian. Anna Haines wrote to the AFSC in Philadelphia about the translation puzzle: 'After six weeks' efforts to achieve a satisfactory Russian translation of "Friends International Service" we have given up the attempt. "Service" was the stumbling block for which there seemed no adequate equivalent. One word expressed a purely material aid, another had too religious a significance, and a third — well, I forget just what was the trouble, but it did not seem just right. I think it was too military. We have finally adopted the following letter head and stamp:

FRIENDS INTERNATIONAL SERVICE

ОБЩЕСТВО ДРУЗЕЙ (КВАКЕРЫ)

ОТДЕЛ ПОМОЩИ ДЕТЯМ

FRIENDS INTERNATIONAL SERVICE

SOCIETY OF FRIENDS (QUAKERS)

DEPARTMENT OF AID TO CHILDREN

'Such a title defines quite accurately the position in which we are at present working in Russia. Everywhere we are known as "Quakers" in so far as popular recognition is concerned'.[112]

---

[112] Letter from Anna Haines to Wilbur Thomas, 13 January 1921. AFSC FSR.

The address given on official papers was: *Central Tsentrosoyuz Warehouse. Perevedenovka, 7 Instrumentalnyi Pereuluk. Moscow. Telephone: 5-91-53.*

The foodstuffs were then delivered by the People's Commissariat for Health to children's hospitals and children's homes in Moscow. In the AFSC Quaker archive in Philadelphia I found a sheet with a touching thank-you letter from children at the Moscow forest school, which said: 'We, the children at Forest School no.1 in the Sparrow Hills, express great gratitude to our dear foreigners for the gifts you have sent us. We liked your presents very much, and the lard is very useful to us, especially now that our rations have been reduced. Receive many thanks from Russian children. We will be delighted if you can travel to see us. The children of the Forest School no.1'.

Oats, fats and underwear were sent to the forest schools where the Moscow children lived. Oatflakes and baby clothes were sent to women's polyclinics and milk distribution points. As there was not much dried milk, it was only provided for children under a year old.

The Quakers wrote to People's Commissar Chicherin in spring 1921 to say that food was being supplied from abroad in sufficient quantities to provide 16,000 children with milk for a few months and enough fats to sustain 30,000 children in the establishments run in Moscow by the People's Commissariat for Health. There were reserves of soap, medicine and clothing. The Quakers expressed their hope that the deliveries would continue and, indeed, increase, so that they would like to extend the geographical reach of their work to include Petrograd and other Russian regions. As other foreign relief organisations had not received permission to enter Russia or could not afford to pay staff in Russia, the Quakers were distributing supplies on behalf of the Save the Children Fund and other organisations.

American Quaker Anna Haines at Forest School in Moscow suburb. 1920

©The archives of the American Friends Service Committee

While the number of foreign organisations hoping to provide food was increasing, getting into Soviet Russia was not at all easy. Given that the country was not recognised by foreign powers, Moscow did not want to let foreigners in. The Quakers were already in Russia and were willing to distribute aid for other groups, but they did need to recruit more staff for the Quaker office in Moscow. For this reason, in April 1921, Arthur Watts wrote[113] to Chicherin at the Commissariat for Foreign Affairs, asking permission for at least four more Quakers to enter Russia, in order to increase their workforce. He informed Chicherin that they would need 20 or even 30 people in the event of an increased flow of supplies, and would also need interpreters.

Chicherin replied the following week, stating that the Quakers 'deserved nothing but appreciation and support from us'.[114] However, the Soviet Commissar explained that the Bolsheviks' good relations with the Quakers did not at all mean that the Kremlin wanted to open the doors of Soviet Russia to all kinds of foreign relief societies and organisations that wanted to do relief work in Russia. Chicherin emphasised that 'the overwhelming majority of these organisations are unfriendly towards Soviet Russia and will not fail to utilise every possibility in order to make their activities a source for all kind of intrigues and anti-Soviet propaganda'. He argued that capitalist countries were strangling millions of Russian workers, their wives and children, through their blockade, and at the same time hoped to use their humanitarian aid to 'mask and cover the most horrible features of the inhuman policy of their countries'. Although he was unwilling to let in

---

[113] Letter from Arthur Watts to Chicherin, 7 April 1921. Moscow. Friends House London archives. FEWVRC-MISSIONS-7-3-9-2_ REPORTS-ACCOUNTS_1921
[114] Chicherin's letter to Arthur Watts, 14 April 1921. Friends House London archives. FEWVRC-MISSIONS-7-3-9-2_REPORTS-ACCOUNTS_1921

random anti-Soviet foreigners, Chicherin did not object to all aid going via the Quakers. He agreed that the increased volume of supplies would indeed necessitate new workers coming to Russia, but he insisted that all potential members of staff should be vetted. Detailed information on each candidate should be sent to Litvinov, who had been Soviet Russia's representative in Estonia.

A new policy of strict control was applied in mid-1921, even towards the Quakers, of whom the Soviet authorities were very supportive. Not everyone gained permision to enter the country, as we saw earlier in the case of Gregory Welch. The People's Commissariat for Foreign Affairs wrote to Lunarcharsky, the People's Commissar for Education, who was wary of the Quakers: 'In answer to your letter of 25 July, ref. no. 5179, I can tell you that at present the People's Commissariat for Foreign Affairs has no objection to Quakers of American nationality participating in giving aid to the sick and needy, and [the Commissariat] retains the right to remove anyone about whom we receive unfavourable reports. You may inform Mr Watts of this'.[115] In August 1921, Commissar Chicherin wrote to fellow Soviet diplomat Leonid Krasin that American Quakers were not allowed into Russia during the period when 'there was a general ban on absolutely all Americans'.[116] Now, though, the ban had been lifted, Chicherin wrote, and there had never been any sort of specific ban on Quakers, in

[115] Archive of the foreign policy of the Russian Federation, fonds 04, series 58, folder 368, file 19, sheets 8-10.
[116] Ibid, fonds 04, series 58, folder 367, file 56059, sheets 68. Copy.

any case. Quakers could now receive entry permits whenever they wanted.

Soon, many Quakers would come to Russia to save people from dying.

The hot, dry spring of 1921 already foretold a terrible disaster, the extent of which the Bolsheviks had not yet realised. Peasants' grain had already been confiscated by the Soviet authorities, leaving them with nothing left to sow on the parched fields which had so recently been the scene of Civil War battles. Famine was looming.

Chapter 6. *Famine in the Volga region. The conclusion of negotiations with the People's Commissariat for Food (Narkomprod) in 1921. The Quakers choose Buzuluk as the centre of their work. Start of the famine relief programme in Buzuluk. American Quakers have to work with the American Relief Administration (ARA). American Quakers open their office in Sorochinskoye. A Quaker centre in Alekseevka. Warehouses in Moscow for Quaker food. The famine passes its peak. Soviet officials ask the Quakers not to leave.*

The famine which began in the Volga region in 1921 has been explained in different ways at different times. Soviet historiography blamed it on weather conditions, the kulaks[117] and the international trade blockade against the young Soviet republic. In recent years, many scholarly works have been published which seek reasons for the famine independently of the political situation.

One of the main reasons for the famine is the *prodrazvyorstka*[118]: the confiscation of grain and agricultural products from peasants by the Soviet authorities, according to a production quota and prices fixed by the state. It was the *prodrazvyorstka* which led to warning signs of the coming famine in Samara province from February 1921, long before the drought. This was when Moscow began to receive worrying news from the Volga region as

[117] [Translator's note: Kulaks were considered by the Bolsheviks to be rich peasants and therefore class enemies.]
[118] *Prodrazvyorstka* was short for *prodovolstvennaya razvyorstka*, meaning 'food allocation'.

a whole, and from Samara province in particular: 'Given the bad harvest in 1920 and the excessive food confiscation to the weight of 10 million *pood*[119], peasants began to go hungry from January 1921 onwards, and in February they began to fall ill due to malnutrition and some died'. By the start of the summer, local authorities reported to Moscow that 'Crowds of thousands of starving people besieged the *Uezdispolkom* (the district executive committee) and are patiently waiting, no amount of persuasion can make them leave, some of them have already died of exhaustion. Urgent assistance is needed'.[120]

The historian Sergei Pavlyuchenkov rightly remarks: 'Until 1920, most of the peasantry still had some surplus of bread that they could barter with. In 1920, however, especially in European Russia, peasant farming turned into subsistence farming for obvious reasons, but the peasants were completely unable to provide food to the cities and the army without harming themselves. During the *prodrazvyorstka* of 1920/21, officials responsible for food confiscation took essential goods from peasants' farmsteads and arable land. The state apparatus had strengthened, while peasants had no money and were weak. "Pumping the peasants" was ordered at the highest level, resulting in the famine of 1921'.[121]

[119] [Translator's note: A *pood* was a unit of mass equivalent to 40 Russian *funt*, roughly equivalent to 16 kilograms or 36 pounds.]

[120] State Archives of the Russian Federation, fonds R-1064, series 1, file 1, sheet 33.

[121] Sergei Pavlyuchenkov. *Krestyansky Brest, ili predystoriya bolshevistskogo NEPa* ['The Peasants' Brest, or the prehistory of the Bolsheviks' NEP policy']. Moscow, 1996. (The title is an allusion to

The Soviet authorities were seriously afraid of mass deaths over a huge territory and the possibility of riots and uprisings by starving people. Pavlyuchenkov notes that 'During the *prodrazvyorstka*, there was no bread left for demobbed Red Army soldiers; when they came home and found their villages in poverty and desperation, they immediately joined the ranks of the rebels. The rebels began to create groups of the captured Red Army soldiers at the very start of March 1921, sending them to fight against government forces. The battles showed the Bolshevik hit squads that the rebels were a force to be reckoned with. Lenin acknowledged at the Tenth Party Congress that the demobilisation of the Red Army had created an 'incredible' number of rebels'.[122]

Due to the famine, the Soviet authorities had to feed many millions of people, mostly peasants, in nearly 35 provinces. The country did not have the resources to feed such a huge number of people. The Bolsheviks had to change their policy, including in relation to foreign aid. Indeed, if they did not ask the West for help, the ex-Red Army soldiers would remove the Bolsheviks from power.

the Treaty of Brest-Litovsk.)

[122] Sergei Pavlyuchenkov, *Rossiya nepovskaya* ['Russia in the NEP years']. Moscow, 2002.

Abandoned Russian child

©*The archives of the American Friends Service Committee*

News about the famine began to reach Europe and the USA in the summer of 1921. The writer Maxim Gorky's appeal[123] to the Europeans and Americans for relief was certainly crucial in getting the news out. The pre-revolutionary Russian intelligentsia, people who had lost their social status as a result of the Revolution and were termed 'former' people, also made appeals to the West: they created the Pomgol (Famine Relief) Committee. (The Soviet authorities mockingly nicknamed the committee

---

[123] The text of Gorky's appeal is available here in English: <http://soviethistory.msu.edu/1921-2/famine-of-1921-22/famine-of-1921-22-texts/gorkys-appeal/>

'Prokukish[124]', an amalgam of the organisers' surnames.) The non-governmental All-Russian Committee for Famine Relief (*Vserossiiskii Komitet Pomoshi Golodayushim*), called VK Pomgol for short, was officially registered on 21 July 1921. It was led by the chairman of the Moscow council, Lev Kamenev[125], and Alexei Rykov[126] was appointed deputy; the writer Vladimir Korolenko[127] was chosen as honorary president. When appeals came from the Bolsheviks, the world outside the Soviet Russia took hardly any notice, but the Pomgol Committee's appeal for aid was paid attention to abroad. In fact, this is why the Bolsheviks put up with Pomgol for a few months before arresting everyone involved. The head of the American Relief Administration (ARA), Herbert Hoover, responded to their request, expressing willingness to help Russia if the Bolsheviks met a series of conditions, including liberating US citizens who were behind bars in Soviet Russia. The Kremlin met all Hoover's demands without delay.

---

[124] Prokukish was similar in sounding with Kukish, the fig sign (a thumb wedged in between two fingers) which is an obscene gesture in Russia.

[125] Lev Borisovich Kamenev (born Rozenfeld; 1883 – 1936) was a Bolshevik revolutionary and a prominent Soviet politician.

[126] Alexei Ivanovich Rykov (1881 – 1938) was a Russian Bolshevik revolutionary and a Soviet politician, most prominently as premier of Russia and the Soviet Union from 1924 to 1929. In 1921 he was the Deputy Chairman of the Council of Labour and Defence of Soviet Russia under Lenin.

[127] Vladimir Galaktionovich Korolenko (1853 – 1921) was a Ukrainian-born Russian writer, journalist, human rights activist and humanitarian. Korolenko was a strong critic of the Tsarist regime and, in his final years, of the Bolsheviks.

When Nikolai Nikolaevich Kutler[128], who had joined VK Pomgol, found out about Soviet Russia's agreement with the ARA, he prophesied: 'Well, we can go home now […] Our work is done. Now [only] about 35% of the population of the famine regions will die, rather than 80% or 70% […] Praise be to the brave Americans'.[129] He was arrested on 27 August 1921, along with all the remaining members of Pomgol. It is no coincidence that the Kremlin had set up a parallel organisation with an extremely similar name, the TsK Pomgol, just the previous month, in July 1921. TsK Pomgol stood for the Central Commission for Famine Relief (*Tsentralnyi Komitet Pomoshi Golodayushim*) and was a governmental body, led by Mikhail Kalinin.[130] Once VK Pomgol had been closed down, only the state-run famine relief organisation, TsK Pomgol, was left in Soviet Russia.

Richenda Scott states in her book *Quakers in Russia*[131] that when information about the famine reached Britain, a meeting was held at the House of Commons to discuss the situation. The Russia Famine Relief Fund was set up, and the executive committee included Henry Noel Brailsford, Colonel Josiah Wedgwood, Harold John Massingham and the Secretary of the Friends

---

[128] Nikolai Kutler (1859–1924) was a Russian politician. After the Bolshevik revolution, Kutler worked at the People's Commissariat of Finance and was a board member of the State Bank of the USSR.

[129] E. Kuskova, 'Mesyats "soglashatelstva"', in *Volya Rossii* issue no. 5, 1928.

[130] Mikhail Ivanovich Kalinin (1875 – 1946), the head of state of Soviet Russia and later of the Soviet Union from 1919 to 1946.

[131] Richenda Scott, *Quakers in Russia*, ch. 18, p.236. London, 1964.

War Victims Relief Committee, Ruth Fry. Nikolai
Klyshko, the representative of the London trade
delegation of Soviet Russia, was invited to the event
and presented Russia's position. A few months
later, all the British organisations involved in aid
work in Russia – the Russia Famine Relief Fund,
the Save The Children Fund and the Society of
Friends – united their efforts under the name of
the All-British Appeal. The money raised went to
one of the three organisations in particular if that
was what the donor specified, or else to whatever
purposes were most important at the time, if the
donation was unrestricted.

Soviet Russia had already signed an agreement
with the American Relief Administration[132] to work
together to deal with the famine, on 20 August
1921 in Riga. A week later, on 27 August, an
additional agreement was signed between the Soviet
government and the International Committee
for Russian Relief (ICRR), also called the Nansen
Committee.[133] On 16 September 1921, the Religious
Society of Friends (Quakers) in Britain and America
entered into an agreement with Soviet Russia's
People's Commissariat for Food (*Narkomprod*).
The agreement stated that 'the Society of Friends,
continuing its work to give aid to children, the
sick and those suffering from malnutrition in the
population of the city of Moscow, pays particular

---

[132] [Translator's note: ARA was called by its initials in Russia too,
but in Cyrillic: 'АРА'.]
[133] [As noted, Fridtjof Nansen, a former explorer, was a
representative of the League of Nations.]

attention to aiding starving people in the Volga region, and also to aiding other region with the agreement of Narkomprom'.[134] Moscow reached a series of agreements with other foreign charities in order to provide food to starving Russians. Here is the full agreement with the Quakers, in the original wording of the English version:

1) The Society of Friends has expressed its wish to help the Russian population with food and clothes.

2) For attaining this aim, the Society of Friends, continuing its work of helping children, invalids and people suffering from undernourishment in Moscow, has mostly given its attention towards the starving districts along the Volga, as well as towards other districts, with the consent of Narcomprod.

3) Narcomprod lets the Society of Friends have, in Moscow as well as at the out stations, lodgings for the members of the Society and stores next to the railway, for food products and articles, that arrive for disposal.

4) The necessary staff for the office, and workmen at the stores are payed [sic] by Narcomprod, and the staff in Moscow must not be more than six people and at the out stations not more than three.

5) For transporting food supplies for the schools, children's hospitals, asylums and colonies, the Society of Friends will have their own garage at Yermolaevsky pereulok no.28.

---

[134] State Archives of the Russian Federation, fonds R-058, series 1, document 5.

*6) Narcomprod represented by the Auto-section, will
provide the necessary staff within the limits of the
confirmed estimates and let the order about the staff to go
through the Auto-section.*

*7) Narcomprod will give out the necessary quantity of
burning and greasing[135] materials through Auto-section.*

*8) The repairing of the cars belonging to the Society of
Friends will be done by Narcomprod at the expense and
resources of the workshop and factories of Auto-section.*

*9) At the end of each month the Society of Friends must
give an account by stated forms, of all operations of their
garage.*

*10) In case the Society of Friends is in need of machines
for the country, it can take such out of the Moscow
garage belonging to the Society of Friends but for not less
than 6 months, or may receive them from the local depot
of Auto-section Narcomprod, in which case the Society
of Friends must give the same number of machines they
took, out of their Moscow garage or bring them in from
abroad for the use of Narcomprod.*

*11) All the goods sent to the disposal of the Society of
Friends through Moscow Narcomprod must be addressed:
"Narcomprod (Society of Friends)".*

*12) On arrival of the goods to the station of destination
they will be examined and received by the representatives
of Narcomprod and the Society of Friends putting all
details down in a special receiving act, signed by a*

---

[135] i.e., fuel and lubricant.

representative of each side.

13) All expenses for loading, unloading and transporting of the goods belonging to the Society of Friends will be covered by Narcomprod.

14) The plans of distribution of goods and articles coming into the disposal of the Society of Friends, will be settled with the agreement of Narcomprod and its local branches in inviting for this work representatives of Narcomprod and Narkompros[136].

15) Lists of all supplies received and distributed must be sent to Narcomprod.

16) Orders for delivering the goods from stores must have the signatures of the representatives of the Society of Friends.

17) The goods are given out to the people gratis, as gifts from the Society of Friends.

18) This agreement is confirmed in 2 copies: one goes to stay with the Society of Friends, the other — with Narcomprod.

Commissioner of the Religious Society of Friends / signature of Arthur Watts/

Members of the Collegium of the People's Commissariat for Food /signature/, /signature/

The post of Soviet plenipotentiary (envoy) was created so that foreign organisations could work well and be coordinated and supported. There was

---

[136] Narkompros was the People's Commissariat for Education.

a plenipotentiary to represent the government of Soviet Russia to all foreign relief organisations, while other plenipotentiaries represented the central government to local governments in the regions. The Council of People's Commissars[137] in Moscow appointed Alexander Vladimirovich Eiduk[138] as plenipotentiary to the ARA and all foreign famine relief organisations. As we saw earlier, Eiduk was a member of the secret police, the Cheka. Another Cheka operative, Martyn Martynovich Karklin, became plenipotentiary to Samara province. His core functions were the following:

1.   Receiving foreign representatives and giving them organisational and other assistance as necessary.

2.   Organising and equipping food distribution points, soup kitchens, storerooms and kitchens.

3.   Registering the population in need, determining the extent of aid, etc.

4.   Safeguarding the rights of the foreign representatives in accordance with the agreement.

5.   Writing regular reports and summaries about the work in progress and its results, financial expenditure and the food distributed.

However, Eiduk and Karklin, being good secret service operatives who saw spies and saboteurs everywhere, began to infiltrate their own agents and informers as soon as the foreign missions started

---

[137] The Councils of People's Commissars, commonly known as the Sovnarkom, were the highest executive authorities in Soviet Russia.
[138] See the introduction to Eiduk in ch.5.

work to save Russians from starving to death. At the end of September 1921, the Cheka sent Lenin a report[139] which mentioned that they had recruited and installed ten secret agents to work at the ARA. Another informer, a woman, was a foreign journalist and a Communist. The person whom the Cheka sent to work as an informer at the Petrograd branch of the ARA was 'a comrade who had been primed in advance with recommendations from the American organisation of Quakers which is located here in Moscow. He is also mandated to recruit secret agents to work for the ARA in Petrograd, if possible'. As we see, therefore, there were also Russian Cheka agents among the Quakers.

The Quakers went to Samara at the end of August 1921 to assess the extent of the catastrophe and work out where the Society of Friends could best concentrate its efforts. Anna Haines from the US and Margaret Thorp, a Quaker from Australia, set off on the trip in the company of a group of Russian doctors. Margaret Thorp wrote:

On the 28th August, I set out for Samara in the Tashkent train. We carried provisions for 10 days, also cooking utensils, candles and a plentiful supply of Keatings powder[140]. Accompanying our party was an influential member of the Russian Foreign Office, who kept us in hand with dignity and quiet perseverance! We had freedom to make our own investigations and were given

---

[139] Russian Centre for Storage and Study of Documents of Recent History (RTsKhIDNI), fonds 5, series 1, file 2559, sheet 31 (both sides).

[140] [Translator's note: An insecticide powder.]

every assistance. On arriving at Samara we paid a visit to the local Soviet authorities where the facts and figures were given to us by the chairman, a thin starved-looking man, with a keen intellectual face, who looked as if he had shouldered responsibility beyond his strength [...] We were motored to outlying villages within a radius of 30 miles of Samara town [...] Most of the people were packing up to leave cause there was no more bread, no more potatoes and the grass had given out. I saw in practically every house, benches covered with birch or lime leaves. These are dried, pounded up, mixed with sunflower seeds or acorns and perhaps little melon peel, some dirt and water, and then baked into a substance which they call bread and which looks and smells like baked manure. The children cannot digest this food and they die.

There are practically no babies, those which survive look ghastly. In some villages as Stavropol on the Volga, the people are eating shale. All the children have inflated stomachs, some are rickety and have enlarged heads. None of them are properly clothed, only a ragged shirt and no underclothes.[141]

As a consequence of Thorp and Haines' trip to Samara, Buzuluk district was chosen as the place where the Quakers – both British and American – would apply their efforts to try to save people from famine. At the start of the autumn, local Pomgol committees were organised in many villages in the district, food distribution points were opened, and deliveries of food were awaited. Many

---

[141] Letter from M. Thorp: A Quaker in Famine-stricken Russia_Sep_1921. FEWVRC-MISSIONS-8-3-9-1_REPORTS-ACCOUNTS_1921

schoolteachers were let out of school to take part in the fight against famine. It was a major problem to transport aid around rural areas, as the beasts of burden had either died or were too weak due to malnutrition. Camels proved to be the most reliable form of transport: they lived off thorns and had a great deal of stamina as draught animals, although they were very lazy.

Camel at the Buzuluk Granary

©Courtesy Friends Historical Library of Swarthmore College

An anthology created in Samara, *On the frontline of the famine*, was published in 1921: 'The Quakers' work began on approximately 10 September this year. Initially, it took the following form: three wagons of food and clothes were received and distributed to the province's establishments for education, health and social provision, with the involvement of members of the society of Quakers.

'As their next task, the Quakers opted to work exclusively in Buzuluk district, where only 5000 portions were being supplied to 45 children's homes due to the absence of food. In their programme, Quakers gave food to 25,000 children, and, depending on the food available, hoped to increase this figure to 100,000 portions in two months. The society of Quakers is carrying out its work with the assistance of the Buzuluk district executive committee, with a negligible number of technical staff in the form of 10 people, funded at the Quakers' expense'.[142]

The Quakers' original plan for distributing food was simple: to only feed the villages where the situation was worst. However, they soon had to change this method: as soon as they heard that food was being handed out in particular villages, peasants from all the villages would abandon their homes and children and go wherever there was food. This led to a sharp increase in the number of children being taken into care in reception centres for children and children's homes. The Quakers therefore decided to give out food in each district, but to the following types of food distribution point:

a) Kitchens (food distribution points). Children selected by the local Pomgol committees were fed in the kitchens. Rations – flour, beans, cocoa, sugar, rice, fat, chocolate and dried milk – were distributed.

b) Children's institutions. Rations were handed out to local state-run children's homes throughout the district, including in Buzuluk itself. These institutions were

---

[142] *Na fronte goloda* ['On the frontline of the famine']. Samara, 1921, p.92.

inspected frequently by the Quakers to check on how food was being distributed.

c) Breast-feeding mothers. Rations were given out to all maternity wards.

d) Babies. Rations were distributed in collective nurseries or to mothers who were at home with their babies.

The list of foods included in the rations was always the same, but the quantities varied. Oats, fish oil and soap were added to the rations for breast-feeding mothers with babies.

As an example, here is a short extract from reports on the Quakers' food distribution in November 1921. This was at the very start of the Quakers' heroic efforts to save people's lives. Food and other goods were being distributed to children's institutions in Buzuluk and to children's homes across the district:

Distribution of food by the Society of Friends in Buzuluk district in November 1921.

Nurseries in Buzuluk: 41 Ufimskaya Ulitsa [Street]: flour (8 pood[143]), rice (1 pood), cocoa (15 funt), soap (30 funt), fish oil (15 funt).

Nurseries in Buzuluk: 20 Pochtovaya Ulitsa: flour (2

---

[143] As mentioned earlier, a *pood* was a unit of mass equivalent to 40 Russian *funt*, roughly equivalent to 16 kilograms or 36 pounds, so a *funt* was roughly equal to a pound.

pood), rice (25 funt), cocoa (7 funt), soap (15 funt), fish oil (7 funt)

[...]

Assorted clothing: [...] children's home no.11
                        Vorontsovka in Tverdilovsk
                        volost - 72

                        children's home no.4 Buzuluk
                        -10

                        children's home no.10
                        Samarskaia Ulitsa - 42

                        children's hospital
                        Teatralnaya Ulitsa - 14

For children of displaced people (Molokans)[144]: flour (18 pood 30 funt), lard (1 p. 10 f.), rice (7 p. 20 f.), sugar (1 p. 10 f.), cocoa (25 f)., soap (25 f.), chocolate (25 cases).[145]

Early in the autumn of 1921, Arthur Watts, the Quaker from Manchester, arrived in Buzuluk, having been working in Moscow since 1920. He became the leader of the 'English' Quaker group, which was extremely small at first. It was Watts who led negotiations with the People's Commissariat for Foreign Affairs, arranging entry permits for more British relief workers to come to Russia.

[144] [Translator's note: The Molokans, or 'dairy eaters', were a pacifist Christian sect, similar to the Doukhobors.]
[145] Central State Archive of Samara Province (TsGASO), fonds R-79, series 1, file 15.

Watts wrote to the London committee at the start of December 1921: 'The population of the Ooyezd[146] is 618,976 of which 252,100 are children. The railway line cuts right through the centre of the Ooyezd, west to east. There are 53 volosts (rural districts) in the Ooyezd. For the purposes of analysing the needs these are divided into 5 categories. The first three have already exhausted the local supplies of food, and it is estimated that the remaining two will exhaust their supplies by the 1st January and 1st February respectively. It will be noted that the worst categories are to the South of the railway. There are organised throughout the whole Ooezd (as in other famine districts) local famine committees, and in most villages, kitchens are arranged for anticipation of supplies'.[147]

The Friends planned to distribute their supplies through the local famine committees[148], using the committees' existing kitchens or getting them to open new ones where necessary. Strict controls were carried out in each district by two supervisors who were full members of Friends' Unit. A contemporary report stated: 'The Ooyezd was divided into 8 administrative areas, 5 of which will have warehouses or supply points (on the railway). A central warehouse in each volost town, run by a manager, distributed food and recipes to villages, got receipts and sent them to the FWVRC. There were three or four kitchens per village, one

---

[146] [District.]
[147] Letter from Arthur Watts to Ruth Fry, 2 Dec 1921. FHL FEWVRC-MISSIONS-8-3-9-1_REPORTS-ACCOUNTS_1921
[148] Ibid.

manager for several kitchens and in each kitchen a child was elected to see supplies given out'.[149]

Local committees decided whom to feed. Sometimes local village councils (soviets) took these decisions themselves, or else the soviet was part of a village committee. Not infrequently, reports from the field and private letters by the Quaker mission workers contained stories of petty theft and fraudulent distribution of food by committees, but these incidents did not threaten the distribution system: the Quakers resolved these issues on the ground with characteristic patience. They considered these irregularities to be due to the character of the Russian peasants, and partly justified by the extremely difficult situation in which villagers found themselves. The Quakers insisted that people on the ground should keep a list of exactly who received food, but they had to be vigilant about staying strict. As Francesca Wilson[150] noted: 'If I made one exception, the whole courtyard was full of similar exceptions the next day'.[151]

People who survived thanks to the Quakers supplies recalled that 'the Quakers' food was of high quality: white bread, meat, condensed milk, various conserves, cereals and fats'.[152]

---

[149] *The Russian Field* issue no. 6, 7 January 1922, FEWVRC/8/3/3 LSF – quote from Luke Kelly, *British Humanitarian Activity in Russia 1890-1923*, p. 202.

[150] Francesca Mary Wilson (1888–1981) was an English schoolteacher, relief worker for refugees and writer.

[151] Francesca Wilson, *In the Margin of Chaos*, p. 150 – quote from Luke Kelly, p. 204.

[152] V.V. Alexeev, *Zemlya Borskaya. Vekhi istorii*. Samara: Nauchno-

The initial plan was for the 'English' group of Quakers to work jointly with the American group, but later it was decided that the Americans should take on sole responsibility for three food distribution points in the eastern part of the district. Three of the eight sites did not have distribution points, so food was delivered directly to them from Buzuluk, Pavlovka or Totskoye.

Cuthbert Clayton, A.P.I. Cotterell and Tom Copeman were some of the first Quakers to arrive in Buzuluk. Questions about administering aid distribution were discussed with the local authorities and resolved fairly quickly. The authorities also provided armed guards to protect the warehouses where the Quakers kept their stocks of food. Arthur Watts, meanwhile, had to keep travelling backwards and forwards between Moscow and Buzuluk.

In order to do fundraising in the West as quickly as possible and raise sufficient money, the Quakers needed to give human-interest reports about the Russian regions affected by the famine. Anna Haines was sent to give speeches around Britain as soon as she got back from Samara. Richenda Scott wrote in her book: 'At a public meeting in the Essex Hall, she gave her quiet, factual statement, avoiding any attempt to dramatize or over-emphasize the seriousness of the position, and on that account making all the deeper impression upon her listeners'.[153]

---

tekhnicheskii tsentr, 2016, p. 337.
[153] Richenda Scott, *Quakers in Russia*, ch. 18, p.238. London, 1964.

The American Friends Service Committee appointed Anna Louise Strong, a left-wing American journalist, as their correspondent, to write regular bulletins in the Western press. Anna Louise, who did not speak Russian, began to write reports for British and American newspapers as soon as she had crossed the border into Russia: 'All the way from Minsk to Moscow were signs of the great spirit that is stirring in Russia in the common fight against famine. Boys in a single garment of hand-woven linen and without shoes, got on the train with official dignity and municipal credentials, selling papers for famine relief or taking collections and giving proper receipts. There were posters in the stations announcing benefit performances of every kind'.[154]

Anna Louise fell ill with typhus on her arrival in Russia, but once she had recovered, she became very active in Samara province. The Samara Province Commission for Improving Children's Lives wrote about her and took her photo for their illustrated journal, in a photo reportage[155] under the heading 'Aid to starving children'. The photo shows 'Miss Stronk [sic] with her interpreter Miss Grokhovskaya among clothing, underwear and presents for donating to starving, ragged children at one of the children's homes in Samara'. There is a photo with the caption 'A representative of the Anglo-American

[154] Ibid, p. 237.

[155] *Na pomoshch!*, illustrated journal of Samara Province Commission for Improving Children's Lives. All money collected to help starving children. Samara branch of State Publishers (Gosizdatelstvo). 1922. p. 12.

Society of "Quakers" and village officials distribute clothing, underwear and chocolate to hungry, ragged children in the village of Novo-Semeikino in Samara province'. A little lower down, there is a photo of 'Miss Stronk personally clothing a boy in a clean shirt and an English suit in one of the reception centres for children in Samara'.

The Russian national newspaper, Izvestiya, wrote about Anna Louise Strong: 'Anna Strong, member of the "Friends Committee for Aid to Russia", wrote [an article] in the Manchester Guardian to stress the 'huge initiative' in Russia to save the country, and noted the extensive organisational work being done by the People's Commissariat for Health'.[156]

English Quaker, A.P.I. Cotterell, returned to the Moscow office after working in Buzuluk, to discuss the situation in the district. After talking with Cotterell, Arthur Watts (who was perpetually on the road between Moscow, Buzuluk and Minsk) wrote to the committee in London: 'The famine conditions there are growing worse every week as the slender stock diminishes and more and more people are becoming absolutely destitute of food'.[157] Cotterell said that feeding children in towns resulted in an ever-increasing number of children being abandoned by their parents and that, if this continued, the overcrowding threatened to become dangerous. He reported that many houses had already earned the name of 'Houses of

[156] *Izvestiya*, issue no. 210, 21 September 1921.
[157] Letters from Moscow. FHL FEWVRC-MISSIONS-8-3-9-1_ REPORTS-ACCOUNTS_1921

Death', since there were more inhabitants than it was possible to feed. Quakers, he said, had come to the opinion that the only course that they could adopt was to feed throughout the whole Ooezd, even if this meant spreading their limited supplies very thinly, as they realised that if they made the conditions in one district visibly better than in others, that district would immediately be swamped by thousands of starving people. Arthur Watts wrote: 'This has placed a very tremendous responsibility upon us [...] We have undertaken a work which we find cannot be limited in the way which we had anticipated. We must feed immediately 30,000 children in the Ooyezd and by Christmas should be feeding 100,000. By January practically all the available local stores will have been consumed and we may have to extend our feeding from 300,000 to 500,000'.

Sorochinskoye. Dorothy Detzer with clothing bales on sled

©Courtesy Friends Historical Library of Swarthmore College

Since the Quakers were guided by their principles, the idea of sharing responsibility for work in the same region with another organisation did not appeal to them much: 'Unless the organisation worked absolutely harmoniously with us a great many difficulties would naturally arise. We had thought of appealing to the American Friends to come and share the district with us but until the position with regard to the Hoover agreement is [clearer] we do not feel that we can do this. The difference in the attitude of the people and officials towards the ARA and ourselves is quite marked. We have a unique position here in Russia and the very fact that we are unconnected with any Government or semi-government organisation has meant a tremendous lot in the development of our work on friendly lines of mutual cooperation. To have two sets of Friends in the same district with one of them limited in its actions and to some extent controlled by a semi-government organisation would, we feel, create a very different position'.[158]

Indeed, the US authorities insisted that American Quakers should work under the umbrella of the ARA. An American Quaker, Murray Kenworthy, wrote home at the start of November 1921 after he had arrived in Russia: 'We, American Friends, had to come in as part of the ARA personnel but were to be given a definite area in which to work; we have however arranged to continue with the English Friends, and will continue to work as the Anglo-American Friends work. We will keep separate

---

[158] Ibid.

books and may have definite distribution points
but will not attempts to keep our rations separate,
nor be very discriminating as to where our workers
are stationed – that is, we may have English and
Americans working at the same point'.[159]

American and British Quakers used short names for
themselves in their dealings with local authorities:
the American ODK group and the English ODK
group. ODK stood for *Obshchestvo Druzei – Kvakerov*,
meaning 'the Society of Friends (Quakers)'.
Sometimes they simply called themselves American
Quakers and British Quakers.

The Quakers wrote in their letters and diaries
about the horrors of famine in Buzuluk and the
surrounding district. These are private accounts
which they did not hand over to the press. American
Friend, Murray Kenworthy, described the situation
in the region: 'The death rate is constantly rising,
frightful conditions incident to famine districts
are here in all their tragedy and horror, it is just
a question of degree. We find more people dead
on the streets, the pile of unburied dead in the
cemetery gets larger every day etc, etc. Miss White,
the girl with whom I was working at first, is in from
her point and reports that cannibalism is now a
fact, a mother killed and ate her nine-year-old girl,
and one family ate an old woman who died in their
home. Yesterday I saw a dog attack a woman and
started to the rescue, but she was able to shake the
dog off before I got far. I do not know that the dog

[159] Letter from Murray Kenworthy to his parents, 5 November
1921. AFSC Archive, FSR.

attacked from hunger or from just crossness. In most villages the dogs are now gone, having been eaten, but there are a good many here in Buzuluk. I have for some time cautioned our people to watch the dogs very carefully. Every time I write I think I'll not say any more about the famine horrors and yet I suppose you wish to know something of the things that are of daily, even hourly occurrence with us'.[160]

The pile of unburied dead in Buzuluk cemetery, December 1921

©*Courtesy Friends Historical Library of Swarthmore College*

The dispatches from local Cheka agents to the centre were even more shocking: 'The famine has reached horrific proportions: peasants have eaten all their food substitutes[161], their cats, their dogs, and now they are eating corpses which they have dug up from graves. Repeated instances of cannibalism

[160] Ibid.
[161] Examples of food substitutes were leather goods (belts, leather boots, saddles, stirrups, bridles, halters and reins), clay and straw.

have been found in Pugachov and Buzuluk district. According to members of the Rural Council Executive Committee[162], cannibalism is widespread in Lyubimovka. Cannibals are segregated from the rest of the population'.[163]

Soviet officials from Buzuluk reported to Samara about how the famine was affecting the mental health of local residents. The executive secretary of Buzuluk district committee of the Russian Communist Party (Bolsheviks), T.F.Ilin, wrote: 'The political conditions in the district up to the 1st January were the following: part of the population were apathetic and indifferent to the authorities and to all their surroundings; the majority had a grudge against the Soviet authorities. This can be explained by the fact that the famine had hit the population very hard by the 1st January [...] As food distribution increased on the ground, and as the Society of Quakers launched its work widely from January, the peasants' mood has changed, and their attitude to their surroundings, apathy and indifference are disappearing, and little by little they are becoming engaged in life in society'.[164]

In the early months, there was only a small number of Quaker workers in Buzuluk and the surrounding district. By January 1922, no more than two or three people were working in the Buzuluk Quaker office;

[162] [the Volispolkom]

[163] Letter, 23 January 1922, Central Archive of the FSB [formerly KGB] of the Russian Federation, fonds 1, series 6, file 461, sheets 183—189.

[164] Samara Province State Archive for Social-Political History (SOGASPI), fonds 1, series 1, file 772, sheet 6.

there were also scattered units in the villages of the district. Due to their limited capacity, everyone lived and worked in squalid conditions. There was no strategy to speak of, and advance planning was simply unrealistic in the circumstances. In an interview in the Quaker journal The Friend, Dr Nansen spoke highly of the Quakers in Russia: 'With their foresight and the efforts they made, they have paved the way, and they did it in a way that no one else would have been able to do. They paved the way for others, for an international mobilisation of effort in order to save millions of Russians from the famine. The Society of Friends arrived in Russia at a critical juncture'.[165]

It is interesting to read a description of everyday life in the Quaker offices in both Buzuluk and Sorochinskoye. Murray Kenworthy wrote home: 'I understand we have very good quarters at Buzuluk. One of the best houses in the city, with a number of rooms and out-buildings'.[166] Soon, Kenworthy and two colleagues would go to the village of Andreevka, 60 kilometres to the southwest of Buzuluk, the district centre. They got there in the Quakers' Ford lorry, while stores of food were being delivered to the Quaker centre there and to other Quaker centres by horse and camel. Kenworthy wrote that his group consisted of two women and himself. One of the women was Irish, 30-year-old Dorice White, who already had almost four years' experience

---

[165] *The Friend*, 7 November 1921, interview with Fridtjof Nansen by John Harris.
[166] Letter from Murray Kenworthy to his parents, 15 November 1921. AFSC Archive, FSR.

of distributing aid in France, Germany, Poland and Russia. Dorice White quickly learnt Russian – in fact, she would be one of the last Quakers to leave the USSR in 1931, after spending ten years working in the country. However, for as long as neither Kenworthy or White could speak Russian, they had an interpreter from Buzuluk with them. The interpreter was a German woman who could not speak English, only German and Russian. She would speak to the local peasants in Russian, and then speak in German to Miss White, who would translate what had been said into English for Murray Kenworthy. The Quakers were responsible for feeding starving people over a colossal territory, so they just did as much as they could while awaiting new staff members. 'We have too much territory here and we hope to have other workers in the very near future, but we are simply going ahead and doing the best we can until we can do better, with people dying we cannot wait until we have all we would like to have', Kenworthy wrote.

English Quakers' Headquarters in Buzuluk in 1921-1924

©Courtesy Friends Historical Library of Swarthmore College

In his letters, he also described aspects of his living conditions in Andreevka: 'When we arrived here our permanent home was not ready, so they put us into a two-roomed house in which 8 people already lived. We took one of the rooms, the back one, their best one, but to get to outdoors we had to go thru their room. The first night there were six of us, three men and three women, and we all slept in the same room, with no ventilation, the windows were double and sealed up with putty or the cracks pasted up with paper. There were six nations = Irish, German, Jew, Russian, Lithuanian and American, sum is an international unit. The room was of fair size but contained a hot stove. We now have very good quarters – for Russia. I have a room all to myself where I now am. This is part of the Hospital. There are five buildings in the compound formerly used for hospital wards etc. and three for various other purposes. We have one entire building'.[167]

The American Quakers opened an office in the village of Sorochinskoye, 80 kilometres from Buzuluk. One of them, a woman called Beulah Hurley, described her new way of life: 'Home and Office. Library building, 26 Trotsky Avenue: 10 minutes from the station. Unused for the last 6 months, but cook stove being built again and is in a good order as is possible with ancient wallpaper and the domestic horror of a kitchen removed from our small dining and living room by long stairway and big upper and lower halls. Excellent heat and light,

---

[167] Letter from Murray Kenworthy to his parents, 25 November 1921, Andreevka. AFSC Archive, FSR.

now that wood and kerosene have arrived. Ground floor: Kitchen & office; above, small living room, one large & two small bedrooms. One large and one small now being used for isolation ward for patient & nurse, the other 2 men sleeping downstairs in the office alcove, the janitress & housekeeper sleeping <u>on</u> the <u>kitchen stove</u>, true Russian fashion'.[168]

Sorochinskoye. The American Quakers' Office is a two-storied building on the left.

©Courtesy Friends Historical Library of Swarthmore College

Foodstuffs which arrived by railway were transferred to the warehouse by the station. A couple of local officials helped out the small group of Quakers: there was a Communist from Sorochinskoye, Konovalov from the Board of Education, and his assistant, a German man called Thomas. They joined the Quakers for some part of nearly every

---

[168] Beulah Hurley on opening the American Quaker centre in Sorochinsk, 27 December 1921. AFSC archives, FSR.

day and helped out with everything from nursing to political affairs. Food was distributed all over the area of the rural council: kitchens were organised, as well as food distribution points, which were nicknamed 'pit-punkty' by the local inhabitants. Quakers gave out food rations in soup kitchens, in children's homes and reception centres for children, and in schools. This helped children learn better: as everyone knows, you cannot concentrate on an empty stomach, or as the Russians say, 'A hungry belly is deaf to teaching'.

The situation was getting steadily worse. Beulah Hurley wrote: 'Buzuluk area is of the worst, but they do manage to <u>bury</u> their dead here though in wholesale lots, 200 to ditch. The shadows that drift by our office windows, and come whispering at our doors wring one's heart and one feels an utter brute to turn from them but what can one do? Feed each one and let the hundreds die?'[169]

There were continuous deliveries of 'Quaker food' to Buzuluk from Britain and America, but money was needed to buy food, and in order to collect donations, people in those countries needed to hear what exactly their donations would be used for. The Quakers on the ground could have written accounts of the horrors of the famine and about the difficult work being done by British and American relief workers, but they already had a lot on their plate. The accounts needed to be written in such a way that the reader would be both horrified and filled

---

[169] Ibid.

with compassion. Good writers were needed, and so journalists travelled out to see the Quakers. The journalist Evelyn Sharp of the Manchester Guardian spent some time in Alekseevka, and afterwards she wrote about how Quakers were saving people from starving to death:

I happened to be in one of the Alekseevka stolovia, or dining-rooms, where the children come for their daily portions of soup, cocoa and milk, chocolate (three sticks a week) and bread. There are 27 of these stolovia run by the Friends' Relief Mission in the volost town of Alekseevka and 15 more for which the local Soviet is responsible. Only some 3000 odd are left of Alekseevka's former population of 8000 (it is impossible to obtain exact statistics of the number of deaths in the famine regions, partly because the total mounts daily, but chiefly because burial has become impracticable in the ordinary way, and it is extremely difficult to keep count of the unburied, who lie in the sheds and unused windmills, and occasionally in churches, as well as in open pits in the churchyards), and the reason why so many stolovia are needed there is that the place is built, like other Russian villages in this part of the world, in a long drawn out line, extending for some versts. Also, there are no large buildings; so the stolovia have to be situated in small houses, each supplying only a limited number of children.

The one we were visiting was typical of the Quaker stolovia, now to be found in all the villages of the Buzuluk Ooezd (or department) of Samara. It was in a peasant's house and supplied about 50 children. A baby slept, suspended from the ceiling in a wooden cradle; older children squatted together on the top of the stove, and peered down at us in silent curiosity. In two large cauldrons the soup and cocoa were boiling; while a still and patient group of children and mothers stood waiting with beautiful old earthenware and metal vessels, shaped like Greek vases in their hands. From a beam in the roof hung a primitive pair of scales, in which the portions of bread, about a quarter of a pound for each child, were weighed under the critical eye of the peasant inspector, a woman chosen by the parents themselves. She looked a lady of the fiercest rectitude, and I would not willingly have been the stolovia proprietor who tried under that searching scrutiny to rob the children of a crumb that was due to them.[170]

Food was delivered to Buzuluk and Sorochinskoye by train from Moscow, after first being sent by goods train from Tallinn in Estonia. Even the Soviet press wrote about this. For example, *Izvestiya* newspaper ran an article on 'The work of the People's Commissariat for Health's goods trains during the famine': 'The other day, the third goods train no.1 left Moscow and took food and clothing to starving children in Buzuluk, provided by the American society of Quakers. Representatives of the society travelled with the train and will lead the distribution of goods on the ground [...]. As well as dispatching the valuable goods trains, the Commissariat for Health's transport department sent separately two wagons of food and clothing provided by the American society of Quakers to

---

[170] Evelyn Sharp, *The Stuff of Life and Death*. Friends House London archives. FEWVRC-MISSIONS-8-3-9-4 REPORTS-ACCOUNTS 1921-1923

Pugachov[171], accompanied by special agents'.[172]

Quaker Ford truck with sacks of grain in front of the American Friends' Mission building in Sorochinskoye

©Courtesy Friends Historical Library of Swarthmore College

It is worth noting that aid to Russia from British charitable funds, including via Quakers, aroused criticism from detractors in Britain. For example, the British newspaper *The Daily Express* doubted the justification for British donors giving money to causes in Russia. Without questioning the honesty of British charities, the newspaper expressed concern about the Russian state's ineffectiveness and Russians' dishonesty, mentioning the unstable situation in Soviet Russia; the worry was that this was bound to affect fundraising in Britain.[173] Given this state of affairs, it was vitally important to carry

---

[171] A town in Saratov province. While Buzuluk is southeast of Samara, Pugachov is to its southwest.

[172] *Izvestiya* issue no. 223, 6 October 1921.

[173] Luke Kelly, *British humanitarian activity in Russia, 1890-1923*. Palgrave Macmillan, 2018, p. 185.

out an information campaign. The London Quaker committee therefore produced a huge number of pamphlets including ones entitled *Facts and figures*[174] or *How the goods reach the famine area*[175]. These booklets were sent to the British media. In these publications, the Quakers drew particular attention to the many checks on the food supply at every point along its journey from London to Riga or Tallinn, and from there to Moscow, and on to Buzuluk. The Quakers also stressed that the level of theft or goods going missing was actually very low.

A member of the Friends' Relief Committee, Gertrude A. Ostler, who wrote for the *Manchester Guardian*, spent some time at the Quaker warehouse in Moscow. The train from Tallinn had just arrived, the wagons were uncoupled, and Ostler, together with Tom Read, the warehouse supervisor, went to inspect the Buzuluk freight train no. 9, which was waiting on the tracks for a locomotive.

There it is with its 32 waggons, crammed with food and clothing for the famine area; we plough through the snow, counting them and admiring the seals. In the middle of the train is the convoy car where our representative will travel with half a dozen soldiers of the Red Army! These people will guard our train, and carry with them a bundle of imperious letters, commanding station masters to see to it that the train is pushed through with all possible speed.

One remembers the good friends who provided the milk

---

[174] *Facts and Figures*, FEWVRC/8/3/2, Publicity, LSF – quote from Luke Kelly, p. 185.

[175] *How the Goods Reach the Famine Area*, FEWVRC/8/3/2, Publicity, LSF – quote from Luke Kelly, p. 185.

and cocoa and beans and wish that they could see for themselves the swift and skilful handling of their gifts.

After starting work in Buzuluk and district in September 1921, the British Quakers in the 'English ODK group'[176] fed 70,000 children and 60,000 adults by February 1922, making a total of 130,000 people. Remarkably, the supply department of the Buzuluk Quaker office consisted of only one Englishman along with four or five Russian staff. Cargoes of food arriving at Buzuluk station were met by twenty or thirty members of the local railway workers' trade union. Although they were given a small quantity of rations for doing this work, these poor workers were sometimes unable to lift sacks or boxes due to their constant hunger. Month by month, the number of people receiving rations from the Quakers increased. When Buzuluk District Commission for Famine Relief sent its report for May 1922 to the Samara Province Commission for Famine Relief, it wrote: 'As could have been expected, the population present is 515,161 people, even though the mortality rate is almost normal, according to more accurate data on the ground received by the Rural Council Executive Committee as of 1st June. Bearing in mind that the almost normal percentage of mortality will only go down, unless there is an epidemic, we can state with certainty that – including evacuees (around 30,000) – the district has lost up to 140,000 people, that is, 21.5% of the population instead of the expected

---

[176] N.B. ODK came from the Cyrillic initials ОДК, standing for Society of Friends – Quakers.

losses of 50%, judging by the proportion of deaths in the population at the start of the famine, especially during November, December and part of January. At present, the District Commission for Famine Relief, with the help of foreign organisations, is feeding 478,772 souls out of the general number of the population in need, that is, almost 100%'.[177] Even with so few staff, the Quakers had succeeded in saving tens of thousands of people.

In June 1922, the Quaker famine relief programme reached its peak – the number of food recipients increased significantly. British and American works on the history of Quaker aid, as well as the Soviet press[178], gave mistaken information which led to a significant underestimate of the number of people helped. With the help of staff from Buzuluk archives, I managed to obtain documents[179] which give the following figures:

English ODK group: fed 264,184 people in 38 rural areas of the northwest part of the district and in the town [of Buzuluk].

American ODK group: fed 147,806 people in 18 rural

---

[177] Branch of the 'State Archive of Orenburg Region' in the town of Buzuluk, fonds 536, series 1, item 2.

[178] 'The most wonderful help from private hands was the help of foreign organisations. I have the figures as of 1st May. ARA is feeding 5,643,387 people. English Quakers are feeding 265,600 people. [...] In total, foreign organisations are feeding 6,549,282 people'. Speech by comrade Kalinin at the opening meeting of the third session of the All-Russian Central Executive Committee, 12 May 1922, reported by *Izvestiya*, issue no. 107, 15 May 1922.

[179] Branch of the 'State Archive of Orenburg Region' in the town of Buzuluk, fonds 536, series 1, item 2.

areas in the southeast part of the district; based in the village of Sorochinskoye.

TOTAL: *411,990 people.*

So, in June 1922, American and British Quakers fed 85% of the population in need in Buzuluk district! Archive documents list the foods which went into the rations:

The English ODK group gives out rations which are the same for adults and children: wheat - 12 funt, beans – 2 f., herring – 1 f., flour – 3 f., rice – 1 f., sugar - ½ f. Conserves – 2 tins.

The American group: 30 f. corn for adults. 18 f. flour for children.

3 ½ f. cereals, ½ f. sugar.

Out of this number [i.e., out of the 264,184 people fed by the English ODK group], the Quakers fed 5500 children in the town [of Buzuluk].

In July, the feeding programme began to reduce. Joint Anglo-American statistics showed that 320,000 people received rations from the English and American ODK groups combined. The peak of the famine was over, summer had come, and hope had been sown too for the new harvest. The statistics for the last months were as follows:

REPORT FOR AUGUST 1922

In August, because of the harvest in progress, the number of people being fed fell to 243,687 people, i.e., the number of people being fed reduced by 50%.

The English group envisages feeding 56,000 people from 1 September, 80,000 in October, 90,000 in November...

REPORT FOR SEPTEMBER 1922

From January 1923 we will need to give food aid to:

141,263 adults, 125,946 children. Total: 267,209 people, which represents 55.1% of the population as a whole.[180]

The local district Pomgol committee clearly feared that the Quakers would leave Russia. Either they had heard worrying rumours, or it was just a reason to write to them:

SOCIETY OF FRIENDS (QUAKERS)

Dear Sirs,

With a feeling of deep respect, the District Commission for Famine Relief expresses our sincere gratitude to you for the aid you have given and your extremely hard work despite known hardships and the risk of danger. Your aid is valued so much by the peasantry of Buzuluk district precisely because it is not for self-interest, but only out of a feeling of benevolence to brothers who, by the will of nature, have fallen into desperate need and suffering. And the importance of this aid is especially great, especially huge, when we stand at the eve of it being ended.

---

[180] Ibid.

According to private information which has reached us, you are intending to leave the district no later than September, in the hope that the ongoing harvest could provide enough filling food without your aid. Fearing that this information might be true, District Commission for Famine Relief has the honour of bringing the following to your attention: the extent of the devastation is so colossal, that it will take at least three consecutive years of good harvests to re-establish agriculture.[181]

A year had passed since the Bolsheviks had opened the gate to foreign relief organisations. The Society of Friends had saved around half a million residents of Buzuluk district. The peak of the famine was over. What form should Quaker work in Soviet Russia take, not that the topic of the famine was no longer on the front pages, even of Soviet newspapers?

---

[181] Ibid.

Chapter 7. *Deaths in the Quaker mission. How the Quakers managed to continue working in Russia after the end of the famine. The history of children's home no. 33 in Gamaleyevka; the village of Kuzminovka; food distribution points in Buzuluk. The campaign against malaria. The merger of the American and English ODK groups. Signing an agreement with TsK Posledgol. The agreement for Quaker tractors. The puzzling meeting with Russian Quakers at Buzuluk station.*

By summer 1922, the number of people in the English ODK group based in Buzuluk had risen to 28, while there were 14 people in the American ODK group[182]. In both groups, many Russians worked alongside the foreigners. As Buzuluk resident V. Melnikov recalled: 'The food distribution base, organised at the trading post of Buzuluk, had four huge warehouses. All the activities were led by two Englishmen. Two teams of Russian ODK workers were always at warehouses no.s 9 and 10, and it was their job to receive and distribute food and check the unloading of the wagons. The staff of warehouse no. 9 included: a former colonel of the Tsarist army, an artist, a violonist, a former priest, a bookkeeper and, as luck would have it, a certain 19-year-old boy. What luck it was that warehouse workers received a monthly food ration consisting of about four pood of various types of food. I'll give an example for comparison: a starving family had <u>to sell a four-</u>roomed house in the centre of town

[182] Central State Archive of Samara Province (TsGASO), fonds 79, series 1, item 21.

just to get two pood of flour. But to get your ration you had to work from 6 a.m. to between 6 and 10 p.m.'.[183]

Members of the US Quaker Mission on their way to
Sorochinskoye: Sam Wetherald, Elma Bliss, Omar Brown

©*Courtesy Friends Historical Library of Swarthmore College*

Samara's archives show[184] that in total the English ODK group served 38 volosts [parishes] in the northwest of Buzuluk district, and the American group served 18 volosts in the south-east of the district. Food distribution was carried out in the following manner: the English group worked in Buzuluk and Pavlovka, while the American group worked in Sorochinskoye and Totskoye. The other areas just

[183] *Pod znamenem Lenina* newspaper [Under Lenin's banner], issue 91, 12 June 1990.
[184] List of volosts served by the Quakers. Central State Archive of Samara Province (TsGASO), fonds 79, series 1, item 41.

ODK checkpoints, without either warehouses or distribution facilities.

Disease arrived together with the famine. Typhus was rampant in the district, no matter whether you were a Russian or a foreigner. People obviously have less strength to fight illness when they're starving, but in the first autumn and winter in Buzuluk, there were several cases of typhus among the foreigners. The first to fall ill, in October 1921, was Anna Louise Strong, the American journalist who had been assigned to write about the Quakers. Nancy Babb then fell ill with typhus at the end of November, but she got better in a few weeks. The head of the American ODK group, Murray Kenworthy, caught typhus, and then his deputy, Beulah Hurley. Two Quakers died. The first was nurse Mary Pattison, who had worked in Buzuluk in 1916 and had come back in response to a telegram from Arthur Watts asking her to help. She was evacuated to Moscow for treatment, but died there in December 1921 in the Haass hospital.[185] Violet Tillard was the second Quaker to die. She passed away in Buzuluk and was buried in the graveyard there in February 1922.

Izvestiya newspaper reported about them: 'Death in service. On 27th December in the hospital of Dr Gaaz in Moscow, Maria-Beatrisa Peterson[186], a

---

[185] This was a famous Moscow hospital for homeless people, named after the 19th-century German-Russian doctor, Friedrich Haass (1780 – 1853). He opened it in 1844 and spent all his money running it.

[186] Her name appears in this way in the newspaper article. Russian documents often distorted the surnames of English and American Quakers, sometimes beyond recognition.

worker in the Samara famine relief organisation, the "Society of Friends" (Quakers), died of typhus. The deceased was born in Manchester (England) and worked in Samara region back in 1916, giving aid to Polish refugees. After the war, Miss Peterson returned to her homeland, but when she found out about the horrors of the famine in the Volga region in July this year, she came back to Samara and began work energetically as a nurse and carer at the hospital for starving patients with typhus. While doing this hard and dangerous work, Miss Peterson fell ill herself, and on 9 December she was taken from Samara to Moscow on the Nansen[187] train. The burial of the deceased will take place at 11 o'clock sharp in the morning on 2nd January at Lefortovsky cemetery'.[188]

Just a few weeks later, *Izvestiya* reported the following: 'The Plenipotentiary Representative of Soviet Russia to all foreign famine relief organisations regrets to announce the death of a member of the Organisation "Society of Friends" (Quakers), VIOLET TILLAR, who passed away from typhus on 19 February in Buzuluk while doing her duty to help starving people. Eiduk, the Government of Soviet Russia's Plenipotentiary Representative to Pomgol'.[189]

Mikhail Kalinin, President of the All-Russian Central Executive Committee, the titular head of

---

[187] [Translator's note: See note in ch.6 about Nansen's famine relief work through the League of Nations.]

[188] *Izvestiya*, issue no. 1, 1 January 1922.

[189] *Izvestiya*, issue no. 42, 22 February 1922.

state of Soviet Russia, remembered the deceased workers in the Quaker mission in his speech to the Fourth Session of the All-Russian Central Executive Committee: 'Comrades, rather a large number of people have died in this campaign, and in the capitalist world their names would not be known, but these names show us that in the capitalist world there are some individuals, the best representatives of the bourgeois world, who themselves died in the campaign to save the population of the Soviet Republic from disaster. I have no doubt, comrades, that their names will be written down in history in the brightest colours'.[190]

Leon Trotsky spoke about the two English women's feat in a speech in Moscow in March 1922: 'The two young Quaker girls, named Pattison and Violet Tillard, have died [...] When you think of these sacrifices, you want to say that, in our bloodstained and at the same time heroic epoch, there are people who, regardless of their class position, are guided exclusively by the promptings of humanity and inner nobility. I read a brief obituary of this Anglo-Saxon woman, Violet Tillard; a delicate, frail creature, she worked here, in Buzuluk, under the most frightful conditions, fell at her post, and was buried there [...] Probably she was no different from those others who also fell at their posts, serving their fellow human beings. [...] Here we count six such graves. It may be there will be more, it is even probable that there will be. These graves are a kind of augury of the new, future relations between

---

[190] *Izvestiya*, issue no. 246, 31 October 1922.

people which will be based upon solidarity and not be shadowed by self-seeking. When the Russian people become a little richer, they will erect (we are profoundly sure of this) a great monument to these fallen heroes'.[191]

The head of the American ODK group, Murray Kenworthy, who had himself recovered from typhus, wrote in March 1922: 'We, who have had the Typhus, certainly appreciate the invitation to take a vacation outside of Russia, but this seems so impossible that we have not availed ourselves of your favour. For those who are in the Buzuluk area it means at least a two-week trip each way and all the trials of travel and borders. […] The better plan seems to be to find a place out in some of our forests where our workers can go for a weekend or more'.[192]

The Quakers had to start thinking about preventative measures, of course, notwithstanding their worries about the convalescing colleagues. Murray Kenworthy wrote in March 1922: 'We find the visiting of kitchens out in the villages a big problem. There is always the risk of disease, we take every possible precaution, and a visitor may be gone from three to five days, on a sledge trip, individual beds and outfit are taken and care is made in selecting sleeping places. Miss Tillard met

---

[191] Trotsky's speech to the ceremonial session of the Moscow Soviet for the anniversary of the February revolution, 12 March 1922. <https://www.marxists.org/archive/trotsky/1921/military/ch77.htm>
[192] Letter from Murray Kenworthy to Wilbur Thomas, 17 March 1922. AFSC FSR.

her death through one of these visits, sleeping in a peasant's home. Her interpreter and driver also had Typhus. It has been proposed that we get this inspection done by Russians who have had Typhus but it is doubtful whether we could find men of the right qualifications'. As for preventative measures, arrangements were made to get a large quantity of lime in order to disinfect the premises. They 'also had at hand [a] quantity of Anti Cholera dope which was to be used when the local doctor [had] the proper time'.[193]

Choosing staff for work in Russia was a serious task. Now that Moscow was placing no obstacles on entrance visas for the mission workers, it became a priority to find enough staff for Buzuluk and Sorochinskoye, but without taking whoever applied. According to British historian Luke Kelly, The Friends War Victims Relief Committee was unsure how to go about selecting new staff and did not develop a systematic staffing policy. Katherine Storr had suggested[194] that informal networks were important for recruitment, particularly among non-Friends. The Committee recommended giving priority to older and more experienced Friends with business ability in the field. 'Workers themselves manifested an anxiety about the "spiritual significance" of the work, something often discussed at relief workers' conferences'.[195]

---

[193] Ibid.

[194] Katherine Storr, *Excluded from the Record*, pp. 39, 157-158 (quoted in Luke Kelly's book – p. 171, footnote).

[195] Luke Kelly, *British humanitarian activity in Russia, 1890-1923*, Palgrave Macmillan, 2018, p. 171.

Murray Kenworthy stressed in his letters to the AFSC in Philadelphia 'that special care be taken to get people physically fit for this field – in this territory good lungs and a steady heart means so nearly everything. In fight[ing] a disease like Typhus, it seems necessary to be particularly careful. People over 40 years of age should not come here for field service (I am 48). Every worker on the field faces the probability of death from one of these diseases'.[196]

Emma Krauss, Dorothy North, Elma Bliss and Alfreda Grundy at the US Friends' office in Sorochinskoye. Russian interpreter Andrei Bartashevich is in the background. 1922

©*Courtesy Friends Historical Library of Swarthmore College*

Arthur Watts was struck down with typhus in April 1922, and for a few weeks he was on the brink

[196] Letter from Murray Kenworthy to Wilbur Thomas, 17 March 1922. AFSC FSR.

of death. Even once he was over the worst, Watts remained very weak and unable to work. English Quaker Tom Copeman wrote about Watts: 'If the impossible has been and is being achieved, it is largely due to his energy, courage and pertinacity. Of an iron construction, with great powers of endurance that have enabled him to stand the strain of working 18 and often 24 hours'.[197] It was decided that Watts should be taken back to Moscow and from there go abroad to recuperate. Watts was still in a bad way and needed to be transported in comfort. A Soviet worker at the Quaker office in Moscow, R. Stein, wrote to Martyn Karklin, the plenipotentiary for foreign organisations in Samara, in June 1922: 'I ask you to provide Watts with the use of a small comfortable carriage which is available in Samara for the Swedish Red Cross. I ask you to let me know in good time whether it will be possible to have use of this carriage or not, and if not, I myself will arrange for a special carriage for Watts to be sent from here in Moscow in good time [...] We are very happy that the representative of the Society of Friends has recovered after a severe form of typhus, and now he must absolutely build up his strength. He was such an indispensable worker in the fight against famine, as his work demonstrated'.[198]

Watts left Soviet Russia, going first to Finland, accompanied by Dr Melville Mackenzie, from there on to England, to his hometown of Manchester, then to the USA, and finally to Australia, to Sydney.

[197] Richenda Scott, *Quakers in Russia*, p. 252.
[198] Central State Archive of Samara Province (TsGASO), fonds 79, series 22.

The money for his trip to the other side of the world had been raised by Margaret Thorp, who had got to know Watts in 1921 while she was in Russia. In August 1923, Arthur Watts returned to Russia and went to Buzuluk, but only for a short trip. In September that year, he went to London, and then back to his fiancée, as Margaret was by now, in Australia. The young couple married on 1st October 1925. However, Arthur left Margaret in 1931 and returned to the USSR. He never went back to Buzuluk.

Interestingly, Arthur Watts' brother, Frank Watts, spent some time in Russia himself, working in the English ODK mission. In summer 1922, Frank explained the anxious reaction of Bolshevik officials to the prospect of the Quakers' departure, even though the ODK was not planning to conclude its work in September. He wrote that the time for the Quakers to leave would only be once the local population was able to feed itself. But it is clear from his letter that, even in that case, the Quakers would be in no hurry to leave Soviet Russia: they wanted to carry on helping children's homes and hospitals until the authorities told them to stop. The disclaimer was that the ODK could not predict how long their work would be able to continue, since their funding depended on private donations. One phrase in the letter sums up the Society of Friends' future work: \We think that in future it will make more sense to help the [Russian] people to stand on their own two legs, than just to hand out food'.[199]

---

[199] Letter to Comrade Ponomarev, chair of Buzuluk district -

Frank Watts wrote about the Quakers' action plan[200]:

1) Setting up workshops for repairing agricultural machinery, if possible

2) Connecting the threshing machines to motors

3) Ploughing the land for those who have no livelihood

4) Reviving handicrafts by importing raw materials

5) Supplying livestock to farms and raising livestock

Frank Watts assured the chair of the Buzuluk district executive committee, that 'The ODK will do everything in its power so that the people we succeeded in saving from famine are able to support themselves after we leave'.

A letter from the American ODK group to the same Buzuluk committee was in a similar vein: 'We hope to stay here for the coming year and use our resources at the discretion of our group, together with the local authorities. Improving the situation depends on helping the population not with food but with clothing, industrial and agricultural equipment, and other work to improve the population's everyday lives and, if possible, widen these forms of help. For this reason, you can be assured that, for our part, we will do everything possible to give real help during the most acute human need'.[201]

---

executive committee, Buzuluk, 26 May 1922. Central State Archive of Samara Province (TsGASO), fonds 536, series 1, item 2.

[200] Ibid.

[201] Letter to Buzuluk Distict Executive Committee on behalf of the American ODK (Society of Friends - Quakers) group, 8 June 1922. Central State Archive of Samara Province (TsGASO), fonds 536,

Incidentally, we should not be deceived by the cordial tone of the Bolsheviks' correspondence with the Quakers. Soviet officials obviously had to be complimentary and praise the foreigners' help in their letters to the English and American ODK groups. However, Soviet documents for internal use reveal that the Soviets' traditional suspicion and dislike of foreigners still reigned. Here are the types of demands made in a secret circular sent from Totskoye Area Committee of the Russian Communist Party on 16 July 1922:

The following abnormalities were found in all village councils [Soviets], and also in the District Committees: when the Society of Friends-Quakers was visiting villages, lots of peasants would appear at the ODK mission and get into conversations. The ODK mission would ask questions about what the harvest would be like, how many livestock there were and lots of other questions. Citizens correctly answered that such behaviour [asking questions] was not acceptable to the district and village councils. The area bureau therefore proposes to secretly get the chairmen of village councils to impress upon citizens that they should not talk to visitors, as the latter must receive all information from the village councils.

The present circular must be put into practice secretly, without disclosing it to citizens, so that it does not become known to the ODK mission.[202]

Realising that the situation was changing, that

series 1, item 2.
[202] Totskoye Area Committee of the Russian Communist Party (Bolsheviks), circular no. 650.

foreign organisations were not going to provide food forever and fearing that they would leave Soviet Russia, Martyn Karklin, the province's plenipotentiary representative to foreign organisations, sent a secret letter[203] to local Communists in August 1922, in which he shared his vision of the future. He cautiously assessed the year of tireless effort by foreign organisations to give famine relief to Russians as work which had had 'fairly positive results', but then regretted that it had been 'not very cheap for the government', and that it would now also 'place a certain burden on the budget of the province'. On the one hand, it was good that they were helping, but we must not forget the other side of the coin: these foreigners had created expenses, and – in Karklin's opinion – they were also exploiting the situation.

Karklin – who was, as we know, a secret police agent – wrote that agreements had been signed with foreign organisations 'under the pressure of the overwhelming famine', which had deprived the Bolsheviks 'of the most basic administrative rights'. Karklin considered that now that things were going better, it was time to review the situation: 'We must be bold in identifying and establishing our line of conduct and tactics concerning them'.

---

[203] Letter from M.M. Karklin, plenipotentiary representative of the government of Soviet Russia to foreign organisations to I.T. Morozov, the executive secretary of Samara Province Committee, regarding the prospects for the work of foreign famine relief organisations. 30 August 1922. Samara Province State Archive for Social-Political History (SOGASPI), fonds 1, series 1, folder 709, sheets 10-11.

Of all the famine relief organisations working in Samara province at the time, Karklin particularly picked out the Quakers, towards whom – by and large, unlike the ARA – the Bolsheviks did not have particular grievances: 'The Anglo-American Society of Quakers do not seem to intend to reduce their work yet, but they are definitely inclined to change the form of this aid, or to put it more clearly – to make a transition to aiding production. They have not been able to approach this question in detail yet, aside from their rather productive work with tractors, which requires a lot of expenses on the part of the state, for example, fuel, materials and all crucial lubricants, which we have managed so far to obtain from the Centre almost free of charge. The Centre still intends to provide us with these materials for a while, but in the future districts which are interested in increasing their agricultural production will have to pay some expenses themselves'.

Martyn Martynovich Karklin explained that this meant that foreign organisations would be hoping to stay on to work in Soviet Russia, but in a reduced form. To get the foreigners to stay, 'we must avoid, as far as possible, problems based on minor, insignificant disagreements (which took place previously), but instead we must take part enthusiastically in drawing up plans for future work and must always know what is going on'. Karklin was going to keep a strict eye on the foreign organisations, and he told local Communists about the secret circular in no uncertain terms: 'I will not tolerate any deviation from the execution of my orders which were sent by telegraph'.

What did ordinary peasants, teachers and children feel, though, and what did they think? It was for their sake that American and British Quakers had come to this famine-stricken place.

We come across extraordinary stories and letters in the archives in Philadelphia and London. They help create a picture of peaceful cohabitation and friendship between nations in this one province.

Here, for example, is an extract from the minutes of a meeting of carers and workers in children's home no. 33 in the village of Gamaleyevka, on 21 June 1922:

We children of Soviet Russia in time will justify all the help from ODK, and we will never forget with our child hearts American proletariats.

1) Hurray for ODK!

2) Hurray for all American proletariat!

3) Hurray for our leaders of Russia, Lenin, Trotsky and others![204]

---

[204] AFSC archives.

Russian interpreter for the US Quakers, Samuel Katzman, in Gamaleyevka

©*Courtesy Friends Historical Library of Swarthmore College*

In the same archive, there is a copy of a letter produced at a general meeting for residents of Kuzminovka, which was the centre of a rural district, on 10 September 1922. 150 people were present.

We, citizens of the village of Kuzminovka, send a thousand big thanks to the Quakers for your help and for your feeding, which has enabled us to continue longer on this earth.

Before your coming we suffered a terrible, yes, and indescribable famine. Neither our fathers nor our forefathers knew such hunger in their day. [...] In the winter before you coming, we fed upon cats, dogs, rats, mice, old hides, harness — but this helped us little... But again, this summer's drought has killed everything, and we are again left without the means of subsistence. And again, we turn with an urgent plea to the Friends, the Quakers. Help us with food. We are ready to do all kinds of work, to do anything that is asked of us.

Help us so that we can cultivate the soil.

And again, we thank you most ardently for all the help already given to us.

Signed: Nekrasov, Chernesov

(Seal of the Soviet).[205]

People from Buzuluk who survived the famine when they were children used to tell the story for many years about how they were saved by the Americans and the English. A resident of Buzuluk, G.A. Aksanov, shared his memories with local journalists in 2004:

English and American Quakers were foremost among the foreigners who stretched out a hand to help [...]. With the donations they received, they bought horses and equipment for working the earth, and in 1922-1923 they organised a supplementary farm which was situated in the region on the left bank of the river Buzuluk from the railway bridge to the railway's water pump, where there is now the Lokomotiv stadium and the 7-7 microregion[206] [...]

---

[205] Letter sealed and stamped from Kuzminovka citizens. AFSC FSR.

[206] [Translator's note: A microregion is a residential area consisting

On road 1 between the train station and the corner of road 9, house 3 or 4, the Quakers had a canteen, or rather a soup kitchen where hot food was given out. We went there several times too, with jars or pots for filling, and they would give us cabbage soup [shchi], potatoes and cabbage.[207]

Formally, the American ODK group was part of a wider programme of famine relief run by the ARA, but there was some friction between Hoover, the head of the ARA, and the American Quakers. Hoover could not tell the Quakers what to do and how to do it, but he never missed an opportunity to give advice to the American Friends Service Committee. Hoover particularly criticised the Quakers for feeding everyone, while he believed that aid should be focussed on a certain number of people. As American historian Bertrand Patenaude wrote in his wonderful book, *The Big Show in Bololand: The American Relief Expedition to Soviet Russia in the Famine of 1921*, Mr Hoover insisted on the policy of selecting recipients of food aid and so advised the Quakers: 'Otherwise it is a question of giving a man his breakfast and letting him die before dinner'.[208]

Quaker stubbornness evidently prompted Hoover to release the American Quakers from the 'shackles' of the ARA, allowing them to work with the British

---

of many apartment blocks. It is a district of a bigger town or city.]

[207] *Vesti ot Partnyora* newspaper [News from the Partner], 21 January 2004.

[208] Bertrand M. Patenaude, *The Big Show in Bololand: The American Relief Expedition to Soviet Russia in the Famine of 1921*, p. 141.

Quakers instead. In February 1922 Hoover gave instructions to Colonel Haskell, the director of ARA work in Soviet Russia, to contact the AFSC representative in Moscow and give the American Quakers permission to go their own way. This was the start of the end of the 'unhappy marriage' between the ARA and the AFSC: it was not until 1st September 1922 that the American ODK group finally withdrew from the agreement with the ARA.

American ODK workers in Sorochinskoye, 1922: Rebecca Timbres, Miriam West, Sydnor Walker, Edna Morris; Cornelia Young, Harry Timbres, Beulah Hurley, Sampson, Emma Krauss; Homer Morris, Parry Paul, Dorothy North

©*Courtesy Friends Historical Library of Swarthmore College*

At the same time, in September, the director of the American ODK group, Beulah Hurley, wrote to the AFSC in Philadelphia about the merger of the two groups: 'This, as you know, is much on our minds and we are all greatly relieved that the Riga agreement is cancelled in actual fact, as it has been inoperative for some time. One of the great needs which I have also felt is that the centre for the entire work Ooyezd should be in Buzuluk, since in the small division we get smaller type officials, and they are [so] unsatisfactory that one must constantly work over their heads to Buzuluk which is most inconvenient in practice'.[209]

To be fair, we must add that collaboration between the American and British Quakers was not a bed of roses either. Now it was the 'English ODK' which often annoyed the American ODK group, who wrote to the AFSC in Philadelphia about the British group's inefficiency and the difference in the temperament of the two units. The opinion was even expressed[210] that the ARA-AFSC split was a mistake. In any case, what was done was done. The two ODK groups had to find a way to work together.

A new problem for the joint Quaker mission was what to call themselves in Russian. Beulah Hurley wrote: 'It occurred to us the other day that one of the points of disagreement in future amalgamation has also been the name Friends International Service. It seems quite a useless controversy and might well be dropped in favour of using the literal translation of that title in Russian, which is Society of Friends, Kwakers. This would cause no difficulty in either

[209] Report no.18 from Beulah Hurley to Wilbur Thomas, 6 September 1922. AFSC FSR.
[210] Bertrand M. Patenaude, *The Big Show in Bololand*, p. 142.

England or America and is the title by which we are known in Russian'.[211]

In a Quaker newsletter called *In the Russian Field*, issue no. 41, an extract was published from a letter sent by May Brinsley-Richards on 5 October 1922 from Buzuluk: 'Friends' Relief Mission, both English and American, to remain out here for the next six months at least, in order to prevent a disaster similar to the one of last year. All the workers I have spoken to are agreed that if we retired from the field now, numbers of people are bound to die of starvation again this winter'. A joint conference of American and British Quakers, held in Buzuluk at the end of August 1922, made this absolutely clear: summer 1922 had been extremely dry; all hopes for a good harvest had been dashed; everything possible had to be done to provide the local population with food. As Robert Dunn wrote in his report on the conference: 'As Karl Karlovich Borders, who is standing in for Nancy Babb in Totskoye while she is on holiday, said, the famine has not gone away, and no one can deny it'.[212]

May Brinsley-Richards also wrote in her letter that Quakers had begun to get particularly interested in a programme of work to develop medicine in the region.

---

[211] Report no.18 from Beulah Hurley to Wilbur Thomas, 6 September 1922. AFSC FSR.
[212] Friends House London archives. FEWVRC-MISSIONS-8-3-9-2_REPORTS-ACCOUNTS_1922

American Quaker mission workers in their own private freight car (teplushka): Edna Morris, Robert Dunn, Russian interpreter Pyotr Narovskii, Karl Borders, Anne Herkner

©Courtesy Friends Historical Library of Swarthmore College

After the two Quaker famine relief workers had died of typhus, a Soviet doctor visited the other mission workers, but he soon left. Only one local medic remained, Dr Petrov, who had a private practice, and there was an unqualified nurse called Miss Swithinbank within the mission itself. A qualified nurse, Miss Yorkston, did not arrive until later. The situation was precarious: if there should be a typhus outbreak among the ODK staff, there would be no one left to save the starving Russians. The FWVRC, the London committee, placed a job advert in the

Lancet medical journal for a doctor specialised in infectious diseases. An English doctor, Melville Mackenzie, who was working in Liverpool at the time, applied for the job. He left his work in England and hurried to Russia, arriving in Buzuluk in May 1922.

Mackenzie's diary entries and letters home are full of interesting details. He wrote: 'The [Quaker] Mission headquarters was a large mansion, three storeys high with a courtyard in its centre, entered an imposing archway. It housed the members of the Unit, forty in number, the servants, the food, drugs and stores. The administration offices were on the ground floor, the residential rooms above. In the rear was stabling for two hundred horses'.[213]

Melville Mackenzie gave a fascinating description of the Quaker mission. All things considered, it was an extremely varied group, and not all of those who had come over from England were Quakers. As a doctor, his description stressed the workers' diligence in following strict hygiene rules, since they had come with the important mission of saving starving people from famine and disease. Alas, the doctor identified various types of people on the staff. Besides the well-informed humanitarians in the mission who understood how vital it was that they themselves lived healthily and looked after their own health, there were 'communists, who were in complete sympathy with the new movement

---

[213] Type-written draft of the book *An English Doctor in Soviet Russia*, courtesy of Melville Mackenzie's son, Andrew Mackenzie, who shared the document with me.

in Russian life [… and] idealists, who thought their lives well spent if lost in the spending for Russia and who would observe no safeguarding measure'. Interestingly, there were also 'kindly, ordinary people who, possessing small incomes of their own, could afford to come out and act as helpers to the Mission, and embraced the opportunity it presented', and no shortage of 'honest adventurers, ex-Service men, who came for the experience to be gained and the taste of danger to be savoured'.

Mackenzie continued: 'In sum: a vital and interesting community containing many individuals of strong character. There was much variety of outlook and opinion, but all were united by the common purpose of befriending Russia'.

Melville Mackenzie set up an excellent mechanism for the campaign against typhus: quarantine facilities were organised at Buzuluk train station and a joint laundry service was set up to serve all the hospitals in the town. Care was also taken to disinfect, clean and delouse the homes of all typhus contacts before they were taken to hospital. This mobile unit was called a 'disinfecting column'. Another mobile unit, a 'flying column of feldshers[214] and nurses', was provided for immediate transport to any area threatened by an extensive typhus epidemic.

The national newspaper *Izvestiya* reported in September 1922 that a new agreement was being drawn up with the Quakers. In an article entitled

---

[214] [Translator's note: A feldsher was a rural medical professional with a level of qualification between that of a nurse and a doctor.]

'Famine relief. Aid by foreign organisations', mention was made of Friends' plans to revive agriculture in Buzuluk district, and the fact that the Quakers were buying 1000 horses for the district. The Quakers' strategic approach to their work in Russia was noted: 'In future they want to supply this region, and other regions too as the work develops, with farming tools, to open a network of agricultural schools in conjunction with the People's Commissariat for Agriculture [*Narkomzem*] and to support the mass dissemination of agricultural knowledge by organising courses modelled on those abroad. In addition, they propose extensive facilities for medical care and food distribution. They do not plan to organise their own facilities, but to run these through our [existing] hospitals and canteens, with one of their representatives involved in running them'.[215]

One important component of the medical programme was the campaign against malaria. This illness was the scourge of Buzuluk district: some years outbreaks were not serious, while other years they were severe. The Quakers opened a malaria clinic in Buzuluk in October 1922, led by an Englishwoman called Ethel Christie.

Ethel was the granddaughter of an organist and musician. She herself showed musical talent from an early age and learnt to play the violin, but she then chose to train in medicine. She went on to work all over the world, including in Borneo

---

[215] *Izvestiya*, issue no. 199, 6 September 1922.

and Malaysia, where she was able to increase her knowledge of tropical illnesses. She spent time working in laboratories in England after working in several countries.

Ethel became restless while doing research in England, though, and decided to go to Russia to participate in famine relief and the campaign against the diseases which went hand in hand with the famine. She concentrated on learning the language, so that by the time she left for Russia she could already speak Russian quite well.

Ethel arrived in Buzuluk on 15 October 1922. She had to wait for two weeks until the laboratory was equipped and ready.

Interestingly, a detailed report on Ethel's work was published in 1924 in the journal *Tropical Medicine and Hygiene*, entitled 'Report on the work of a clinic in Buzuluk district run by the Society of Friends'.[216] Ethel wrote this report as part of her preparation for giving a presentation in Russian at an all-Russian meeting of malaria doctors in Moscow.

Every day, people queued outside the clinic in Buzuluk, hoping to receive a lifesaving dose of quinine. The clinic, which saw up to 2000 people a day, was housed in the building of the former Hotel Metropol which had been owned by a local merchant called Pyotr Stepanov, on Samarskaya

---

[216] 'An Account of the Malaria Work done in Buzuluk Ooyezd by the Society of Friends', *The Journal of Tropical Medicine and Hygiene*, vol. XXVII, issue 13, 1 July 1924, by Ethel Christie of Buzuluk Malaria Clinic.

Ulitsa [Street]. In fact, the clinic was directly opposite the English Quakers' office. Ethel Christie later recalled the long, sad queue of people who needed medical help. Many of them had had to walk a long distance through the night to receive medicine. Initially, the decision was taken that the ODK only had enough quinine for the clinic to serve the town of Buzuluk. As Ethel Christie wrote, however, news travelled incredibly fast in such a small town. Villagers who came to Buzuluk on market days (of which there were two a week) found out that the Quakers were curing people and so went to see them for medicine. Ethel Christie remembered how peasants used to lie, saying that they lived in town but somehow having difficulty giving an address in Buzuluk. As quinine was only dispensed in the clinic (patients had to take the medicine in the presence of a doctor) and a course of treatment took a week, many peasants stayed with people they knew or rented a room so that they could have the medicine.

Buzuluk resident G.A. Aksanov recalled: 'In 1922, my little sister, who was born in 1915, fell very ill with malaria. My brother and I took her to the hospital which was being run under the care of the Quakers. They gave her quinine and then a piece of chocolate. They gave me a piece of chocolate too, as I'd come with her. My brother stayed outside on the street. He was 11 years old and was very shy. I shared my piece [of chocolate] with him'.[217]

---

[217] *Vesti ot Partnyora* newspaper [News from the Partner], 21 January 2004.

Every month the clinic in Buzuluk cared for 20,000 to 30,000 people, and soon enough it was obvious that one clinic was not enough to meet local needs. In spring 1923, Dr Mackenzie managed to collect enough money to open and equip a bacteriological laboratory for overcoming malaria. The Quakers managed to open seven new malaria stations, and later they were even able to increase the number to eleven. These medical establishments were one of the Quaker mission's most important achievements. Ethel Christie selected staff personally for the medical stations and was very pleased with the appointments, as the new employees were hardworking and attentive.

As well as their food programme and medical services, the Quakers began a new initiative. In her article, Brinsley-Richards referred to it as the 'Horse and Ploughing' programme.[218]

Soviet officials wrote the following about this: 'The Quakers bought 1380 horses in Turkestan to work in the fields in the springtime. Some of the horses were passed on directly to local Executive Committees, which handed them over to peasants with little land. The Americans, meanwhile, set a condition that horses should be given to families of at least five people and which had a harness, a cart and the necessary food for a horse. The Quakers' representative is currently in Orenburg buying 600 more horses. As for tractors, ten have already

[218] *In the Russian Field*, issue no. 41, October 1922.

arrived and nine more are in transit. Tractors work exclusively on the land of the poorest peasants. An expedition has also been sent to Khiva [in Uzbekistan] to buy up to 3000 horses'.[219]

The plenipotentiary to foreign organisations affirmed his loyalty to the Quakers and his respect for their integrity once again in the same document: 'Considering that the Quakers are fulfilling the agreement in full and that in some respects they are exceeding their programme, that they pay great attention to assisting production and are loyal to the Soviet authorities, and that [our] expenditure on them is very small, I consider that this organisation should continue to work until the

American ODK group and their Russian interpreters in Sorochinskoye, 1923

©*Courtesy Friends Historical Library of Swarthmore College*

---

[219] Information about famine relief by the Society of Friends (Quakers) in Samara province in 1921-1922. Russian State Archives of Economics (RGAE), fonds 478, series 1, folder 2120, sheets 89-92.

end of the agreement'.[220]

In his secret report about the work of foreign aid organisations, produced in June 1922, Karl Lander, plenipotentiary of Soviet Russia (RSFSR) and the Ukrainian Soviet Socialist Republic to all foreign organisations in Russia, stated categorically: 'In view of the benefits of the activities of the organisation in question from the economic point of view, without any political damage at all, and also considering that this organisation began its work in Russia long before the famine, during the civil war, there is no basis for liquidating their activities, which are worthy of extensive cooperation on our part in the future'. [221]

In autumn 1922, the Soviet authorities announced that the famine was defeated, but had consequences. Instead of TsK Pomgol, the Soviet central committee for famine relief, the All-Russian Central Executive Committee established a new committee on 7 September 1922, TsK Posledgol – the central committee for the campaign against the consequences of the famine of 1921. M.I. Kalinin, who had previously been the head of Pomgol, became the head of Posledgol.

A new agreement was signed between the Quakers

[220] Ibid.
[221] From the report by K.I. Lander: "About the activities of foreign charitable organisations in Russia". Top Secret. Archive of the Foreign Policy of the Russian Federation (AVP RF), fonds 04, series 58, file 372, folder 56147, sheets 9-11, 17-18, 21-32, 37-39. Quote from *Sovetsko-Amerikanskiye otnosheniya. Gody nepriznaniya 1927-1933 [Soviet-American Relations. The years of non-recognition 1927-1933].* 'Demokratiya' International Fund, Moscow, 2002, p. 296.

and the Bolsheviks on 25 October 1922 in Moscow. Karl Ivanovich Lander, the plenipotentiary of the Soviet government to foreign famine relief organisations in Russia, signed on behalf of the Soviets, and two Quakers signed on behalf of their groups: William Albright for the English ODK group and Walter Wildman for the American ODK group.

The agreement, which was four pages long, covered the period from October 1922 to 31 July 1923. The Quakers promised to do the following over those nine months:

1) The feeding of a number of children and adults in the Buzuluk and Pugachev ouezds in need of relief, estimated to be about 200,000.

2) To purchase of from 500 to 1000 horses for ploughing. These horses to be lent free of cost to the peasants on a plan which the mission has adopted with success in other countries to be carried out in cooperation with the local representative of the Posledgol.

3) To spend about £20,000 on clothing and the establishment of Kustar industry, particularly weaving and spinning and the manufacture of clothing for use in the Buzuluk and Pugachev ouezds where the clothing is urgently needed.

4) To spend about £10,000 on medical work, including help in the establishment of quarantine stations and assistance to hospitals.

In order to carry out this program the Society of Friends

proposes to furnish 16,000 tons of food, 1,000 tons of clothing and from 15 to 20 tractors.[222]

The Russian Government confirmed that Society of Friends staff would benefit from all necessary arrangements for entry into and exit from Russia. It said that while Quaker workers were in Russia, the government would accord them full liberty to come and go and move about Russia on official business, and provide them with all necessary papers, such as safe-conduct and laissez-passer to facilitate their travel. The number of staff was to be fixed by a special agreement. The Quakers were given complete freedom to select their Russian employees. Posledgol would cover all expenses connected with paying salaries to the Russian staff of the Society of Friends. It also committed to paying expenses connected with transportation from Riga and Reval (Tallinn) ports to the Russian boundary, supplying storage facilities at bases at its own expense and providing the transportation needed for supplies, petrol and lubrication oil for motor transport, and tractors – at quotas to be fixed by special agreement.

Paragraph 19 stated that the relief was to be distributed without regard to race, religion or social or political status. The Society of Friends was banned from engaging in any political or commercial activities. In the event of a serious violation of the agreement in full or in part, each side had the right to refuse to continue to keep this

[222] Agreement Lander – Albright – Wildman. 25 October 1922. AFSC FSR.

agreement. In this case, a two-month period had to be given to the Society of Friends to liquidate its activities, but the foreign staff of the Society of Friends would still have the right to leave Russia freely and take along personal luggage as well as transport, office and any other supplies belonging to the Society of Friends.

As for tractors, on 1st November 1922, the American Quakers reached an agreement about transporting tractors – nicknamed 'iron horses' at the time – into Soviet Russia to plough the land. The agreement stipulated that the tractors would later be bought out by local districts and agricultural schools in the area where the Americans worked. The Quakers proposed this payment scheme in the awareness that a gift is treated very differently to a purchase:

The tractors, plows and equipment furnished by the Kwakers [sic] are to remain Kwaker property until paid for in full. Payment is to be on the following terms:

(a) November 1, 1923 — First payment to cover one half the cost of the tractors, plows and equipment. Payment is to be in grain or its equivalent. Cost of tractors, plows and equipment to be figured at market price in Moscow, grain to be figured at local market price.

(b) November 1, 1924 — Second payment to cover one half the cost of the tractors, plows and equipment. Payment to be on the same basis as section A.

(c) November 1, 1925 — Third payment to cover one fourth the cost of tractors, plows and equipment. Payment to be on the same basis as section A.

All payments received by Kwakers or their successors is to be used for relief or reconstruction purposes in the American District.[223]

Tractor school in Sorochinskoye. Parry Paul in the front row, second from the right

©*Courtesy Friends Historical Library of Swarthmore College*

The American ODK group opened a mechanics workshop in Sorochinskoye, the village where the American tractors were kept and where Parry Paul had set up a tractor school. He was one of the longest-serving American Quakers: he had arrived in February 1922 and did not leave the country until early 1923. For the occasion of his departure, a festive evening with dancing and pies (pirogi) was organised in the Quaker house in Sorochinskoye. Fellow American Robert Dunn recalled the event: 'Our little bookkeeper Ermolai Kopylov rose nobly to the occasion and, in a flight of oratory, bade Godspeed to Parry and wished his quick return with a hundred tractors to plough up thousands

---

[223] Tractor Contract of 1 November 1922, AFSC FSR.

of dessiatins[224]. In a trice, Parry was heaved to the shoulders of his admiring pupils and three times raised with a hurrah'.[225]

An intriguing story relates to this period of the Quakers' work in Buzuluk district. It is found in the diary[226] of Tom Copeman, who was one of the first Quakers to arrive in the English ODK group. He described attending a prayer meeting where the people called themselves 'Quakers'. The meeting was held next to Buzuluk station. Around a dozen Russian 'Quakers' took part, as well as a few British and American Friends, including Beulah Hurley. None of the foreigners spoke Russian, so they had to rely on the Russian chauffeur who had brought along English Quaker Alfred Cotterell. The chauffeur, a small man called Semyon, translated the prayers as best he could. Gertrude Swithinbank recalled that a ten-minute sermon in Russian was translated laconically into English: 'By God, we love peace' (Ei Bogu, my lyubim mir). Another Russian participant in the prayer meeting then gave another sermon, which lasted even longer. It was translated equally concisely as: 'By Jesus Christ, you are right'. The British and American Quakers spread this story by word of mouth so that it became apocryphal that there were secret brothers in faith somewhere in Russia, and indeed many of them.

---

[224] [Translator's note: A *dessiatin* or *desyatina* was a unit for measuring land area, roughly equivalent to 1 hectare or 2.7 acres.]
[225] Parry Paul's Party by Karl Borders. December 1922. Friends House London archives. FEWVRC-MISSIONS-8-3-9-2_REPORTS-ACCOUNTS_1922
[226] Tom Copeman's diaries.

One of the mysterious 'Russian Quakers' gave the Quakers a book of hymns which had been sung at the meeting. Some of the hymns were translated by the Moscow Quaker office, who believed they contained an exceptionally deep spirituality, as Beulah Hurley wrote.[227] I came across these type-written sheets in the archives of Friends House in London. There were the words of two hymns: one had the refrain 'Come, we are all brothers, give me your hand', and the second began 'Listen, the word is blossoming, the hour is coming'. The first hymn or poem[228] was 'We are brethren' by the Scottish poet Robert Nicoll, in a translation (Vse lyudi bratya) by A. Pleshcheev, while the second was by Olga Tolstaya.

My research[229] has led me to conclude that the people the Quakers chanced to meet probably belonged to the 'Dobrolyubovtsy' sect. Members of the sect were pacifists, lived in Samara province, and their prayer meetings were often held in silence. It is well known that the Russian Orthodox Church had a negative attitude towards sects, and indeed a missionary priest, Mikhail Alexeev, warned the church authorities in Samara about the existence of the Dobrolyubovtsy as early as 1916. He referred to them as 'Quakers' in his letters denouncing them to the diocese of Samara. Alexeev wrote that 'At the Quakers' religious meetings there are no fixed activities at all: no set prayers, readings, singing, or

[227] Beulah Hurley, *Quaker Meeting in the Volga Valley*. AFSC FSR.
[228] <https://www.bartleby.com/360/1/236.html>
[229] Sergei Nikitin, 'A Russian Tale'. *The Friend*, 16 February 2018, p. 10.

sermons, only reverent silence, sometimes broken by an enraptured speech by one of those present who felt a special movement of the spirit'.[230] Although the leader and founder of the sect, Alexander Mikhailovich Dobrolyubov, left the steppes of Samara for good in 1915 and moved to Siberia, his followers, the Dobrolyubovtsy, stayed behind. They called themselves 'Brethren'. In 1918 the 'Brethren' organised two communes near Samara, in the villages of Alekseevka and Galkovka, and in 1919 they even organised their own settlement, which they named 'Worldwide Brotherhood' [Vsemirnoe bratstvo]. Perhaps, when they left that famine-stricken area in 1921 to search for food, they were destined to encounter the British and American Quakers at Buzuluk station.

---

[230] Russian State Historial Archive in St Petersburg, fonds 821, series 133, folder 318.

Chapter 8. *Changing from feeding programmes to re-establishing agriculture and rebuilding villages. Meetings with Bolshevik officials. Religion in an atheist state, seen through the Quakers' eyes. Providing peasants with horses. Nancy Babb's business plan and the hospital she built in Totskoye.*

The hot spring and summer of 1922 had affected crops. The harvest was poor, so the Soviet authorities were afraid the famine would continue. For these reasons, as can be seen from the correspondence between the Bolsheviks and the Quakers, it was important to the Communists to supply the district for autumn 1922, and winter and spring 1923, with the Friends' help. The Quakers were clearly happy, on the whole, with their relations with Soviet officials and the local population. Indeed, it was the Quakers' wish to help the local population which could explain their strategic approach to their own future activities. As historian Luke Kelly rightly notes, the mission's famine relief workers were not motivated to help Communist Russia (although some of them did have this motivation), but to try to put into practice the Quaker idea of enlightened, international citizenship. The Quakers realised that the peasants would eventually be able to feed themselves again at some point. It was important not to stop there, though, but to help Russians to provide for their future, putting into practice the ideal of friendship between nations. The Quakers wanted to help organise health facilities, the mechanisation of agriculture and education, including professional training.

Ruth Fry, the secretary of the Friends War Victims Relief Committee, during her visit to Russia in 1923, met Maxim Litvinov, who was then second-in-command of the People's Commissariat for Foreign Affairs. She wrote in her diary: 'I asked him to tell me quite frankly whether they wanted us to continue helping. He said that even if the famine were over there was any amount of work and the Quakers (he did not know those from America) were the first people they wanted, as they always trusted them. It was not, of course, he said exactly in his department, and we ought to see Kameneff and Kalenin [sic]. They should consult together, and each would say it was not for him to decide. But he said that I might quote him as saying that he personally hoped we should stay'.[231]

As we recall, the Quakers placed no conditions on Moscow about whether they should have the right to spread information about the Society of Friends, or what the Communists called 'religious propaganda'. Even in 1921, Friends reached an agreement among themselves that Russians should judge their faith by their actions: first help suffering people, and only talk about faith if people asked. They did not hide their intentions to talk to kindred spirits, with brothers and sisters in faith, and they regularly discussed this with the Bolsheviks. During <u>her meeting</u> in the Commissariat for Foreign

[231] Ruth Fry's journal about her second journey to Russia from 12 Apr to 19 May 1923. AFSC FSR.

Affairs, Ruth Fry spoke to Litvinoff very frankly about the fact that the Quakers' work was based on religion and that they could not be silent about it. She wanted him to understand that the Quakers did not want to stay if they were to be silenced, because Friends believed in goodwill and friendship between nations.

As an example of such communication with the authorities, here is a curious episode which took place in the Tashkent express train when Ruth Fry was travelling from Moscow to Buzuluk with five more Quakers. No one in their delegation spoke Russian except one Englishman, Edward Balls, who had already spent some time working in Russia. Ruth Fry later recalled: 'The other interest of the afternoon was a long visit from the Provodnik (conductor) whom we found most intelligent. E.K. Balls most cleverly told us what he was saying. He was rather troubled that we had no outer sign of being Christians, for suppose we were to die in an unknown place, no one would know our religion. He explained the sign of the cross as "Enlighten our minds, clean our hearts and give us strength". He said that when God was denied, great disaster must follow and referred us to the passage in Timothy about [the] Anti-Christ coming and said that he believed that was coming now. He was evidently interested in Balls's account of our beliefs and thought them good'.[232]

Ruth Fry was late to her meeting with Kalinin in

---

[232] Ibid.

Moscow, so she only got to talk about the prospects for Quaker work in Moscow with Olga Kameneva. 'We went into the building of the Executive Council and directly to see Madame Kameneff [sic], who I am told is Trotsky's sister. She impressed me as an able and charming personality and was very friendly. She preferred to speak through an interpreter although she knew French. In answer to my question as to the attitude of the Government to our staying on, she assured me that the Quakers were the foreign organisation that they most wished to remain as our ideas of relief – such as medical and agricultural – were most in the line with their views. She said that of course their plans would now be changed as the Posledgolod might be abolished and they would be quite unable to spend the money on facilitation for foreign agencies as up till present'.

The day before meeting Kameneva, Ruth Fry met Nikolai Semashko, the People's Commissar for Health: 'We had a pleasant talk with him and he told us that he, and the Government, asked us to stay and that we were quite free to either to take charge of institutions, to give help in one special department such as anti-malarial work, or to help a special district'.[233]

Wilbur Thomas[234], executive secretary of the AFSC, took part in this trip. He too supported continuing Quaker work in Russia. He was always completely

---

[233] Ibid.

[234] Wilbur K. Thomas (1882-1953), a Quaker born in Indiana, was executive secretary of the American Friends Service Committee from 1918 to 1929.

loyal towards the Bolsheviks in his notes and letters. Thomas's clear sympathy towards the Soviet authorities makes you wonder whether he was seemingly so gullible out of naivety or caution and his wish to avoid criticism, realising that the Soviet authorities were probably reading the Quakers' correspondence.

Thomas, in his letter to the American Quaker Alfred Garrett Scattergood in spring 1923, wrote: 'We had the opportunity of meeting quite a number of the prominent men of the Government and I have been very much impressed with the brains back of what is going in Russia. The men in the Government Departments are very able and are doing the best they can under the terrific handicaps that have been imposed upon them. There is no doubt at all that they are succeeding. One of the officials said the other day that in one sense it was a real blessing that the Allies had isolated Russia because otherwise Russia might have been hopelessly in debt. They had to struggle along without the material help that they might have had from Allies and perhaps it has been a real benefit to them'.[235]

While the Quakers' overly optimistic impressions of meetings with Bolshevik officials and civil servants could have been down to not knowing the language and being willing to take everything at face value, their assessment of the situation regarding freedom of religion is undeniably surprising. Wilbur Thomas seems to have considered the Soviets'

[235] Letter from Wilbur Thomas to Alfred Garrett Scattergood, 9 May 1923, AFSC FSR.

actions justified, even though – as he admits – he was unable to judge for himself whether or not the persecuted religious figures were guilty: 'No doubt you have had a great deal in the papers recently about the "religious persecution" that has been going on in Russia. It is my impression that there is no religious persecution here other than, of course, where some local official has a grudge against the church or against someone who is opposed to the present policy of the Government. The impression prevalent in the Government circles here is that the men who have been tried had really been actively opposing the enforcement of law. Any Government must protect itself under such circumstances and the wonder to me is that there has not been a great deal more trouble of this sort. I have no information as to the guilt or innocence of the men who have been tried, but remembering what the Church has been in Russia and how closely it has been associated with all Government activities, it is no wonder that the people have turned against it and say that Church and State must be separated'.[236]

Ruth Fry seems to have been somewhat confused when she wrote about the situation of the church in the Soviet state. Rees Williams, a pro-Kremlin American journalist and writer, who was living in Moscow at the time, took her to the Third House of Soviets where the 'First Renovationist' or 'Second All-Russian' Council was being held.[237] The great

[236] Ibid.

[237] In 1922, there was a split between the old Russian Orthodox Church and the 'Living Church' which was supported by the Soviet secret service. For further details, see: <https://en.wikipedia.org/

number of bearded men in cassocks made a strong impression on her: 'And a wonderful sight it was! One felt one might have got back to the Council of Nicaea. A crowd of long haired, often bearded, long robed priests, many with fine thoughtful and peaceful faces. [...] Apparently there was entire freedom of speech, but the position now is a puzzling one when, though the Government do not uphold religion, the 'New' and Living Church is in some way connected with them'.[238]

Russian Priest

©*Courtesy Friends Historical Library of Swarthmore College*

Some noteworthy correspondence relates to this time. Sergei Kelep, a railway man who was a pump operator at Novosergeevka station, near

---

wiki/Renovationism>
[238] Ruth Fry's diary. Friends House London archives.

the village of Sorochinskoye, tried to understand what was motivating American Quakers to come all the way across the ocean to save Russian people from dying of starvation. He wrote a letter to the American ODK group, since Novosergeevka was in the area under the care of the Americans: 'I have heard many different opinions with regard to the question why you are feeding the hungering of Russia. Some people pretended you would receive in remuneration for your relief work some Russian gold, or Russia will have to give up Kamchatka to America. Others denied it and thought we were helped just by such workers as we ourselves are. However, I personally did not believe in any of these explanations as I see that all people, not excluding our politicians, are partial and unjust, seeking only to maintain their power and position'. Confused, the railway man asked the Quakers to tell him 'your aims, aspirations, measures and ways of spreading out your belief, your attitude towards politics and your general ideas on the world, on Christ, on God, etc. I shall be deeply grateful for your letter. Sergei Kelep'.[239]

An interesting comment made by Dorice White relates to the same year, 1923. Writing from Sorochinskoye, she told William Albright that 'people believe us to be disinterested and know that we are here in a spirit of sympathy and love'.[240]

---

[239] Letter from Sergei Kelep to the American ODK group, 12 May 1923. AFSC FSR.
[240] Dorice White to William Albright, 26 March 1923. FEWVRC-MISSIONS-7-4-5, various letters 1921-1923.

But let us get back to Sergei Kelep. The Americans considered for a good while how best to respond, especially regarding explaining Quaker faith. The thing that the Quakers had been expecting – a Russian asking about their faith because he had seen their works – had finally happened. On the other hand, the state's attitude towards the religion was no secret for the American Quakers who had already been living in Russia for some time. Edwin H. Vail was entrusted to reply. He was a person with a clear talent for writing, as can be seen from his diaries. In one of the paragraphs in his letter back to Kelep, Vail outlined the history of the Society of Friends, stressing their rejection of violence and war: 'Many of their young men when called to the army, refused to go, believing that the inner law of their conscience was above the authority of the State'.[241] Later, Vail explained that the awful aftermath of the First World War made Quakers go to help citizens in France, Austria, Poland and Germany, since the Quakers 'recognised no enemies and no enemy country': all people were brothers.

Vail continued: 'Then came the terrible famine here in Russia which you have witnessed. The fact that people were dying brought the Quakers here. The nationality, religion and political beliefs of the people had no weight one way or the other. So you see, the Quakers are simply trying to put in practice the way of living which Jesus taught'.

Edwin Vail ended his letter to Sergei Kelep with the

---

[241] Edwin Vail's reply to Sergei Kelep. Gamaleyevka, 11 June 1923. AFSC FSR.

words: 'The Quakers do not actively try to increase their membership. They are interested in bringing new spirit into the world rather than building up an organisation'.

Indeed, Edwin Vail, who was working in Gamaleyevka, prepared a few posters to put up at food distribution points in each village. He noted in his diary in May 1923: 'It is meant to give the peasants an idea of who the Quakers are, and in what kind of a spirit they are doing the work. It goes like this: The food which you receive here is a gift of the American people to the hungry of Russia. It is distributed by the Quakers, Religious Society of Friends, in the only aim to help suffering people and thus put in practice the belief of Quakers in the brotherhood of all people'.[242]

American Quakers and Russian peasants in Gamaleyevka

©Courtesy Friends Historical Library of Swarthmore College

---

[242] Edwin Vail's diary, 18 May 1923. AFSC FSR.

Wilbur Thomas would doubtless have been distraught to know that Sergei Kelep, who was deeply religious, was arrested in 1928 and accused of setting up an anti-Soviet organisation. After a while he was released, then arrested again, and shot in 1937. Kelep was posthumously rehabilitated in June 1989, like many other innocent victims of Communism.[243]

Russian interpreter Andrei Bartashevich playing balalaika to peasants standing next to a Quaker Ford truck

©*Courtesy Friends Historical Library of Swarthmore College*

While realising that the threat of a serious famine had passed, the Soviet authorities in Buzuluk believed that the Quakers' exit from Russia would seriously complicate life for the local peasants. The American and English ODK groups had saved hundreds of thousands of Russians from dying of starvation, and were continuing to provide

[243] *Mucheniki i ispovedniki Orenburgskoi eparkhii XX veka* [Martyrs and Priests of Orenburg Diocese in the Twentieth Century], vol.3, pp. 124–127. Compiled by Father N. Stremskii. Orenburg, 2000.

peasants with food, but they were now expected to give practical help to re-establish agriculture. That meant machinery, working livestock, rebuilding collapsed bridges, roads, hospitals, polyclinics and schools.

The Quakers already had quite a number of tractors but, firstly, there were not enough, and secondly, Russians were not yet ready to trust 'iron horses' (tractors) to replace peasants' horses. In July 1922, the Buzuluk authorities wrote to Comrade Lander, the plenipotentiary representative of Soviet Russia to all foreign relief organisations in Russia: 'The Quakers have definitely given a lot of help, working with 18 tractors on public land, and transferring the gross yield of bread to the poorest peasants. In addition, this organisation has taken part enthusiastically, doing almost 20% of the following tasks: reconstructing bridges, schools, health facilities, etc. They are now suggesting large-scale purchases of working livestock'.[244]

The Pomgol [Famine Relief] Executive Committee in Buzuluk reported back to the Samara Province Commission for Famine Relief to give the dreadful statistics on the reduction in livestock:

There is a huge loss of livestock. The peasants do not have the means to obtain more livestock.

---

[244] Central State Archive of Samara Province (TsGASO), fonds 536, series 1, item 1.

	Horses	Oxen	Camels	Total
Spring 1921	97,725	7,304	1,347	106,456
June 1921	34,607	2,679	1,569	42,663

"With this number of working livestock, the district can prepare the ground for the winter and spring planting for 1923 over no more than 300,000 desyatin, which is off course insufficient for increasing agriculture. The Pomgol Executive Committee has addressed a special letter to the OD [Society of Friends], asking them to continue to help the population of the district in the future, but not by giving food directly to the population, but by supplying the district with agricultural equipment, tractors, breeding stock, etc. which are crucial to farming and which are available in the Quakers' homeland.[245]

In answer to this letter, the Pomgol Executive Committee received from both the English and American ODK groups 'agreement in principle to continuing work in our district in the field of re-establishing agriculture, and a final decision regarding this issue depends on the decisions of the Quakers colleagues abroad, whose representatives here hope for a positive decision'.

The head of the American ODK group, Murray Kenworthy, wrote about supplying horses in a letter to the AFSC in Philadelphia from Sorochinskoye in 1922: 'Russia needs horses, many of them, seven years of war and two years of famine have terribly reduced the number. I at first thought that the money spent in shipping them over might buy more horses here in the East, but I am told they are

[245] Central State Archive of Samara Province (TsGASO), fonds 536, series 1, item 2.

not there now to be bought. Eiduk[246] says to send them'.[247]

Tractors were one thing, but horses were still needed as they were what the peasants wanted: people longed to have working livestock again after losing them in the years of famine. Of course, there are many reasons why you cannot just hand out horses. The Quakers knew that anyone might look after a horse differently if they had bought it themselves than if they had received it as a gift, and as they were not made of money, they realised that with the proceeds of selling one lot of horses they would be able to buy the next lot. The Society of Friends therefore drew up a scheme like this for distributing livestock.

At the same time, the People's Commissariat for Agriculture [*Narkomzem*] in Moscow was sending instructions to the Executive Committee in Samara province to help the Quakers in the charitable endeavours to provide peasants with horses:

RSFSR [Soviet Russia]

People's Commissariat for Agriculture

7 June 1923

No. 4533

---

[246] Alexander Vladimirovich Eiduk, whom we encountered in previous chapters, was plenipotentiary to the ARA and all foreign famine relief organisations in 1921-1922.

[247] Letter from Murray Kenworthy to Wilbur Thomas, 17 March 1922. AFSC FSR.

Because of the Narkomzem's existing agreement with representatives of the Friends (Quakers) from England and America, in which they expressed their agreement to work to supply peasants in Samara province with horses, the ODK must now do this in practice as soon as possible.

Considering too that the agreement to re-establish agriculture is extremely desirable, and remembering that the Society of Friends from England and America are friends of Soviet Russia, and that the money which they will use is collected by them voluntarily among their supporters, the Narkomzem of the RSFSR asks the Province's Executive Committee to take the following measures to support this work:

1. Help the representatives of the ODK to distribute these horses among the peasants to whom they are being made available.

2. Take measures to ensure that the price of the horse received is paid promptly, so that it is possible for the ODK to continue the work it has begun.

3. Encourage all departments of the Province's Executive Committee to establish a close relationship with the representatives of the ODK and make them feel that they are indeed among friends.

People's Commissariat for Agriculture

Official of the Central Administration for Horse Breeding and Livestock Breeding.[248]

---

[248] Central State Archive of Samara Province (TsGASO), fonds 79, series 1, item 166.

At the start of 1923, the American Quakers were able to reach an agreement with Ilya Andreevich Tolstoy. He was a great expert on horses, as well as being the grandson of Lev Tolstoy and the son of Andrei Tolstoy and Olga Tolstaya, the only Russian Quaker. They committed to a trip to Siberia to buy 500 to 1000 horses and transfer them to Buzuluk and Sorochinskoye. In accordance with the agreement with the Soviet authorities, no taxes were payable on the horse purchases, meaning that peasants could afford the prices.[249]

Tolstoy went to Siberia with Alfred Smaltz, a representative of the American ODK group, and an Englishman, Ralph Fox. In the space of a few days, they managed to buy horses at various fairs. Haggling is not easy, especially for a foreigner, so Tolstoy always made the final decision about purchasing any livestock.

A herd of horses arrived in Orenburg at the end of June 1923. By then, the Quakers had decided to replenish the stock of working horses to 70% of their pre-famine levels. They decided to allocate $10,000 to buying horses so that they could sell them to peasants at cost price. The proceeds would be used to ensure the lowest possible prices would be charged, so that most peasants could buy a horse, not only those who were better-off. Quakers asked the Narkomzem for a representative 'with full authority to act as a liaison officer between the Society of Friends and the local governments'

[249] Agreement between the Quakers and the town of Orenburg. 26 February 1923. AFSC FSR, 1923.

and for transportation, inspection and taxation issues to be facilitated on their behalf. Since the horses would remain under Quaker supervision for projects in Buzuluk and Sorochinskoye, they also asked 'that the horses be exempt from military service or government mobilisation'. [250]

'Within a week the Agriculture Department accepted the Quaker offer, asked them that the programme be expanded but could make no guarantees with respect to exemption of the horses from the mobilization', wrote the American historian David McFadden.   He highlighted that 'the Department promised to facilitate the transportation, inspection and taxation issues, and during the subsequent two years, the government did not mobilize any of the horses'.[251]

The head of the American ODK group, Walter Wildman, told a joint meeting of the English and American Quakers in Buzuluk held in June 1923 that in order to make Friends' work more effective, the Soviet authorities had appointed a special representative to look after their interests, had granted the privilege of using government veterinary assistance, and were issuing special mandates to facilitate the work of the mission members involved in the horse programme. Everything was being done to secure cheap freight rates and exemption from tax on all purchases. When peasants bought

---

[250] Proposal from Quaker Service to the Department of Agriculture. 31 May 1923. AFSC FSR, 1923. Quote from David McFadden et al, *Constructive Spirit*, p. 97.
[251] Ibid.

a horse, a contract was drawn up and signed by a government representative.[252]

In his letter to Wilbur Thomas, Alfred Smaltz described the epic trip with the horses: 'The success or failure of the expedition was chiefly in [Ilya Tolstoy's] hands. This imposed upon him a responsibility well beyond his years, but he has fulfilled it to a gratifying degree. His responsibilities not only called for endurance of physical hardship but also the careful handling of difficult and delicate situations which have been a severe test of his energies and abilities. Besides his knowledge and love of horses which made that phase of the work agreeable to him, he has a genuine appreciation of the spirit that inspired Quaker efforts and he has been able in a simple and dignified way to convey that message to all whom we have met'.[253]

The Quakers now faced the question of creating a scheme for distributing horses. The American ODK group in Sorochinskoye met to examine two options: paying by labour (i.e., paying by grain), or paying a price for a horse in money (i.e, paying in chervonets). To explain, a monetary reform took place in Soviet Russia over 1921-1923: the country went over to hard currency, instead of having banknotes and prices expressed in millions. The new currency was the chervonets, equivalent to the

---

[252] News Release for AFSCRCO by Jessica Smith, 1 July 1923. AFSC FSR.
[253] Reply from the People's Commissariat for Agriculture to the Society of Friends from England and America. 7 June 1923. AFSC FSR. Quote from David McFadden et al, *Constructive Spirit*, p. 97.

ten-rouble gold coin from the Tsarist era, and for whatever denomination it was guaranteed to 25% of that amount in gold, other precious metals and foreign currency. It was this fact that prompted the Quakers to implement option 2: selling horses in chervonets.

Prince Sergei Golitsyn and American Quaker Dorothy Detzer – supervising horse distribution in Sorochinskoe, 1923

©The archives of the American Friends Service Committee

This plan had various advantages. It would create a revolving fund which would allow the Quakers to supply more horses to the district. It would be simpler to control, and the whole process would be built around business relationships. After a long discussion, the Quakers decided to go for this second option, which could be summed up in the following points:

1) All valuations to be made with a gold rouble as basis

2) One fourth the purchase price to be paid at date of purchase

3) These on present list to be given first opportunity to purchase

4) Horses to go to Volost showing smallest percentage of horse.

5) Very poor families to be encouraged to pool resources.

Alfred Smaltz explained how the prices of horses worked: 'The price of horses on the local market is two or three times as much as the price at which the Quakers are able to sell their horses (cost price plus 10% for losses). That is why the peasants are flooding the Quaker offices with requests to buy. Although no payment is required until the receipt of the horse, over 250 peasants have already made their first payment of a billion roubles'.[254]

American Quaker Edwin Vail described how horses were distributed in Gamaleyevka in July 1923:

On Monday morning all the peasants from my district were in to receive the horses that I promised would be ready when they paid the required one-fourth the week before. But there had been many hitches in the examination,

---

[254] News Release for AFSCRCO by Jessica Smith, 1 July 1923. AFSC FSR.

classification and pricing of the 450 horses, besides the usual annoyances and hindrances of the Russian plenipotentiary who is supposed to help us out. As it is just the busiest time with the rye harvest, and the peasants had walked in thirty or fifty versts, we were anxious not to keep them waiting over too long. The drawing began in the middle of the afternoon. I wish you could see that eager crowd of men dressed in all sorts of descriptions of clothes and rags gathered together to draw for a horse which in this country is bread, clothing, and life itself. With great fumbling fingers, they drew in turn from the basket the little white slip which gave the number branded on the horse which was to be theirs. The contracts were all filled in and ready by eight o'clock in the evening and a few minutes later we were out at the corral. The men were already there, and most of them had located their horse. No one was greatly disappointed for, on the whole, the horses were very good.[255]

An American Quaker, Nancy Babb, took an active role in developing the programme for distributing horses. She worked in isolation, away from the other Quakers, in Totskoye, halfway between Buzuluk and Sorochinskoye.

Miss Babb was an outstanding Quaker worker, living in Russia for almost ten years. Numerous documents and letters show that she was an unusual and awkward person, and that neither the American nor the English Quakers got on with her.

Born in 1884 in Virginia, Nancy Jones Babb came to Russia for the first time in August 1917. At that

---

[255] Edwin Vail's diary. AFSC archives.

time, she went with five other American women to Buzuluk, to help the first Friends' mission which was working with refugees in the district. The Quaker mission left Buzuluk in 1918, and Nancy Babb went to the east of Russia with most of the remaining Friends from the Buzuluk mission. She worked for some time for the American Red Cross in Omsk, where she saved a huge number of refugees, then in October 1919 she returned to the USA. Soon, Nancy came back to Soviet Russia: she started work in Moscow in August 1921, helping Arthur Watts and Anna Haines distribute humanitarian aid to children in Moscow children's homes and other institutions for children. When the famine began and the Quakers headed to Buzuluk, Nancy Babb was one of the first to go there.

Miss Babb's difficult character made for a tense atmosphere wherever she went. Murray Kenworthy, the first head of the American ODK group, described his fellow American in a letter home: 'I also have a task of acting between this person (a woman) who has irritated every member of the English staff and keep peace in our own family. I shall do the best I can. She is with me on this trip. And is now in my compartment. If her tongue was ever still, I suppose it was when she was asleep. She also has decided opinions of her own and does not propose to yield them in defence to others'.[256]

Nancy was transferred from Buzuluk to Totskoye. Murray Kenworthy wrote again to the AFSC in

[256] Letter home by Murray Kenworthy, 24 November 1921. AFSC FSR.

Philadelphia about the conflicts which seemed to follow Nancy Babb wherever she went: 'So far we have a congenial bunch, with one exception, and we entertain great fears on account of Nancy Babb, the facts are we may ask her to resign. It is so unfortunate that she antagonises everyone, I think there are no exceptions [...] She is in Totskoye alone — except Russian helpers — and it may be that on account of her reputation — that of being hard to get along with — we may have to leave her alone in spite of the increased personnel. She might make it all right, if she could dominate her associates'.[257]

Nancy Babb checking the bridge repairs done by the Red Army soldiers near Totskoe

©*The archives of the American Friends Service Committee*

The volosts [parishes] of Pronkino, Markovka, Totskoye, Bogdanovka and Baklanovka in Buzuluk district were all under Nancy Babb's care.

---

[257] Letter from Murray Kenworthy to Wilbur Thomas, 17 March 1922. AFSC FSR.

Nancy Babb's five-year plan for Totskoye can be seen in a few lines from the report she wrote in 1928, after her departure from the USSR:

a) Famine relief — supervisor of feeding programme

b) After Famine relief – reconstruction organisation

c) Medical relief — malaria epidemics, children's clinics and feeding undernourished children, orphans etc

d) Establishing, building, organising and equipping a new hospital centre and reconstructing a demolished summer sanatorium with farm attached and supporting both […] through salvage of supplies.[258]

An American Communist, Robert Dunn, who also worked with the Quakers in the area, described one of Nancy Babb's projects in autumn 1922:

Nancy Babb way last spring announced to the peasants in Totskoye volost that she would exchange old clothes for wool. The wool came in quickly. It was handed over to skilled valenki experts who worked for a Quaker 'special workers pyok'. The Cooperative Society of Totskoye offered its shelves and counters to facilitate the transactions, over five hundred pairs of children valenki is the result. In Bogdanovka volost, to the south, over 1200 children will be <u>valenkied</u> according to a similar scheme carried out under the direction of Miss Babb in cooperation with the local Russian Famine Relief Committee. A thousand more children will be skipping about over the white snows of Pronkinskaya and Baclanovskaya and Markovskaya volosts. Altogether something like five thousand children

---

[258] Quote from David McFadden et al, *Constructive Spirit*, p. 80.

in the district of which Miss Babb is Supervisor will be wearing the finished product within a month. And there are enough reserves on hand to give them a change to a second pair when they have worn out the first sometime in the middle of the long winter.[259]

Children's home in Totskoe - orphans wearing the Valenki (felt boots) made in Quaker workshops

©*The archives of the American Friends Service Committee*

Nancy Babb's final task in Totskoye was the hospital building. She wrote in a letter: 'The Narkomzdrav [People's Commissariat for Health] will take all possible steps to get the 50% promised by the Government to furnish and equip same. You will probably be interested to know that it is the first large building of its kind since the war and our little village is quite proud of the fact that they have it here built from their own bricks made in the

---

[259] *The Finished Product* by Robert Dunn, 1 Nov 1922. Friends House London archives. FEWVRC-MISSIONS-8-3-9-2 REPORTS-ACCOUNTS 1922.

village'.[260]

The hospital was opened in November 1927. The building is still standing today, in the centre of Totskoye, on Karl Marx Ulitsa, and is now the House of Children's Creativity. I went there in 1997 with David McFadden, the American historian and expert on Quaker relief work in Russia. We met an 86-year-old pensioner, a retired teacher called Ivan Leontevich Terentiev, who lived next door. He could still recall the day the hospital opened: 'I remember that it had been pouring with rain for a few days. All the roads around here were impassable with mud. But on the morning of the opening day, the sun came out and lit up the brand-new beds, the tiled floor and the shiny taps'.

Nancy Babb left Totskoye in 1927. The medical staff of Totskoye hospital wrote her a letter of thanks: 'The protection of the health of babies; the preschool age and the mothers, the maternity home, the hospital ward; drug stores, children's sanatorium, day camp for tuberculosis; and the plan of lectures, each of these departments you have placed on a firm basis. In addition to the above, you have been able to erect of newly made red bricks a splendid hospital — the best of district'.[261]

---

[260] Letter from Nancy Babb to Wilbur Thomas, 22 October 1926, AFSC FSR. Quote from David McFadden et al, *Constructive Spirit*, p. 106.
[261] Ibid, p. 107.

Totskoe hospital built by Nancy Babb. 1927

©*The archives of the American Friends Service Committee*

Ivan Terentiev recalled that Nancy Babb returned to Totskoye once more, just as a tourist, in 1937. 'She was welcomed like a queen, and nearly picked up and carried', he told me. My conversations that day convinced me that Nancy Babb's memory was still alive. When I asked some women who were selling milk at the little local market whether they knew that an American woman lived there in the 1920s, they answered: 'Of course we do!' and pointed to the building where Nancy Babb had lived 70 years before.

Chapter 9. *The Quakers' project for agricultural schools in Oomnovka. Plans for further collaboration in both Moscow and Buzuluk. The Quakers' gradual withdrawal from Buzuluk. American Quaker Anna Haines' medical projects. Anna Haines' summons to OGPU. Could the Moscow office be the future Quaker centre in Russia?*

In his book *Constructive Spirit. Quakers in Revolutionary Russia*, American historian David McFadden[262] comments that the bold plans that the Quakers had drawn up in 1923 already seemed to be under threat in the summer of 1924. Funding from Britain and the USA began to decrease, now that the famine had passed its peak, Soviet Russia was trading in grain again, and the Bolshevik state's New Economic Policy (NEP)[263] was improving people's wellbeing. The Friends service committees in London and Philadelphia thought that their aid programmes in Russia were dragging on too long. There was no need for foreign food aid anymore, and the Bolsheviks were gradually turning into arrogant and picky recipients. More and more often the communications from officials were in a certain tone: just give us money and we'll work out what to do with it ourselves. The People's Commissariat for Health changed its policy: People's Commissar Semashko now refused to finance work that had already begun on an equitable basis. Instead,

---

[262] David McFadden et al, *Constructive Spirit*.
[263] [Translator's note: NEP was Lenin's strategic, temporary, reintroduction of aspects of a free market and capitalism in 1921.]

the rent the Quakers had to pay for buildings and communal services was increased, and the Bolsheviks demanded increased wages for Russian workers in Quaker hospitals and outpatient clinics in Buzuluk district – but with the foreigners paying, of course.

The regional director of the American Friends Service Committee (AFSC), Vincent Nicholson, was pessimistic about the very existence of Quaker work in Russia. He believed it was essential to stop giving charitable aid and cease participating in the work to re-establish agriculture and healthcare, prioritising instead the setting up of a Quaker 'embassy' in Moscow, which would allow the Quakers' values and ideals to become known to the general public. In his opinion, further work could then be rebuilt from scratch, in a centralised way, and on a long-term basis.

At this stage, the idea arose of opening a Quaker agricultural and technical training school in the village of Oomnovka[264] in Buzuluk district. The initial plan was to open an agricultural school in Borskoye[265], too, as there were so many orphan children in that region. In the end, the Quakers decided just to concentrate on Oomnovka. They drew up a proposal at the start of 1924 for the school to be a joint project with Buzuluk district executive committee for ten years. The Society of Friends

[264] Oomnovka is now the settlement of Krasnogvardeets in Orenburg region.
[265] Friends House Library archive. FEWVRC-MISSIONS-8-2-1-1_REPORTS-ACCOUNTS_1923

would commit to provide 440,000 golden Soviet roubles of funding for the technical and agricultural school in the centre of Oomnovka farm, Buzuluk district, Samara province. The school would teach crafts, agriculture and domestic management to children aged 14 to 18, while the Quakers also wished to find 'a way to teach moral principles and develop qualities in these children which will make them worthy members of any community in which they live'.[266]

Buzuluk's *Ispolkom* (local executive committee) did not agree. They wanted more control and a monopoly on the educational process, just as the Quakers were trying to reserve the right to teach children themselves. The Society of Friends' representatives stated that they hoped to teach in the school 'in accordance with the demands of Soviet laws and with the approval of the head of the Department for General Education'.[267] The sticking point was the Quakers said that they were only willing to fund the school if they knew that the education there would be in accordance with its values. Edgar Nicholson, head of the Quaker centre in Moscow, said on their behalf: 'The Society of Friends, which has been giving active aid for the last seven years, and has clearly indicated its association with the Russian people and its wish to help them during the years of hardship, proposes

---

[266] State Archives of the Russian Federation, fonds 3385 (the Commission for Foreign Aid within the Presidium of the All-Russian Central Executive Committee), series 1, folder 25, sheets 1–4.
[267] Ibid.

that it has the right to ask for a guarantee that the general education provided at the school will not deviate from its principles. We do not think that the central Friends committees will agree to opening the school if the agreement does not include a paragraph giving such a guarantee'.[268]

What lay behind this sticking point?

The Quakers wanted the following sentence, clause 15, within the text of the agreement: 'The present agreement prevents the teaching of anti-religious and atheist ideas in any department of the school'.

The Quakers' old ally, Olga Kameneva, chair of the Commission for Foreign Aid within the Presidium of the All-Russian Central Executive Committee of the USSR, also got involved in the argument. She wrote to the People's Commissariat for Education (*Narkompros*) and received a curt reply from the head of its advisory board:

The Advisory Board of the People's Commissariat for Education finds these proposals unacceptable on the following grounds:

1) The principles of the organisation of the school in question are entirely unacceptable for Soviet Russia [the RSFSR], on whose territory all schools are run using a single system of educational plans on a scientific and natural basis. This system inherently includes anti-religious elements.

2) All teaching staff in schools in Soviet Russia must

---
[268] Ibid, folder 56 (1-2).

be approved by the relevant branches of the People's Commissariat for Education; the planned exemption for the Society of 'Quakers' is inadmissible.[269]

As the historian David McFadden writes[270], Olga Kameneva assured the Quakers that their request would be met as long as they did not insist on putting it in writing, meaning that they should omit clause 15 of the agreement. For a while, the Quakers were even willing to let atheism be taught in the technical school: 'the fact of anti-religious teaching being given in the school might not debar Friends from giving their help in other departments, but rather might be a challenge to them to show faith in the efficacy of their own beliefs'.[271] Ultimately, the Quakers decided not to compromise on their principles, and shelved the idea of setting up a technical school.

Medicine was another important component of the Quakers' practical work. By summer 1923, the Quakers realised that the Bolsheviks were going to get rid of foreign organisations gradually, as the threat of famine receded. Exceptions were made for foreign organisations involved with health issues. In April 1923, Walter Wildman, the regional director of the American ODK group, wrote to

---

[269] Ibid. Correspondence with the "Society of Friends – Quakers" foreign organisation about the organisation's work in the USSR. Part 2.

[270] David McFadden et al, *Constructive Spirit. Quakers in Revolutionary Russia*, p. 141.

[271] Attention of Executive and Russian Committees, 8 May 1924. FSC RU/1 Friends Service Council Records. Friends House London archives.

Wilbur Thomas of the AFSC: 'There is a great need for medical relief, especially to combat malaria and other epidemics. The Russians are lacking in efficient and capable personnel as well as in supplies and equipment. They are glad to receive all medical supplies possible and we have recently received a request for additional supplies of quinine from the Gubernia Medical Department'.[272]

Russian doctor Zinaida Saukke worked in Totskoe

©*The archives of the American Friends Service Committee*

Putting these proposals into practice depended on whether additional funding could be received from London and Philadelphia, and whether the Soviet authorities would agree to Quaker work continuing, with Russian doctors and Moscow specialists who were willing to travel to Buzuluk.

---

[272] Letter from Wildman to Thomas_14_Apr_1923_RUS. AFSC FSR.

The key parts of the work plan that the Quakers presented to the Soviet authorities in August 1923 were as follows:

WORK PLAN

ODK IN THE FIELD OF HEALTH IN BUZULUK DISTRICT.

10 August 1923

Hospitals

a) The ODK commits to repair existing hospitals and supply additional inventory for them, so that they are in better condition in order to give wider medical help. The town's Accident and Emergency Department and epidemic hospital must stay under the ODK's full control, as previously.

b) The District Health Department will provide all essential goods for the health facilities as far as they are able, and the ODK will provide anything which is missing, especially for special diets.

c) Given that District Health Department is able to meet 50% of the demand for medicines and dressings, it is desirable for the ODK to meet the remaining 50% of the demand.[273]

As well as hospitals, the ODK would take responsibility for medical facilities in the countryside: 'The ODK will aid medics and nursing staff in rural medical points'.

---

[273] Central State Archive of Samara Province (TsGASO), fonds 79, series 1, item 167.

The local authorities had noticed an increase in venereal diseases and so made a request to the Quakers: 'It is desirable for the ODK, if it is able, to open a venereal department at the district hospital, funding it themselves and committing to equip it fully'. As part of the campaign against tuberculosis, there was an expectation that 'the ODK [would] help the District Health Department to open new facilities by providing inventory and distributing rations to sick adults and children'.[274]

Besides the points listed above, the Quakers were ready to carry out additional work concerning providing medical assistance in Buzuluk district:

- *Assistance in the repair and further equipment of existing hospitals and sanatoriums of a permanent nature and the supplying of medicines and other medical supplies.*
- *The organisation of consultations for mothers and children in existing institutions and at other points mutually agreed upon between the ooyezd[275] medical authorities and the Society of Friends.*
- *The opening of day nurseries during the summer months in rural districts where the need is indicated.*
- *Assistance to the oozdrav[276] in the programme for health education and sanitation through use of books and materials.*
- *The continuance of the present malaria clinics in Buzuluk and Sorochinskoye and the opening of*

---

[274] Ibid.
[275] [District.]
[276] District Health Department.]

additional ones.
- *The maintenance of all doctors and nurses brought into the ooyezd for the carrying out of the medical programme.*[277]

The malaria clinic and outpatient clinic that English Quaker worker Ethel Mary Christie had opened in Buzuluk gave a head start to the project to spread malaria outpatient clinics throughout the district. Interestingly, this building is still in use for medical purposes today: it is now the children's municipal polyclinic in Buzuluk. In the 1920s, the British and American Quakers had their main office in the clinic's building, at 63 Samara Ulitsa [Street], which is now named Gorky Street. In 1997, the doctors there proudly told me that there was still an outpatient clinic in the neighbouring building, where Ethel Christie had had her outpatient clinic.

Two doctors worked in the Quaker mission in Buzuluk: Melville Douglas Mackenzie and Elfie Richards Graff, who arrived after Mackenzie. It was they who drew up the plan for medical work in Buzuluk district, together with Walter Wildman. They needed to increase the number of doctors and nurses, provide additional places in in-patient wards for patients suffering from tuberculosis, malaria and venereal diseases, and provide new batches of medicines and other essential products.

---

[277] Letter from Walter Wildman to the President of the Foreign Relief Commission, 12 September 1923. AFSC FSR, 1923. Quote from David McFadden et al, *Constructive Spirit*, p. 121.

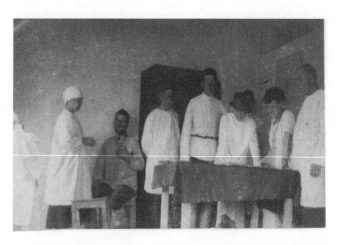

Russian doctor Ivan Gusarov, Dr Elfie Richards Graff and Mabel C. Phillips in Totskoe sanatorium. 1925

©*The archives of the American Friends Service Committee*

Alice Davis, head of the American ODK group, wrote in an AFSC report[278] from Sorochinskoye that in June 1924 they had closed the old programme, and were now concentrating their efforts on polyclinics where they were going to continue medical work. Only nine polyclinics now remained open in Sorochinskoye volost.

The Quakers' promising programme to supply agricultural machinery to peasants in Buzuluk district was wound down at the end of 1924. Edward Kent Balls, director of the Quaker representative office in Moscow, wrote to Parry Paul, former head of the tractor programme, who was now back in America: 'A good deal of the Sorochinskoye and

---

[278] From the AFSC's report on its work in Russia, 20 August 1924. AFSC Archives, FSR.

Buzuluk transport has been sold, they have only a small garage left. The tractors are working in Sorochinskoye area and 5 in Totskoye area, and 3 are out of order. I dare say some of the others are too by now. The general work you probably knew about from the Committee is practically all medical, with the exception of Nancy's industries and some garden work that has been done in both Totskoye and Sorochinskoye'.[279]

Graduates from the Tractor School in Sorochinskoe Willard Blackburn on the left. Alfred Wetherald on the right

©*The archives of the American Friends Service Committee*

Earlier in the same year, the Quakers had reported that:

2658 children were under treatment in the clinics, and 705 home visits were made. Visits to the clinics totalled 24,298. Malaria clinics are now operating only in villages where

[279] Letter from E.K. Balls in the Moscow office to Parry Paul. AFSC Archives, FSR.

there are children's clinics. In June 4,092 patients were under treatment. In Sorochinskoye a prenatal clinic was opened on June 13. The service which is being rendered is very much appreciated. In the middle of June, a day camp for the treatment of tubercular children was opened in Sorochinskoye. There are already 30 children under treatment. The camp is in a shady, sandy place near a branch of the river. The children have a regular regime of rest, feeding and exercise carried out under supervision of the nurse in charge.[280]

Friends stressed how vital it was to increase the number of tuberculosis sanatoria during the summer months, in order to prevent patients' health getting worse.

The Quakers planned to work with the People's Commissariat for Health in Moscow, as well as in Buzuluk. This was American Quaker worker Anna Haines' idea. Anna was a veteran of Quaker work in Russia: she had come to Buzuluk in August 1917, like Nancy Babb; she left Russia in 1919, but came back to Moscow in 1920, travelling to Samara in August 1921. Anna returned to Russia once again in 1925, after training as a nurse in the USA. It was already her third visit to the country.

Richenda Scott, the English researcher into Quaker history in Russia, wrote that Anna Haines, drawing on her own experience and her visits to hospitals, 'discovered that the status of the nurse and standards demanded for her work varied considerably from

---

[280] From the AFSC's report on its work in Russia, 20 August 1924. AFSC Archives, FSR.

hospital to hospital. There was no independent nursing organisation, no recognised routine of duties and responsibilities'. Anna 'was more than convinced that the only way of improving matters and raising the standard of education and of work demanded from nurses would be through some foreign agency setting up a modern training school, where the requirements for admission, the hours of duty, the division of labour and the introduction of scientific nursing techniques could be standardised and demonstrated'.[281] She believed that the Society of Friends was ideal for this role, and decided to take the initiative in setting up a new system of nursing training.

In Moscow, Anna Haines worked as a volunteer nurse in the Moscow children's hospital run by Vera Pavlovna Lebedeva, as well as being the American Quakers' representative in the Moscow Quaker centre, alongside British Quaker, Dorice White. As David McFadden writes, 'Because of her background and experience, and the confidence of American Quakers in her, Anna Haines functioned as the director of Quaker programmes in Russia during the transition year of 1925-1926'.[282]

It was Quaker mission worker Dr Elfie Graff who had first contacted Soviet doctor Vera Lebedeva in Moscow. At her instigation, Ruth Fry met Lebedeva in May 1923, noting in her diary that, 'Dr. Lebedeva was anxious for our help but would

---

[281] Richenda Scott, *Quakers in Russia*, ch.19, p.267.
[282] David McFadden et al, *Constructive Spirit*, p. 125.

like it in money rather than anything else'.[283] Vera Pavlovna Lebedeva was a famous figure in the Soviet health service. She had set up the Institute for Maternal and Infant Healthcare, where she led the Department of Social Hygiene for Mothers and Children. After meeting her a second time, Ruth Fry made the following diary entry: 'On 20 January 1925 Dr Graff and I went to see Dr Lebedeva with whom she works so closely. She is the doctor in charge of the maternity and child welfare part of the Ministry of Health and runs the great big hospital of Solyanka which I saw before. We had a pleasant talk with her, about our present and future work, and she would very greatly welcome more help from our staff, which we hope in any case Anna Haines will give. Then we saw over her training school for nurses, towards which we are giving help in the way of salaries. There are nearly 400 girls there, but the condition is very crowded, and we saw them studying in their bedrooms'.[284]

Anna Haines was responsible for work with Lebedeva's department at the hospital. She collected data and contact details, as well as giving tips and making plans for improving nurse training. Together with the department's senior medics, Haines prepared a presentation about the state of nursing in Russia and new methods for teaching young nurses. She wrote to the AFSC in Philadelphia that the Russian doctors' commitment to working

[283] Ruth Fry's diary about her second trip to Russia, 12 April - 19 May 1923. AFSC FSR.
[284] Ruth Fry's diary about her third trip to Russia in 1924. AFSC FSR.

on the joint Russian-American presentation was a 'rather big step in a small way in international relations [...]. It rather confirms my feeling that peace is after all by-products of constructive work for better social conditions and not a thing to be too noisily worked for in itself'.[285]

In 1925, Nikolai Semashko presented the Quakers with a certificate attesting that the Society of Friends (Quakers) was providing medical help to the population of 'our Republic' and supporting several medical facilities. The document confirmed that all Quaker work of this type was being carried out with the agreement of Soviet Russia's People's Commissariat for Health. The following year, in 1926, Semashko signed a certificate given to Anna Haines as an individual. It said that she was working 'on issues connected with healthcare' and asked those concerned 'to give the aforesaid person assistance in these tasks'. Anna Haines warmly recalled the support she had received from People's Commissar Semashko: the certificate he had given her had 'made it possible for me to enter without previous announcement hospitals, day-nurseries, sanitoria and other medical institutions in the remotest parts of the country'.[286] The same year, in issue 2 of *Care of Mothers and Infants*, a journal for midwives edited by Vera Lebedeva, a long article appeared by Anna Haines entitled 'Childcare in

---

[285] Letter from Anna Haines to Wilbur Thomas, 27 June 1925. AFSC FSR. Quote from David McFadden et al, *Constructive Spirit*, p. 125.

[286] Anna J. Haines, *Health Work in Soviet Russia*. New York, Vanguard Press, 1928, p. 5.

Russian and American health facilities'.

Everything seemed to be going extremely well. Anna Haines was full of enthusiasm. She hoped the Quakers would collaborate successfully with the People's Commissariat for Health. However, one institution in Soviet Russia viewed the foreigners' sincere desire to help with nothing but suspicion.

In the summer of 1926, a summons from the OGPU[287] arrived at the Quaker office at 15 Borisoglebskii Pereulok. Certain comrades wished to see Anna Haines. These comrades were responsible for the campaign against counterrevolutionaries and spies, and it was their job to protect state security and combat any elements which were alien to the Soviet authorities.

Richenda Scott describes Anna Haines' trip to the Lubyanka as follows:

Next morning Anna Haines set off for the GPU headquarters, outwardly calm, inwardly shaken with fear. The sentry on duty hurried her through a side wicket and she was then led by a maze of dark and narrow corridors to a small room, furnished only with a table and a few straight-backed chairs. Here a tall, and rather sinister individual presently entered, introducing himself as Secretary for Religion to the GPU. he knew that Anna Haines spoke some Russian but asked if, on this occasion, she would like to have an interpreter. She at once replied

---

[287] [Translator's note: OGPU, the Joint State Political Directorate, was the name of the Soviet secret police from 1923 to 1934. Later it was called the KGB and today the FSB. All have been based in the Lubyanka building in central Moscow.]

in the affirmative, first to make sure that her answers would be understood, secondly to gain a little time to collect her thoughts while the translation was in progress. A pleasant young man with an excellent command of English was called and the interrogation began. She was questioned on the beliefs of the Quakers, on the work they were doing and had done in Russia, on how this was financed and why they had undertaken it, to all which she replied readily. The secretary for Religions then said that he recently seen her at the opera to his surprise, for he thought that all good Quakers eschewed the theatre. Throughout the interview he remained polite and correct in manner and bearing and ended it by saying that now Anna Haines could see for herself that the GPU was not so black as it was painted. She replied, with her customary frankness, that if everyone called to it had her experience it would scarcely have gained the reputation it enjoyed. 'At this he smiled and said I might go. I had a queer feeling in my shoulder blades, for there were legends of people being shot from behind in that building. However, I got away and home safely and thankfully, and never heard any more from the officials'.[288]

I sent an enquiry to the Lubyanka in 1997: did they have any record of having questioned an American woman, Anna Haines, in 1926? The FSB (successor to the OGPU) sent a curt reply to say that they did not.

The same summer, Anna Haines outlined on paper her proposal for setting up a nurse training centre and sent it to the Soviet authorities. The proposed

---

[288] Richenda Scott, *Quakers in Russia*, ch. 19, p. 268.

nursing courses would last two or three years, and the aim was to extend the project in the future. If all went well, the project could be the model for other medical establishments.

The People's Commissariat for Health asked Dr Lebedeva to look at Haines' proposal, since Vera Pavlovna was, after all, head of the Department for Mothers and Children, and knew the American personally. Vera Lebedeva rejected the proposal, responding that if the Quakers were really interested in developing nursing in Russia, they should just give financial aid to the nursing schools which already existed. Essentially, give us money and we'll be the ones to decide what to do with it. Being a Soviet official, Dr Lebedeva did not really understand fundraising, even though she had spent some time abroad: she had worked in Geneva from 1912 to 1917, as an intern in the university gynaecological clinic under Professor Beitner. Nevertheless, Anna Haines, together with Fred Tritton, who was acting director of the Moscow Quaker centre at that time, was able to persuade Vera Pavlovna of the necessity of setting up a separate structure, since that would make fundraising abroad much easier. Lebedeva finally agreed and recommended several buildings within her scientific research institute to the Quakers. However, the buildings were in an abysmal state – it would cost $22,000 just to repair them. Haines signed an agreement with the People's Commissariat for Health about setting up the nursing school and contacted the AFSC in Philadelphia to ask if it would be possible to raise that much money.

At the end of July 1926, the American Friends Service Committee (AFSC) was willing to start fundraising and already had an arrangement with two donors for $15,000. Suddenly, though, the AFSC decided to reconsider its position and informed Wilbur Thomas, secretary of the AFSC and a big supporter of Quaker work in Russia, that it was not reasonable to fund such large projects under the conditions that had been proposed, especially as funding would have to be guaranteed for five years. London too reacted cautiously to the proposal, letting it be known that British Quakers were unable to commit to any funding at that time.

The AFSC in Philadelphia told Anna Haines that there was no money for her project and nor would there be any in the future. She began to despair. The project she had dreamed of and in which she had invested so much energy and hope was now falling apart. She begged the committee not to reject her plans and suggested going over to the USA to give talks to the general public and take part personally in fundraising. She wrote to Wilbur Thomas: 'It is a tremendous pity […] to allow the opportunity to open the training school to go by the boards for lack of funds to operate it. The type of nurse […] we think it could produce is greatly needed in Russia, especially in the villages. We are the first foreign organisation allowed to establish such an educational institution for Russians. It is a work which could be carried on here in Moscow.

[…] We are all of us agreed technical aid as a demonstration of our friendship toward Russia. […] No stone should be left unturned in the attempt to find funds to carry about the plan of the school'.[289]

There it was: the People's Commissariat for Health gave the Quakers a unique opportunity in 1926 to open a foreign educational establishment in Soviet Russia, but disagreements among AFSC staff and American Quakers' growing dissatisfaction with Wilbur Thomas' style of leadership (exacerbated by disagreements between the British and American Quakers), ruined Anna Haines' plans.

Anna had little reason to stay in Soviet Russia anymore. Her hopes had been dashed. American Quakers rightly had reservations about contributing a significant amount to a project which might have been closed or taken away from the Quaker representative overnight. The Bolsheviks had nothing to lose when they set these financial conditions: either the Americans will agree, in which case that is excellent, or if they refuse, it is no great loss. In retrospect, this turn of events did not do Soviet nursing any favours, since it slowed down the development of nurse training. On the other hand, there is no doubt that Anna Haines' 'baby', her training centre, would have been taken away from her within just a few years and, at that point, she would have been lucky if they had just expelled her from the country. They could equally have accused her of sabotage, Trotskyism, deviationism

[289] Letter from Anna Haines to Wilbur Thomas, 26 July 1926. AFSC FSR. Quote from David McFadden et al, *Constructive Spirit*, p. 129.

and other crimes, and either shot her or sent her to a camp. As it was, Anna Haines left the USSR on 18 October 1926.

There was a last glimmer of hope for Quaker involvement in medical projects in the Soviet Union in 1928. In the centenary of Lev Tolstoy's birth, the Quakers tried to obtain permission to open a nurse training school as part of a programme initiated by the Soviet authorities to set up an educational centre in Yasnaya Polyana. They knew that his daughter, Alexandra Tolstaya, had opened a village school that year which was named after Tolstoy.

The same year, an American Quaker called Emma Cadbury[290] travelled to Yasnaya Polyana:

There was a possibility that Friends could be of help in connection with a new hospital which is being built by the government as a memorial to Leo Tolstoi, in this year of centennial of his birth, at Yasnaya Polyana – near to his home. In connection with this I spent a few days at this most interesting place and also had an opportunity to see a bit of peasant life. We actually slept in his house although this is now to be a national museum, and we ate our meals at a cooperative dining room in what was formerly a barn on the estate. His daughter, Alexandra Tolstoi, lives here much of the time and is keenly interested in the community

[290] Emma Cadbury [junior] (1875 - 1965) was the daughter of Joel and Anna Kaighn (Lowry) Cadbury. She graduated from Bryn Mawr College in Pennsylvania in 1897 and received an honorary degree for humanitarian work from Wilmington College in Ohio in 1962. Cadbury was committed to Friends' international work and was American secretary of the Friends' International Centre in Vienna from 1924 to 1938.

life. She took us to visit two schools which owe very much to her untiring devotion. One school takes especially the boys and girls of intellectual promise and prepares them for the University while another one, in Telyatniki, keeps those children whose development seems most likely to be promoted by training of the hand as well as the brain. The spirit of freedom is very evident, and the children are conscious of their responsibility to their community. The character of Tolstoi and his teachings cannot fail to influence these young people.[291]

Although they knew their chances of success were slim, Friends endeavoured to build a constructive relationship with the Soviet authorities, offering their services, experience and knowledge, and proposing to transfer equipment to the hospital which was meant to be being built in memory of Lev Tolstoy. If they succeeded, Anna Haines was willing to return to the Soviet Union to take an active part in the new project. However, the Bolsheviks showed little interest in foreign involvement in the work in Yasnaya Polyana. The Quakers' suggestions were rejected.

The Quakers' work in Buzuluk was wound up in summer 1926. Only Nancy Babb remained in Totskoye, used to working by herself and relying on local peasants. The last people to leave the Quaker mission in Sorochinskoye were Alice Davis and Nadezhda Danilevskaya. They both arrived in Borisoglevskii Pereulok in Moscow in January 1927, at the address where the Quaker office was located.

---

[291] Emma Cadbury's memoirs. AFSC archives, FSR.

Quaker Centre in Moscow - Borisoglebskii, 15

©*The archives of the American Friends Service Committee*

Since November 1922, the Soviet authorities had been letting the Quakers rent a small, detached house which appeared to have a single storey from the road, but actually had two storeys. The extra storey only covered part of the building. The wooden, plastered, building, was constructed in 1817, and it still stands on Borisoglebskii Pereulok today. The road was called Pisemskii Street for much of the Soviet era, from 1962 to 1994. At the height of the famine, when the Quakers moved to this house from 43 Bolshoi Nikitskii (where they had shared a building with other organisations), quite a number of people were working in the Moscow office, so it was the right time to move. The delay in providing an office was due to the shortage of living space in the capital. The house had enough space for office rooms and bedrooms – indeed, not only for the Quakers, but also for the Baptist and Mennonite relief agencies. The building was well located, in the heart of the city but in a quiet lane, in a part of town where there were embassies and consulates. All the staff, both foreign and Russian, spoke very highly of living conditions in the Moscow office: it was spacious and warm, even in those years.

The Quakers saw the house on Borisoglebskii Pereulok as the future Quaker embassy, or – using the later terminology – as the Quaker centre.

Theodore Rigg, who was head of the Quaker mission from 1916 to 1919, had developed the idea for a Quaker embassy back in 1918, with great enthusiasm. He used this term for a particular reason.

The Council for International Service (CIS) was formed in London in 1918 by the Yearly Meetings in both London and Dublin. In many ways, the new body was similar to the American Friends Service Committee, the AFSC. Carl Heath became head of the new Council. He had become a Quaker in 1916, only a couple of years before taking the post, but was already well known to Friends as he had spent eight years working as secretary of the National Peace Council. Carl Heath was convinced that peacebuilding work should have a religious basis. This was necessary, he believed, in order to counteract patriotic nationalism. The idea of Quaker embassies in various capital cities came from Carl Heath, as did the term. He believed that the embassies' work should be coordinated by a Quaker 'Foreign Office' in London, and that Quaker 'ambassadors and attachés' would work in the overseas missions of the Society of Friends. His bold vision for the Quakers was considered highly ambitious, but Friends liked the idea. Instead of using the word 'embassy', though, they decided to use the term 'centre', and instead of referring to a Quaker 'ambassador', the new term was 'representative'.

Carl Heath's attitude was that, after all the horrors of war, the Quakers would be respected throughout the world thanks to their definite pacifist position. In his view, this would enable them to do successful peacebuilding work. In terms of practicalities, he suggested that 'ambassadors' should be sent abroad for two-year terms of service. The Quaker houses would become unique aid centres and initiators of social reforms; they would enable the creation of international political institutions for the cause of peace. Carl Heath also saw a role for Quaker offices as centres of adult education, as organisers of children's camps, and as a place for holding conferences. Heath proposed that students could be appointed as attachés at the Quaker embassies, travelling to serve in them as interns.

The first Quaker International Centres, set up as a cooperation between Irish and American Friends, were set up in regions where relief work had been done after the war. Three offices were opened in

Germany (in Berlin, Frankfurt and Nurenberg), and later four more were set up, in Paris, Vienna, Warsaw and, eventually, Moscow.

As for the Moscow Quaker embassy, things did not work out there as in the other cities. The staff of the Moscow office realised that British Quakers had got naïve fantasies into their heads since they could not understand the Soviet reality. The Quakers in Moscow tried to explain to the London committee why it was hard to work in Russia. The then head of the Moscow office, Edward K. Balls, wrote to Heath: 'I am afraid it will be hard to make anything of the centre here in Moscow, for we have not truly the liberty to do those things which Friends want to do'.[292]

British Friends could not grasp what Soviet life was like and thought there must be some reason why Quaker workers in Russia did not like the idea of an embassy. In every single letter they sent to Russia, even if it was about opening a medical centre, a nursing school, a rural medical point or the hospital in Yasnaya Polyana, Carl Heath always devoted a few lines to the idea of a Quaker embassy. In 1925 he wrote to Dorice White who was at the Moscow mission: 'Our work is primarily one of international life, reconciliation and understanding. It is only in a secondary sense that we are concerned for a health centre or health service work. […] What we are aiming at is a […] place where such a touch

---

[292] Letter from Edward Balls to Carl Heath, 29 April 1925, FSC RU1. Friends House London archives. Quote from David McFadden et al, *Constructive Spirit*, p. 151.

may be maintained with the heart of Russia as comprehension of the men and women who are shaping the destinies of modern Russia'.[293]

Carl Heath's obsession with the idea of a Quaker centre led to him convincing London Friends to reject the proposal by the AFSC and Anna Haines in 1926 to open a school for training nurses and their further plans to set up rural medical points in local areas in Russia. His intransigence also prevented funding for the hospital to be built in Yasnaya Polyana.

So, while the work in Buzuluk district came to an end, the Quaker office in Moscow stayed open, even though with a minimal number of staff. What could such a small outpost of Quakers do in practical terms, in the midst of the anti-religious campaign and increasingly militant atheism? Ruth Fry, who had travelled to Moscow from London in January 1925, met up with Olga Davidovna Kameneva, who had known the Quakers for a long time and was sympathetic to their concerns. Kameneva wanted to know what exactly the Quakers were going to do next. Ruth Fry wrote in her diary afterwards: 'We rather gathered that she is to explain our continued presence and I don't think she knows too well about our work. She says she has always spoken well of our work, as I believe she has, and wants us to stay, but she dwelt on the terrible need for houses and hinted that it might not be possible for us to keep ours'.[294] Later the same year, the Quakers' attempts

[293] Ibid, p. 152.
[294] Ruth Fry's diary, December 1924 – January 1925, entry for 10

to open a library and arrange English-language teaching were halted due to the Soviet authorities' negative reaction.

The Moscow office had materials in Russian which talked about the Society of Friends, but there was no reading room or fixed place for the Quakers' meetings for worship. One of the British Friends suggested that fellow mission workers could give English lessons as a way of giving information to Russians about the Quakers' activities. Edward K. Balls, who spoke Russian well, evoked the idea of giving English lessons and setting up a library at a meeting with the authorities. He noted: '[A Soviet official] did not object to our teaching the professors [...] English, but said that, as a precedent, it was a bad thing, and could it not be arranged privately. [...] He thinks there will be no difficulties in the way of the library, but was a little wary of anything that might look like Quaker propaganda'.[295]

As well as Olga Kameneva, Ruth Fry met Theodore Rothstein[296] (named Fyodor Aronovich Rotshtein in Russian) in 1925, who was one of the main Soviet censors: 'As to our reading room, he says he should very much like to meet us over it, and will see what

---

January. AFSC archives, FSR.

[295] Letter from Edward Balls to Alice Nike, 9 February 1925. AFSC archives, FSC RU1. Friends House London archives.

[296] Fyodor Aronovich Rotshtein (1871-1953) had been a left-wing activist in Great Britain before becoming an émigré in Soviet Russia for political reasons. He was a Russian revolutionary, an Anglo-Soviet diplomat, journalist and writer, and a member of the Advisory Board of the People's Commissariat for Foreign Affairs.

can be done'.[297]

Quakers who had experience of working in the Soviet context understood the nuances of cooperating with the Bolsheviks: they would never give unambiguous agreement to any project initiated by foreigners. The thing is, who was to know how the party line might change later, and which Moscow comrade would want to be answerable for having had a short-sighted policy regarding some religious people? However, Theodore Rigg, Arthur Watts and Edward Balls' talent and knack for negotiating with Soviet officials brought results which, unfortunately, the Friends in London considered inadequate because they were unable to grasp the reality on the ground in Moscow. As David McFadden writes[298], it would later transpire that one reason for the Soviet authorities' refusal to give permission not only for the English lessons, but also to the opening of a library and reading room, was the London committee's insistence on getting official permission for everything. Edward Balls wrote: 'I feel that Friends need to be very patient with the slow development of their work in Russia and be content for some years to come, to be allowed to continue the material aid which we have been able to give in the past few years. The only possible message of our work here, is to live Quaker lives and by our contacts with everyone around us to continue to inspire the trust and friendship which, so far, we seem to have succeeded in doing here in

---

[297] Ruth Fry's diary, entry for 23 January 1925.
[298] David McFadden et al, *Constructive Spirit*, p. 149.

Russia. For the continuation of our work here, we must have funds and a clear programme of useful work'.[299]

The time had come when the Friends would have to teeter on the brink: they could either do openly what they considered right, which would definitely mean being shut down quickly, or keep an island of Quaker values in the centre of Bolshevik Russia. The price would be making compromises, keeping under the radar and staying out of trouble.

---

[299] Letter from Edward Balls to Carl Heath, 17 April 1925. FSC RU1. Friends House London archives.

Chapter 10. *The survival of the Moscow Quaker office until its closure in 1931. Attempts on the part of individual Quakers to work with Soviet Russia: the stories of Arthur Watts and the Timbres family, Alexander Wicksteed, Margaret Barber and William Wheeldon.*

Alice Hamilton, an American physician, research scientist and author, travelled to Moscow in 1924 at the invitation of the People's Commissar for Health, N. A. Semashko, to find out about occupational health in practice in the USSR. In her autobiography she described everyday life in the Quaker Centre on Borisoglebskii Pereulok [Lane], where she was staying. 'We were four in one fairly large room, with four army cots, one tin wash basin, and a great porcelain stove which served as chimney for the stove on the first floor and was always warmish so that one could thaw out one's hands against it and dry one's towel. Even in October Moscow was bleak and cold and I remember no sunny days. There was, however, one warm room, which served as living room and dining room, and there we could have an open fire of birchwood. All Moscow was heated with wood, we saw great piles of it around the buildings of the Kremlin. As for food, I can remember only that I was hungry a good deal of the time, that I got the most satisfaction out of the heavy, damp, strong-tasting black bread; that kasha, a queer sort of cereal, was rather horrid; but most of all, I remember that the tea was not tea and the coffee was not coffee'.[300]

As the volume of relief work decreased, there was less need for such a large building. In 1924, the number of staff reduced, the Mission's cars and lorries were sold, and unused rooms were handed over to American and British correspondents. In 1925, the Quakers decided to reduce the area they used, keeping just the upper storey of the building, where there was a dining room, kitchen and three bedrooms, and keeping only one large room – the office – and the bathroom on the ground floor.

In 1928, the afore-mentioned American Quaker, Emma Cadbury, described the Quaker office as follows: 'The Quaker Centre to which they took me is a small two-storied house nearly half of which was rented to an American newspaper correspondent and his family who have been to Russia several years. His knowledge of inner and foreign politics was another advantage of the environment which helped toward a broad and friendly understanding of the people among whom I had come'.[301]

As we said above, there were now fewer staff, so in April 1926 the head of the office, Irish Quaker Dorice White, let part of the office to the family of an American journalist, William Chamberlin[302].

---

[300] *Exploring the Dangerous Trades - The Autobiography of Alice Hamilton, M.D.* New York. 1943, p. 237.

[301] Emma Cadbury. Impressions of a trip to Soviet Russia [notes]. 1928. Emma Cadbury papers, Haverford College Quaker & Special Collections, Call Number: Coll.1017.

[302] William Henry Chamberlin (1897-1969) was an American journalist and historian.

This subletting was a sensible idea: in 1927, Chamberlin paid the Quakers 100 roubles a month in rent for three furnished rooms, a kitchen and bathroom. As well as the financial support from their neighbours, the Quakers also benefitted from relative safety, since William Henry Chamberlin, who worked as the Moscow correspondent for the Boston newspaper *The Christian Science Monitor* from 1922 to 1934, was a Marxist with entirely pro-Soviet views. This was bound to improve OGPU's impressions of the inhabitants of Borisoglebskii Pereuluk. The Bolsheviks probably felt less warmly towards the Quaker house's other visitors: Olga Tolstaya, who was the first Russian Quaker, and the only one at the time; Vladimir Chertkov, who was a leading Tolstoyan; and other Tolstoyans. The Russian employees of the Quaker house were also likely to have been watched closely by the secret police.

One of the people who worked for the Quakers in the mid 1920s was Maria Alexandrovna Mansurova (née Rebinder), formerly lady-in-waiting to the Russian tsarina. Her husband, Nikolai Nikolaevich Mansurov, had been executed by the Communist forces in 1918, together with Maria's brother, Alexander Alexandrovich Rebinder. When Maria Alexandrovna's daughter Katya was arrested in 1924, Olga Tolstaya got involved, contacting Ekaterina Pavlovna Peshkova, Gorky's first wife, who was the chair of *Pompolit*[303]:

[303] "Assistance to Political Prisoners", shortened to Pompolit or Politpomoshch, was an organisation which made enquiries into the whereabouts of political prisoners on behalf of their relatives,

Most respected Ekaterina Pavlovna, I send to you Maria Alexandrovna Mansurova, whom I know well, and ask you to treat her with your full trust. She is a wonderful person, pure as crystal, full of nobility and simplicity. She works for the Quakers, where she is respected by all.

Her daughter, aged 20, was arrested on Thursday of Holy Week. M[ay] b[e] you can help her clarify the circumstances of the case and what she is accused of. [...]

Bear in mind in conversation with Maria Al[eksandrovna] that she is hard of hearing.

Yours faithfully,

O. Tolstaya[304]

The Quakers would end up helping Maria Mansurova and her daughter after her daughter's release: in September 1926 they had the chance to live in Totskoye, where the Quakers paid them to work in the children's sanatorium opened by Nancy Babb on the grounds of the kumis sanatorium[305] run by Dr Gusarov.

---

gave them material assistance and petitioned the authorities for their release. It was based at 16 Kuznetskii Most Street, near to the OGPU headquarters in the Lubyanka.

[304] State Archive of the Russian Federation (GARF), fonds 8409, series 1, folder 41, item 130. Handwritten document.

[305] [Translator's note: A kumis sanatorium treated tuberculosis by giving fermented horse milk, *kumis*.]

Medvedka clinic near Sorochinskoye. Alice Davis seated on the left

©*The archives of the American Friends Service Committee*

Another member of staff in the Quaker office was Nadezhda Viktorovna Martynova-Danilevskaya. She had come to Moscow from Sorochinskoye with American Quaker Alice Davis. Everyone called her simply Nadya Danilevskaya. Another American, Edwin Vail, who had worked with Nadya in Sorochinskoye and Gamaleyevka, wrote about her in his diary in 1923:

Mrs Danilevsky feels hard from the loss of her husband and her prison experiences. She works like a trojan to speed time away to the relief of death. And then she wants to make retribution to the peasants for their sufferings [for] which she, as one of the upper class, feels partly responsible. As I have perhaps mentioned before, she had the rank of countess. Her stories of the former life with its luxuries and continual round of pleasure is as fascinating as it is unbelievable from what one sees now.

She used to be a great sportswoman and held the women's tennis championship of Russia. Her language gifts and personality make her invaluable in the work. [...] She has an almost fanatic loyalty to the Russian people, and since she has lost her husband and her son, only wants to work. Still, she realizes that it will be very difficult when we leave, as jobs for the former aristocracy are very scarce. She says she [would get] some enjoyment in going to jail when she knows she has done nothing, but is afraid she may be exiled to Archangel.[306]

Nadezhda Viktorovna was indeed the best Russian tennis player of the early 1910s. She was a member of the Moscow Lawn Tennis Society and Champion of Russia from 1910 to 1912. After the Revolution she worked for the Quakers in Buzuluk district, and later in the Moscow office and in medical facilities in Moscow.

What did staff of the Moscow Centre spend their time doing, once work in Buzuluk district had come to an end and fewer staff were working in Moscow? According to a report by the American Friends Service Committee (AFSC) for 1927:

In Moscow, Dorice White has carried on the work of the Centre which acts as a service and information bureau for foreigners, helps individual Russians, and establishes friendly relations and valuable contacts in the city of Moscow. Alice Davis and Nadya Danilevsky have been studying at the Moscow Professional Educational Department to equip themselves more thoroughly for service in the Soviet Health Department. Anna Haines

---

[306] Edwin Vail's diary, AFSC archives, FSR.

continued her services as nurses' instructor in the department of Motherhood and Infancy until June 1926. The unit worked out, with the National Health Department, plans for a nurses' training school for public health workers and Anna Haines returned to America in December 1926, to help raise the funds for establishing the school. It is expected that this will be the next piece of work for Friends to do in Russia.[307]

Since diplomatic relations between the USSR and Great Britain, which had begun in 1924, were interrupted in May 1927, and there were no diplomatic relations with the USA until 1933, the Quaker Centre sometimes functioned as a representative office for Britain and America. A letter[308] I found in the AFSC's archives gives a typical example of these activities. The letter arrived in Borisoglebskii Pereuluk from the village of Kuryeva Slobodka in 1927. Efrosinya Petrovna Shmel, who was semi-literate, asked the Quakers to look for her husband, Emelyan Artemovich Shmel, who had left their village for America in 1914, and persuade him to contact her. Since he had left, Efrosinya Petrovna wrote, she had had no word of him, while her father-in-law regularly received letters from his son. The unfortunate woman complained that she was looking after their two sons by herself, and in all these years she had received just two money transfers for the paltry sum of 40 roubles, via her father-in-law, for her sons Ivan and Panteleimon.

[307] Tenth Annual Report of the American Friends Service Committee, June 1, 1926 to May 31, 1927.
[308] Letter to the Moscow Quaker Centre from Efrosinya Shmel. 1927. AFSC archives, FSR.

This was by no means enough for their upkeep. 'I ask you therefore not to refuse me if it is possible to help me and to influence my husband to behave as he should to his legal wife and his legal children. I also ask you to help me to influence my husband to send the necessary sum for us to leave for America to join him there', ended Efrosinya Petrovna Shmel's letter to the Quakers.

In August 1926, Dorice White, who was working at the Moscow Quaker Centre, reported:

This month there has been a continuous flow of visitors to Moscow and owing to the absence on holiday of some of the permanent residents of the Moscow flat, it was possible to take in two or three guests at a time. During the month eight visitors stayed in the house, six of whom were there more than a week. In the early part of the month twenty members of the Sherwood Eddy party under the leadership of Sherwood Eddy[309] himself, visited Russia. Arrangements for their entertainment were made chiefly through the Bureau of Cultural Relations and they were received anywhere as very distinguished guests. They had a very full programme. Three of their members stayed at the Friends' Centre and others called from time to time; some of them we were able to put in touch with people of interest or authorities on some particular subject of which they were making a special study. Two of the members of the party who stayed at Borisoglebsky Pereulok were young

---

[309] George Sherwood Eddy (1871–1963) was a leading American Protestant missionary, administrator and educator. He made 15 trips to the Soviet Russia. He admired the Soviet system and refused to believe reports of famine of 1930s; in 1937 he agreed that the victims of Stalin's show trials were traitors as charged.

University graduates who had been attending the World YMCA conference at Helsingfors[310].[311]

In the second half of 1926, Dorice White, head of the Moscow Quaker centre, sent London day-by-day lists of events, visits and guests to the house on Borisoglebskii Pereuluk, in addition to the monthly reports about work in Moscow. Olga Tolstaya and Vladimir Chertkov were frequent guests. There were also some idiosyncratic regular visitors: Dorice White complained to the London committee that two American women, Miss Graves (who had been living in Moscow for two years), and Mrs Fletcher (who had only been in the capital for a few months) could not stand Russian food, so both of them 'practically insist on coming here regularly to lunch and dinner respectively'.[312] They were taken in and fed, before eventually being refused on the grounds of staffing issues, since the number of staff had been reduced to save money.

In early 1927, Dorice White received a letter from London asking her to close the Moscow centre for a few months to save on paying rent. This extremely naïve suggestion showed once again the British Quakers' complete lack of understanding of Soviet reality. White replied: 'With regard to the suggestion of the Committee that we should close in September "for a few months", this seems altogether unfeasible from every point of view. In

---

[310] [Helsinki.]
[311] The Moscow Centre report, August 1926, AFSC archives, FSR.
[312] Letter from Dorice White to Alice Nike, 17 November 1926, Friends House London archives, FSC-RU-1-5.

the first place according to the house agreement, we cannot renew the lease for a period of less than a year so that if we were to close at all, we should have to do it immediately, i.e., before the 1st June. Even then we should probably have to pay two months' rent as, according to the old agreement, we have to give two months' notice beforehand'.[313]

Dorice White grumbled to the London committee about the poor coordination between British and American Friends. She quoted a telegram from the AFSC in Philadelphia which said: 'Committee urges renew lease Moscow house. Opening Medical School next year'. The fact that the London committee was saying the opposite was surprising, Dorice wrote.

Being a very practical person, she made a list of the reasons why she believed they should stay:

It seems to us that there are four main reasons for keeping on this house over the winter:

(1) If we officially withdrew, it might be impossible for Friends to come back again at all.

(2) Owing to the extreme shortage of housing in Moscow it would be impossible to get such suitable quarters again. Even if we took just one room in a hotel the rent alone would come to about 100 roubles a month.

(3) There is large quantity of equipment here (not only what was in this house but also stuff from Sorocky[314] [sic]

[313] Letter from Dorice White to Alice Nike, 10 May 1927, AFSC archives, FSR.

[314] The Quakers often shortened Sorochinskoye to Sorochi, Soroki

and Totskoye) which would have to be stored somewhere in the meantime. In short, the expenses involved in closing down and opening again would be greater than if we reminded here.

(4) The AFSC was in any case undertaken to support Alice Davis and Mrs Danilevskaya during their training and it is cheaper for them to live here than it would be elsewhere.[315]

Dorice White continued to account for literally every kopeck and try to keep expenses to a minimum, so as not to waste the unique opportunity of having an office in the centre of Moscow. She did not give up hoping that the very fact of having a stable Quaker presence in Moscow would be beneficial to Friends. With contacts in the capital already established, it would be easier to look for ways to fulfil the Quakers' mission. Any potential partners the Friends contacted would say: 'Well, if you must have foreigners, those foreigners are ok'. They had been in Soviet Russia for almost ten years already and had not been driven out. You could do business with them.

It might seem surprising that the Moscow authorities had no objections to the Quaker office being sublet. Besides the afore-mentioned Chamberlin, staff of the Greek embassy contacted the Quakers about a sublet. Dorice White wrote: 'Some time ago the Greek Consulate asked us if we could give up our

or Soroka.
[315] Letter from Dorice White to Alice Nike, 10 May 1927, AFSC archives, FSR.

office to them. At that time of course it was not possible for us to do so. I went to see the Consul this morning about it. He says that at present they do not want it, but that in about ten days they will be having a new first Secretary and he thinks it is just possible that he may perhaps need it. But if they did not wish to do so, the Chamberlins are anxious to have it and they would pay half the rent plus half all overhead expenses'.[316]

Alice Davis and Nadya Danilevskaya, who were living in the Quaker house on Borisoglebskii Pereulok, also paid their share of the sublet, which came to 30 roubles a month. Dorice White counted up that if the Greeks came to live there too, they would pay 70 roubles a month. In total, 200 roubles – the rent for the office – could be covered by the lodgers. Dorice White herself did not need to pay any living expenses: her share was covered by a separate payment from the Chamberlins for the use of the furniture in their rooms. Davis and Danilevskaya's share was covered by income from the American Friends Service Committee in Philadelphia, which sent them $75 a month, while London sent $55 a month. Altogether, from 1 June 1926 to 31 May 1927, Philadelphia sent Moscow $12,106. A significant portion of this sum went to Buzuluk, Totskoye and Sorochinskoye. Nancy Babb stayed in Totskoye until November 1927. In Sorochinskoye and Buzuluk, the American funding was used to pay Russian doctors' wages, in accordance with the Quakers' agreements with the

---

[316] Ibid.

People's Commissariat for Health.

Thanks to these savings, Dorice White managed to continue to employ a few Russian workers in the office, with some changes to their job contracts:

Then we could dispense altogether with the office staff for those few months, or if we took Alexandra Tichonovna and she consented to come at about half the salary she is receiving at present, we might arrange to do that. I should hate parting with Mrs Boiko, but I am sure Anna Haines would take her on again if the Training School were in Moscow as she is such a tried and valuable worker. We could also dispense with both servants if we had Alexandra Tichonovna's help for house and office work. If I remained as representative of the Friends, if we did not withdraw officially, there would still be a fair amount of correspondence, contacts, etc., I could also have from time to time some English lessons and by that means I could entirely cover all my living expenses. In this way we could reduce expenses to the minimum, that is, about $70 to be paid by the American Committee for Alice Davis and Mrs Danilevskaya and about 55 dollars for the general upkeep for joint expenses by London alone if they considered me as from the London Committee.[317]

She attached a list of Russian staff and their wages to her letter:

1) Natalia Boiko	Bookkeeper, typist and interpreter	160,80 roubles

---

[317] Ibid.

2) Alexandra Tichonovna Krasotkina	Courier	110,40 roubles
3) Sasha Matveeva	House worker	43,20 roubles
4) Janitor	Part time	10,50 roubles
Total		324,90 roubles

The AFSC annual report about the Moscow Centre's work for the period ending in May 1928 stated:

There has been less Friendly activity in Russia during the past year than at any time since the work was begun in 1916. This is due to the fact that during the year we concentrated our efforts upon a plan to found a Nurses Training School in Moscow or some other prominent center in Russia. It was felt that by making a demonstration of public health work as carried on in America and England through a Nurses' Training School that Friends could make a great contribution to the Russian people. We were not able to secure sufficient funds to guarantee the success of this undertaking, and the plan has been abandoned.

In the meantime, Alice Davis and Nadya Danilevsky [sic] have completed their course of study in a Russian Nurses' Training School in Moscow. They expect to be associated with the Tolstoi Memorial Hospital which is being built and equipped by the Soviet Government at Yasnaya Polyana. While they will not be able to do as much toward developing a nurses' training course as was contemplated under the other scheme, they will be able to make a considerable contribution to public welfare work in Russia. We expect to make contributions toward the equipment of this hospital so that their work can be more effective.

L. Dorice White has been serving as head of our work in Moscow. She has been doing a great deal of teaching and thus has been able to support herself. She has been of great service to travelers and to other foreigners in Russia.

The work at Totskoye in the old famine area has been completed, and Nancy J. Babb has returned to America. About $1000 worth of equipment has been purchased in Germany and shipped to the hospital. This money represents the proceeds of the sale of embroidery work and linen which has been produced by peasants in the Totskoye district.[318]

Alice Davis was not very keen to work at the Centre. She wrote to the new secretary of the AFSC, Clarence Pickett[319]: 'Most of what I am doing is just childish boasting about our achievements'.[320] She refused to accept financial support from the AFSC, since she believed that what she was doing 'was not really honest work'. Nadya Danilevskaya found poorly paid work at the Committee for Aiding Prisoners, while Davis earned a pittance translating

[318] Eleventh Annual Report of the American Friends Service Committee, June 1, 1927 to May 31, 1928.

[319] Clarence Evan Pickett (1884-1965) served as Executive Secretary of the American Friends Service Committee (AFSC).

[320] Gregory A. Barnes, *A Centennial History of the American Friends Service Committee*. Philadelphia, PA: Friends Press, 2016, p. 80.

documents for the Russian Red Cross. Reflecting on her difficulties with work in Russia, she admitted in her letter to Pickett that she was 'nearly at the end of my rope', and that she wanted Anna Haines to come back to Russia to 'take hold of things'.[321]

Friends at other Centres were aware of the situation at the Moscow Quaker Centre. Gilbert McMaster[322], who had been living in Europe for a long time and was head of the Berlin Quaker Centre, did not see any reason for alarm: 'I do not think that Alice Davis' life is in danger [...] she would simply [rather] be put out of the country'.[323] However, the AFSC wanted Alice to come home, and Alice's mother even went to Russia to try to persuade her daughter to leave. Nancy Babb also wrote to Pickett about the 'hopeless situation in Russia', mentioning 'Alice's desire to leave only when she can escape with Mrs D'.[324]

According to the AFSC's 13th annual report[325] for 1 June 1930 to 31 May 1931, Alice Davis was mostly doing translations over this period, while Nadya Danilevskaya was involved with assisting prisoners (we deduce that she must have been

[321] Ibid.

[322] Gilbert McMaster, also spelt MacMaster (1869-1967), started work in 1920 on the large-scale relief program across Germany. Over 1925-1930, McMaster was occupied mostly with relief and interpreting work at the Quaker Centre in Berlin, with occasional trips into Russia.

[323] Gregory A. Barnes, *A Centennial History of the American Friends Service Committee*. p. 80.

[324] Ibid, p. 81.

[325] Fourteenth Annual Report of the American Friends Service Committee, June 1, 1930 to May 31, 1931, p. 6.

working with Peshkova at Pompolit). Dorice White went to England on holiday in June 1930, but when she tried to come back a few months later, she was refused an entry visa.

Carl Heath, British head of the Council for International Service (CIS), wrote a letter to the Soviet authorities, reminding the Bolsheviks of Dorice's 'useful work jointly with Soviet institutions'. Heath mentioned in his letter that two work plans by the Friends in the areas of infant health in the USSR had been rejected by the Soviet government, but in 1929 the Quakers agreed to a proposal by the People's Commissariat for Health to donate equipment to a children's clinic in Moscow. Katherine Edwards was appointed for this mission and prepared to travel to the USSR with Dorice White at the end of August. However, when White's visa for her return to Moscow was refused, it was impossible to continue this work.

Carl Heath wrote in his letter to Maxim Litvinov: 'If the Soviet authorities notify us that Friends' presence in Russia is no longer desirable, then it remains necessary to dismantle our centre, which would require our representative to spend a few weeks there'. In Heath's words, this work could not be entrusted to anyone else: 'The Society requests permission for Dorice White to enter the USSR to continue her work or, as the Soviet government wishes, to dismantle the work'.[326]

[326] Archives of Foreign Policy of the Russian Federation, fonds 0129, series 12, folder 120, file 306, sheet 145. Quote from *Sovetsko-Amerikanskiye otnosheniya. Gody nepriznaniya 1927-1933*

The Quakers' correspondence with the Soviet authorities bore fruit: Dorice White received an entry visa to the USSR in January 1931, but only for one month. In February she was refused an extension to her visa and so left the Soviet Union, after working in the country for ten years. After her departure, Floy George worked for a time in the house on Borisoglebskii Pereulok. She was married to Paul George, an American Quaker who was a specialist in tractor construction. He had come to the USSR as a contractor. It was Floy who wrote to the London committee when the Quaker mission was asked to vacate the premises by 10 July 1931.

The AFSC's report for 1930-1931 stated that Dorice White had left Russia for good, and that Alice Davis and Nadya Danilevskaya were probably going to leave too, on extended leave in order to study in America. The report said that opening a nurse training school had not worked out, but that Anna Haines was willing to return to Russia the next summer if it became possible after all.

[Soviet-American Relations. The years of non-recognition 1927-1933].
'Demokratiya' International Fund, Moscow, 2002, p. 358.

*Sorochinskoye workers with Alice Davis, Nadia Danilevsky
and Dorice White (in a hat)*

©*The archives of the American Friends Service Committee*

Nadezhda Danilevskaya spoke excellent English
and had good enough connections to receive an
exit visa from the USSR, which saved her from
being arrested. The American Friends Service
Committee agreed that Nadya could enrol at Bryn
Mawr College. Danilevskaya and Davis left Moscow
in May 1931, and with that their hardships came to
an end.

The address of the Quaker office appeared in the
Moscow phone book every year from 1922. The
last mention of the Quakers is in the phone book
for 1931. In the entry for 1931 under 'Societies for
giving assistance' on page 119, there are just three
lines:

Society of Friends 'Quakers'. 15 Borisoglebskii Pereulok, tel. 3-35-06. Representative: Dorice White.

On page 593 there is an entry for White, Lucie Dorice, with the same telephone number and address: it was both an office address and residential address.

A short article was published in *Pravda* newspaper on 31 July 1931 entitled 'The Quakers are leaving the USSR':

London, 28 June.

The Moscow correspondent of The Observer reports:

The sole foreign charitable organisation continuing to work in Soviet Russia – the Quaker 'Union of Friends' – is leaving the USSR in July. The reason for the departure is the refusal of the People's Commissariat for Health to renew the agreement which gave the Quakers a noted freedom of charitable activity.

The Quaker organisation worked in Russia from the time of the war and saved many thousands of lives during the famine of 1921.[327]

This was rather a distorted translation of the original article in the British newspaper The Observer. Aside from the parts which were adapted for the Pravda article, the rest of the original was as follows:

It is not Soviet policy to encourage the work of foreign

[327] *Pravda* newspaper, 31 July 1931. The article can be seen here: <http://old.russ.ru/ist_sovr/express/1931_26.html>

religious bodies, and the long existence of the Friends here is attributable to the fact that they never carried out religious work but confined themselves to social service.

The work of the Friends in Russia, in which British and American representatives took part, began during the War with the care of refugees evacuated from the fighting zones. The Friends provided food in Buzuluk county in Samara Province during the famine of 1921 and subsequently furnished medical aid to this country.[328]

The committees in London and Philadelphia speculated about the circumstances: 'It is true that White has been refused a visa to return to Moscow. The probable reason is that Rosinsky [sic], who was employed by us as an interpreter during the famine days, has more recently been employed in the [Soviet] foreign office and has continued to show an interest in Friends and frequently visited our centre'.[329] Indeed, Yulii Oskarovich Rozinsky was arrested in 1929, and in 1930 he was sentenced to be shot, accused of spying activities. The sentence was carried out on 14 January 1931.[330]

It was hardly just because of Rozinsky, though. The Soviet authorities' patience had run out. Even if the Quakers' activities did not bother them at all, by 1931 no one wanted to have a foreign-run office in

---

[328] 'Quakers to Leave Russia: Closing of Headquarters', *The Observer*, 28 June 1931.
[329] Gregory A. Barnes, *A Centennial History of the American Friends Service Committee.* Philadelphia, PA: Friends Press, 2016, p. 79.
[330] Sakharov Centre, Martyrology of those shot in Moscow and the Moscow district. The entry on Rozinsky can be seen here: <https://www.sakharov-center.ru/asfcd/martirolog/?t=page&id=13131>

the centre of Moscow anymore.

And so the story of the Quaker office in the capital of the Soviet Union in the first half of the 20th century came to an end. A new Quaker office would open in the USSR almost exactly sixty years later.

However, the history of Quakers in Russia did not end in July 1931. The same year, English Quaker Arthur Watts came back to Moscow. He had worked in the capital and in Buzuluk over 1920-1923. After suffering from typhus, he left, first for England, to his hometown of Manchester, and from there to the USA and on to Australia. In Australia he got married to Margaret Thorp, whom he had met in Buzuluk in 1921, and they went to the USSR together as tourists in 1930, before settling in Sydney. In 1931, though, Arthur Watts left Australia. Having lived there a few years, he made up his mind for good that Russia was the country where he could fulfil the motto of Ackworth, his old school, a Quaker school in Yorkshire: Non sibi sed omnibus [Not for Self, But for All]. Watts returned to the USSR and divorced Margaret Thorp, sending her notification of their divorce by post. He began work as an engineer in the town of Novomoskovsk, which was still called Bobriki at the time. He took Soviet citizenship when the Second World War broke out.

In 1957, Arthur Watts met several young British Quakers who had travelled to Moscow for the World Festival of Youth and Students. Two of those who took part in this meeting, Phillip Morris and Irene Jacoby, recalled that Arthur Watts said that 'in the USSR he felt free to give his whole self to the service of the community, which he had felt unable to do while working for an employer in a capitalist system. He felt "free as an artist is free to paint a picture with his whole self, even he has to be poor"'.[331]

Another of those who took part in the meeting with Watts, David Harper, jotted down some notes after their conversation in Moscow:

Arthur looked like any Russian artisan, though it soon became obvious that he had retained an English head upon his shoulders. He was glad to see us — partly because he felt he had something to offer to us. During the course of our conversations, I wondered how far disappointments with the Soviet regime he had been compensated by the return to his Quaker faith, and did not like to ask whether he was or had ever been a C[ommunist] P[arty] member. I think I detected a slight note of tragedy in his voice, but over this lay a considerable amount of praise for the achievements of the Soviet Union and an appeal to us to try and understand the Russians' point of view by really imagining ourselves in their position.[332]

Arthur Watts died in 1958. He never travelled back to England, fearing that he would be arrested there.

A Quaker family, Rebecca and Harry Timbres, arrived in the Soviet Union from the USA in 1936. They had already worked in Sorochinskoye from April to September 1922. Harry was a doctor, a

---

[331] Memorandum about Arthur Watts. No. 1 — Phillip Morris and Irene Jacoby. Author's personal archive.

[332] Memorandum about Arthur Watts. No. 2 — David Harper.

specialist in tropical diseases, and in 1936 got a visa with great difficulty and for a short stay. He travelled to Russia by himself and wrote detailed letters home to Rebecca, who was waiting for Harry to tell her and their two daughters when to join him. He was enchanted by how wonderful life was in Moscow, where he had met up with some old acquaintances – a young couple from Sorochinskoye who had come to live and study in the capital. He also met up with Arthur Watts, who had gone native as a Muscovite by that point.

Harry and Rebecca Timbres fundraising dance. USA 1930s

©The archives of the American Friends Service Committee

Harry finally managed to get permission for his wife and children to enter Russia. The family was allocated to move to the Mari Republic (on the Volga river near Kazan) and work on a project called 'Marbumstroi' [Mari Paper Construction] to build a pulp and paper factory. Life in semi-starvation, in dreadful living conditions, the reality of Soviet labour for practically no pay... we can imagine that the Timbres family's enthusiasm did not last long. The 'Marbumkombinat' [Mari Paper Factory] opened in 1938, but Harry did not live to see it in action. In 1937, he had suddenly fallen ill with typhus and died. He was buried in the Mari Republic, and Rebecca went back home with their children. In her book *We Didn't Ask Utopia*[333], Rebecca Timbres Clark describes in detail life in the woods near the town of Volzhsk. I was lucky enough to meet her when she was living at Medford Leas senior care community in New Jersey in the USA in 1996. She was almost 100 years old, blind and very hard of hearing, but it was obvious (as the nurses caring for her confirmed) that she was pleased to meet a guest from Russia. We chatted for a long time, and then I asked Rebecca if she remembered any Russian words at all. 'Teplushka' [a boxcar with a small stove against the back wall for when live cargo was carried], she said clearly. She signed a copy of her book by feel, and we hugged when we said goodbye.

Alexander Wicksteed, an English Quaker, arrived in Russia in April 1922. He worked at the Quaker famine relief mission and then, as nearly all the Quakers were leaving the country, Alex decided to stay in the USSR. The American doctor Alice

---

[333] Harry Timbres and Rebecca Timbres Clark, *We Didn't Ask Utopia: A Quaker Family in Soviet Russia*. New York: Arno Press, 1970.

Hamilton, who met him in October 1924 at the Moscow Quaker Centre, described him as a great admirer of Soviet Russia. She recounted the speech which he gave to the newly arrived foreigners: 'It is the only country in which life is really free'.[334] Miss Hamilton recalled that everyone present gasped at that, as Edward K. Balls, the then director of the Moscow office, who spoke Russian well, had only just warned the foreign arrivals that each of them would have a personal spy following and reporting; that careless words even in English might cause grave danger to others if not to themselves; and that they must 'walk on egg[shell]s always'. But Wicksteed seemed to have his own way of understanding freedom: 'Oh well', Wicksteed answered, 'if you are thinking of politics, all right, but I care nothing for politics. The Russian mind is so open and free from inhibitions that talk about real things can be freer than anywhere. If in England I am asked to dinner and accept, I must remember to go that particular night whether I feel like it or not, and I must be on time. Here I can go or not and at the hour I please. Ten chances to one my hostess has forgotten she asked me, and the meal is never on time'.

Alex Wicksteed earned his living teaching English in a higher education institute in Moscow. American journalist Negley Farson wrote about Wicksteed in his book *Caucasian Journey*[335]: every year, when his students began their holidays in May, Alex took all

[334]Alice Hamilton, *Exploring the Dangerous Trades: The Autobiography of Alice Hamilton*, M.D. Northeastern, [1943], reprinted 1985, p. 328.
[335] Negley Farson, *Caucasian Journey*. Evans Brothers Limited, 1952.

the money he had saved up over the winter, stuffed a rucksack with provisions, and went to the Caucasus for the whole summer. He lived in a tiny room in one of the hostels in a working-class neighbourhood of Moscow, where the toilets were at the end of a long corridor. Wicksteed's whole garret was full of furniture, Farson recalled, with a huge samovar on a table in the centre. Wicksteed, who did not speak Russian, tried very hard to look Russian by shaving his head and letting his beard grow, and went about Moscow wearing a tattered shirt and high boots. In his attempt to become Russian, Wicksteed had practically no contact with foreign diplomats and journalists, but Russians did not consider him one of them either. He died of chronic bronchitis, alone in his room, in the summer of 1935, and his body was not found for some days. The newspaper The Scotsman reported on Wicksteed's death.[336] Alex Wicksteed was one of those Quakers who preferred to live in Soviet Russia than return to the West: he liked everything in Russia and wrote about it in his two books: *Life Under the Soviets* (1928) and *Ten Years in Soviet Moscow* (1933). It may seem surprising, given Wicksteed's devotion to the Bolsheviks, that these books were published in the West but not translated into Russian. We can only assume that even the Kremlin censor did not think it wise to torment Soviet readers with a foreigner's fantasies of what the Soviet Union was like.

Another Quaker who decided to stay in Russia was Margaret Barber from England. She had worked

---

[336] *The Scotsman*, 31 July 1935, p. 13.

in Buzuluk district in the first Quaker mission from 1916 to 1918. She was adored by the local population and looked after people in Lyubimovka in 1916, where she ran the local hospital. Once she had left Buzuluk in May 1918, Margaret Barber went first to Moscow, and from there to Astrakhan, where she worked as a nurse in a hospital. After many adventures, she eventually managed to reach England via Constantinople.[337] In 1922 she returned to Soviet Russia, this time forever. Margaret went to Lyubimovka, where she already knew her way around, and worked first in the hospital and then on a collective farm, where she married a local resident and had a son. When Margaret fell ill with tuberculosis, it was the Quakers who saved her life. As she recalled: 'They sent horses for us, and we all went to them. They gave my husband work and put me and the baby in the hospital. Later we went to Nancy Babb's sanatorium in Totskoye. By the end of the season, we were strong again'.[338] Margaret and her family soon left the area, moving first to Uralsk and later to Azerbaijan. Although she was already a nurse and midwife, she did additional training in Russia to become a physiotherapist. Richenda Scott wrote that Margaret Barber was still working in the USSR in 1961, living on the Black Sea coast. Her husband had already died, and her son had died at the front, in the Battle of Stalingrad.[339]

---

[337] Margaret H. Barber, *A British Nurse in Bolshevik Russia.* London: A. C. Fifield, 1920. [Translator's note: Constantinople is now Istanbul.]

[338] Richenda Scott, *Quakers in Russia*, p. 259.

[339] Ibid.

Englishman William Wheeldon had less luck in life. A member of the Quaker mission, he too decided to stay in the USSR. William was a pacifist and a Marxist, and after serving numerous prison sentences in England for being a conscientious objector, he was unable to get a good job in his homeland. So William, who was not a Quaker, went to Buzuluk with the Quaker aid service and helped Russians in the aftermath of the terrible famine. He fell in love there, and his Russian wife was called Zinaida Ivanova. Town resident V. Melnikov still remembered many years later: 'In 1923 Wheeldon married Zina Ivanova, an office typist. As the bride's parents wished, they were married in the cathedral according to Christian rites. Zina invited me [to the wedding], and as I was best man, I held the crown over her head during the ceremony'.[340]

The Soviet authorities referred to them as the Vildony, the Wheeldons. Will and Zina Wheeldon travelled from Buzuluk to Samara, and then on to Moscow, where they lived in a hotel for foreign Komintern[341] staff. Wheeldon started work as a translator for Komintern.

However, he was arrested by the secret police on 5 October 1937, accused of spying and preparing acts of sabotage, and sentenced to be shot. William Marshalovich Wheeldon was shot at Christmas

---

[340] Pod *znamenem Lenina* newspaper [Under Lenin's banner], issue 91, 12 June 1990.
[341] [Translator's note: The Komintern was the Communist International, an organisation founded in 1919 to promote world communism.]

1937.[342]

---

[342] Russian State Archives of Social-Political History (RGASPI), fonds 495, series 198, file 537.

Chapter 11. *Were Quakers 'useful idiots' for the Bolsheviks or stubborn optimists?*

As well as Arthur Watts, Margaret Barber, Alex Wicksteed and William Wheeldon who opted to stay in the Soviet Union, there were other Quaker workers too who fell under the influence of communist ideas, during both the first (1916-1919) and second (1920-1931) Quaker missions. Most of the Quakers who had worked in Russia and had genuinely sympathised with the Bolsheviks eventually left the country, but they remained in thrall to their imagined idea of communism.

John Rickman and his wife Lydia Rickman (née Lewis), for example, were convinced that the Communists had good intentions, and in March 1918 they even registered their marriage with the Buzuluk Council of Deputies. They believed that registering their marriage with the Bolsheviks would be a symbol of their confidence in the new government. Historian David McFadden quotes a letter from John Rickman, who felt that their marriage registration enabled the Quakers to persuade local communists to stop lynchings in Buzuluk: 'Having witnessed the executions, Rickman anguished over how to oppose the killings, without endangering the Quaker relief efforts. He wrote to his mother: "We therefore quite calmly resolved to go to the Tribunal and tell them that we had witnessed the scene of the afternoon and we knew how they would feel at having justice sacrificed to mob law. [... We] came to the conclusion that the best way we could show them that we really did have confidence in them and that we did not go to them [only] to criticize their action was to go to them to be married"'.[343]

After the Quaker mission in Buzuluk closed, the Rickmans went to Vladivostok, sailing from there to the west coast of the United States in October 1918. John and Lydia went to Washington with the aim of telling the capital what was happening in Soviet Russia. The Anglo-American couple, who sympathised with the new government in Russia, were counting on the fact that people in Washington would be interested in what they would say. However, they were given a polite but dismissive reception. Throughout their subsequent journey to London, the Rickmans were eager to tell literally everyone what was really happening in Soviet Russia, but every time they tried to paint the Bolshevik experiment in a positive light, they encountered prejudice and distrust. In their later writings, speeches and articles, they continued to adhere to the same pro-Soviet point of view.[344] Immediately upon his return, in 1919, John Rickman published the book *An eye-witness from Russia*[345], followed in 1950 by *The People of Great Russia*.[346]

Two American women, Anna-Louise Strong and

[343] D. McFadden et al. *Constructive Spirit* p. 30.

[344] Richenda Scott. *Quakers In Russia*, p. 218.

[345] *An eye-witness from Russia* pamphlet. People's Russian Information Bureau, 1919.

[346] *The People of Great Russia: A Psychological Study*. Chanticleer Press, Inc., 1950.

Jessica Smith, were also fans of the Soviet regime and all things Soviet. They were not members of the Society of Friends, but had been invited by Quakers to go to Russia as journalists and write articles about Friends' work, doing what we now call PR.

Anna-Louise Strong, born in 1885 to a family of missionaries in the Congregational Church, had been fighting for workers' rights and denouncing the ulcers of capitalism from an early age. A keen wordsmith, she wrote several religious texts (such as *The Psychology of Prayer* and *Boys and Girls of the Bible*) before turning to issues of social injustice. In 1921, Strong went to the Quaker mission in Poland, and from there to the country where her dreams were coming true: Soviet Russia.

Strong was a diligent worker, producing very well written reports from the Volga. At the same time, though, her love for the new regime and her admiration for everything she saw in Soviet Russia was growing at a tremendous pace. She sang the Communists' praises in a letter to America in December 1921: 'In the midst of the ruin and desolation, there is an organizing life. It consists in the comparatively small group of Communists, devoted, self-sacrificing, working themselves to death, not merely to reconstruct Russia but to reconstruct it on entirely new lines'.[347]

Strong went on to work in the Soviet Union and

---

[347] Letter from A-L. Strong of December 19, 1921. Friends House London archives. FEWVRC-MISSIONS-8-3-9-1_REPORTS-ACCOUNTS_1921.

founded the newspaper *The Moscow News*, before leaving for the People's Republic of China. There she admired the Cultural Revolution and the Red Guards, and even made friends with Mao. She died in China in 1970 and is buried in Beijing at the cemetery of the Martyrs of the Revolution.

Born in 1895, Jessica Smith went from the US to Soviet Russia in February 1922 and worked for the Quakers until January 1923. She wrote innumerable accounts and short notes during this time and travelled all over, visiting villages and farms located in the work area of the ODK's American group. After returning to the United States, Smith became editor of the publication *Soviet Russia Today*, which was the mouthpiece of 'Friends of Soviet Russia', a pro-Soviet organisation. During the Second World War she founded the National Council of American-Soviet Friendship, and remained an enthusiastic admirer of Soviet Russia, travelling there many times after the war. Almost fifty years after her first stay, she even went back to Sorochinskoye, as A.T. Sinelnikov, director of Sorochinskoye Local History Museum, gladly recalled when I met him in 1997. I have also read an article written by Jessica Smith in *Krestianka*, the Soviet magazine on rural life, in which she wrote enthusiastically about the remarkable successes of Soviet Russia – as it seemed to her from the distant United States, at least.

Although Jessica Smith and Anna-Louise Strong spent some time living in the USSR, they were both pro-Bolshevik optimists who looked at the reality around them through rose-tinted spectacles. They were not alone in their sympathies with the Bolsheviks. Reading archival materials, I have repeatedly come across instances of some Quaker mission employees giving a biased picture when describing Soviet reality, finding explanations for certain shortcomings, and emphasising the positive aspects of life in the country. There was often a prosaic reason for this: their lack of knowledge of the Russian language and their faith in official Bolshevik propaganda. But Smith and Strong are extreme cases. Anna-Louise Strong, for example, happily quoted the assertions of Soviet propaganda, reporting that 'Even in this situation of uncertainty, Russia will allocate more funds for education in its budget for the next year than for military expenses. This is the only country in the world about which that can be said'.[348]

Alice Hamilton, the American doctor and labour safety specialist mentioned above, met both Anna-Louise Strong and Jessica Smith during her trip to Russia in 1924. The latter's views made Hamilton despair:

'One evening we got to discussing the universal espionage and I said Russia could never hope to have a united people till she got rid of it and restored people's trust in each other, that mutual suspicion and mutual betrayal spoiled human relations.' She insisted it was necessary. 'But,' I said, 'don't you value at all a sense of honor, respect for

---

[348] Ibid.

truth-telling, loyalty?' She smiled in a pitying way. 'Petty bourgeois ideology,' she said. 'And you are not revolted at all by the cruelty, the midnight arrests, the shooting without real trials, of hundreds?' 'Certainly not,' she said. 'The one question I ask is, 'Does that help the Party?' If it does, it is right; if not, it is wrong'.[349]

When Wilbur Thomas, Executive Secretary of American Friends Service Committee (AFSC), visited Russia in 1923, he wrote: 'We have had the opportunity of meeting quite a number of the prominent men in the Government and I have been very much impressed with the brains back of what is going on in Russia. The men in the Government Departments are very able and are doing the best they can under the terrific handicaps that have been imposed upon them. There is no doubt at all that they are succeeding'.[350]

After working for a year at Sorochinskoye, Edwin Vail, an American Quaker, remembered Wilbur Thomas' trip and speech: 'Thomas stressed the meaning of our work in both America and Russia, not only in terms of material relief or suffering, but in terms of international brotherhood and love of human people. With both the commercial press and religious press damning Russia, who is going to show friendship and thereby gain friendship?'[351]

---

[349] Alice Hamilton. *Exploring the Dangerous Trades - The Autobiography of Alice Hamilton, M.D.*, 1943.
[350] Letter from Wilbur Thomas to Skattergood, 9 May 1923, AFSC Archives, FSR.
[351] Edwin Vail's diary, AFSC Archives, FSR.

By that point, after a year in Russia, Vail had an astute idea about what was going on in the country. His diary is full of interesting comments and anecdotes:

It is not a communistic state. It is not that now, and under the New Economic Policy gets farther away from it every day. State capitalism, I think, is the expression that comes nearest toward describing of the present organisation. Communism was the opposite point of the pendulum swing from hated oppression of the rule of the autocrats and foreign capital, and therefore an impracticable extreme. As has often been the case in history, reformers revert to the old evils and justify their action by the law of necessity as did those who preceded them. At the first [year] of the Revolution the death sentence was abolished, but now it is even used for bribery, and the hated Cheka espionage system still spies but has another master. The present government is no more humanitarian than the old. As you probably know, the government has no use for the church, and does everything it can to kill it by confiscation of valuables, taxes, etc. It is only natural that they should want to destroy it because it was an instrument of oppression and a stronghold of the reactionaries. But I think their policy is a very short-sighted one because it has no constructive side. They make it a point to teach atheism in all the government schools.[352]

At the same time, Edwin Vail also noted in his diary that, 'I am having a desperate time to rise above a passionate consideration of the Revolution and Communism, and gain a clear-eyed historical

---

[352] Edwin Vail's diary, AFSC Archives, FSR.

perspective... The Revolution whatever it is, is a great event in history, and should be studied with fairness necessary in all historical research'.[353]

Of course, in retrospect, it is all too easy to be scathing about the Quakers' gullibility, given that we know how events unfolded in the USSR after their departure, once Stalin came to power. We can smile wryly at Vail's conclusions, set out in his diary, immediately after the announcement of Lenin's death: 'Lenin's death at any time would have great political significance and consequence, but especially so now when the conflict within the Communist Party is at its height. His death now will probably quiet the opposition for several weeks and with Trotsky sick and on vacation, it will be a good opportunity for the Central Executive Committee to crush the opposition entirely or at least make it less effective. However, the later reaction may be all the greater, and it is probably foolish to forecast. It will be interesting to watch the political events of the next few months'.[354]

As adherents of a religion whose main principles include honesty and candour, the Quakers sometimes perceived events in Russia rather naively, or only saw what they wanted to see. Like many others, they were misled by the slogans proclaimed by the Bolsheviks in 1917: 'Power to the Soviets' and 'Land to the Peasants'. Leninist philosophy, with its ideas about the reconstruction of society, the elimination of all oppression and social inequality,

[353] Ibid.
[354] Ibid.

was quite in tune with Quaker principles and very similar to the Bolsheviks' declared aims. Among the Religious Society of Friends – a church of peace and non-violence – Lenin's argument that the First World War was unfair to all parties and was alien to workers' interests went down well. On the other hand, Lenin's calls for turning an imperialist war into a civil war and for workers to use the war to overthrow their governments clearly contradicted the Quaker approach to confronting injustice in this world. But Lenin did call[355] on the Russian Social Democratic Party to participate in the anti-war movement, using pacifist slogans. Quakers were therefore very useful for him too, with their strivings for peace and their refusal to take up arms: this would create a gap in the imperialist armies, even if only a small gap. This is what Lenin joked in a playful note to his colleague N.A. Semashko: 'My dear Semashko! Don't get cross, my old dear! We'll leave the Quakers for you, just for you. Don't be jealous of Kuskova'. This remark is about the defeat of the Pomgol All-Russian Public Committee, one of the leaders of which was Ekaterina Dmitrievna Kuskova, whom Lenin mentions. But the archive documents confirm the fact that the Quakers were fairly well known to the Soviet authorities in the 1920s, and these authorities stressed repeatedly that the Bolsheviks had no objections to the Society of Friends.

As an example of a positive story about Quakers, we

[355] I.V. Lenin. *Socialism and War (The Attitude of the Russian Social Democratic Labour Party towards the War)*. Collected Works, vol. 26, pp. 307- 350.

can quote from a national newspaper: in the January 1922 issue of *Izvestia* newspaper, a respectful note 'The Activities of the Society of Friends (Quakers) in Russia' was published, which gave a very brief overview of the history of relations between Quakers and Russia: 'The activities of the Society of Friends began in Russia long before the famine in the Volga region. In 1916-1918 the Society of Friends in England and America united to give help to refugees who had been transferred from the front to Samara province. The activities of the joint Anglo-American society continued for a while after the revolution but soon had to come to an end since the society was prevented from receiving supplies from England'.[356]

Noting the help given by British Quakers to children in Moscow and Petrograd in 1920, the article went on: 'In the period from February to September 1921, the Society of Friends of the American [Friends] Service Committee and English Friends of the Committee for Assisting Victims of War united into one whole and distributed about £150,000 sterling in Moscow alone. In this way, some 14,000 children were continuously supplied with milk, while the rest of the medicines and food were distributed to children's prison colonies, hospitals, orphanages and schools; clothes were distributed directly from the society's warehouses. Now, the Anglo-American Society of Friends has shifted the centre of its activities to Buzuluk district'.

---

[356] *Izvestiia* newspaper, issue 16, 22 January 1922.

The Kremlin's sympathies with the Quakers increased from the summer of 1921, as the Communists realised the tragic scale of the forthcoming famine in the Volga region. They saw that Quakers were already engaged in humanitarian work in Russia, helping children's institutions in cooperation with the People's Commissariat for Health. That summer, the Bolsheviks were therefore forced to put a temporary brake on their traditional suspicion and hostility, letting about twenty foreign aid missions into the country.

Gregory Welch, who had travelled to Moscow in the summer of 1920 just before the famine in order to help Watts, who was already working with the People's Commissariat for Health and the People's Commissariat for Education, wrote about what is now called the 'war of the Kremlin towers'. During his month-long stay in Moscow, the Soviet Foreign Ministry repeatedly tried to expel the Englishman from the country, but the GPU (the political police) leapt to his defence. The Lubyanka was unusually supportive because Welch met many like-minded people during his visit, such as Tolstoyans, and so unwittingly helped the secret police by shining a light on his contacts. It did not occur to him that there was a need for caution.

As we saw above, Welch, who was refused an extension to his Russian residence permit in 1920, was afraid that Quaker assistance to the communist country might be misunderstood by the world community, and by the Kremlin itself: 'Watts takes rosy view of Soviet Government, is a communist himself, and under his auspices our efforts would be construed as an expression of sympathy with the Soviet Russia. ...Arthur Watts does not talk Russian therefore takes what is told him and does not yet see that [Bolsheviks] are falling far from their expressed ideals'.[357]

However, the attitude of Arthur Watts and his allies in both London and Philadelphia prevailed, thanks to the idea that Quakers should not remain indifferent to the suffering of ordinary people, and that Christian principles did not require checking documents before reaching out to brothers and sisters in distress.

The subsequent work carried out by Friends in Soviet Russia proved this approach to be correct. The Quakers, though generally trusting and friendly, have nevertheless been vigilant about how their supplies are used, where the food goes, and who the final recipient of clothing and food is. Trust, but check. Occasional incidents of theft or unauthorised distribution of rations did occur, of course. One such incident is described by Dorothy North, a member of the American group of the ODK and the head of the Quaker post in Grachyevka. The chairman of the local committee in Pomgol was accused of distributing Quaker rations without prior discussion with Quakers. The guilty party was contrite, promising, 'You may cut off my head with a knife, you may put me in jail for ten years

---

[357] Letter from Lucy Biddle Lewis to Wilbur Thomas, 29 September 1920. AFSC archives.

instead of three [the time he was liable for], if I ever disobey instructions again or take advice from any but the Quakers'.[358] Someone growled: 'Remember the Soviet is the government of Russia and not the Quakers'.

A similar story is told by the English nurse Muriel Payne, who worked in Borskoye, 60 km from Buzuluk. In her letter to Ruth Fry in London, Muriel wrote that over the last two months, in the six volosts [parishes] under her care, almost all the members of the two local Pomgol (Famine Relief) Committees had been arrested 'for most outrageous stealing of our food. In a third Volost the Chairman has been arrested and given five years sentence for prolonged stealing of food and 2/3 of the clothes issued for Children's Home. He was really a most impressive person to talk to! Two other Volosts have been selling the rations for 15,000 Roubles each to pay the Ooyezd tax, stopping the ration if people can't afford to pay'.[359] Muriel Payne wrote that if Quaker work in Russia continued, Friends would need to reach a completely new, tougher agreement with the Soviet authorities, to prevent the misuse she encountered in Borskoye.

Another case of a scam, about which Muriel Payne wrote[360] to her mother in June 1922, began

---

[358] Dorothy North. *In the Quaker House in Grachevka*. Friends House London archives. FEWVRC-MISSIONS-8-3-9-2_REPORTS-ACCOUNTS_1922.

[359] Letter from Borskoe from Muriel Payne to Ruth Fry in London on 24 May 1922, FEWVRC-MISSIONS-8-3-9-2_REPORTS-ACCOUNTS_1922.

[360] Muriel A. Payne. *Plague, Pestilence and Famine*. London: Nisbet

when she received some out-of-date corned beef from England. As she saw that the tinned food was very old, the decision was taken to bury the tins outside the village. However, Muriel had previously established a rule that if any foodstuff in the Quaker rations turned out to be poor quality, it would be exchanged for an equivalent, good-quality foodstuff. Some Borskoye residents found the place where the outdated tins were buried, dug them up and took them to the Quaker warehouse, demanding their replacement. Muriel's assistant, Henry Goldey, realised quite quickly that they were being tricked. He had to dig up all the buried tins and mark each one so that no one else would be tempted to try the scam.

The local Communists in Buzuluk district, too, had a strong dislike for foreigners. Their irrational hostility towards the Quakers was typically based on so-called class instinct mixed with rigid patriotism. In the summer of 1922, for example, Walter Wildman arrived in Sorochinskoye to succeed Beulah Hurley, who had left for the United States, as director of the ODK American group. Beulah told him about the strained relationship between the American ODK and local Communist Konovalov. Like many Bolsheviks, he did not believe in the good intentions of the Americans in general, and the Quakers in particular. In the summer, ten days before the sowing season, for example, he told the American group of the ODK that foreigners would have to pay for the grain for sowing, which should have been free of charge according to the agreement between the Soviet authorities and the ODK. Intervention from Moscow stopped the local Communist's arbitrary rule, and Konovalov was soon expelled from the party.

There is no doubt that the secret police, the Cheka, watched all foreign organisations, and the Quakers were no exception. In fact, Soviet Russia's representative for foreign famine relief organisations, A.V. Eiduk, and from the summer of 1922 K.I. Lander, were both Cheka members. The regional representative responsible for work with foreign aid organisations in Samara province, Martyn Martynovich Karklin, was also in the Cheka. Incidentally, both Eiduk[361] and Karklin[362] were shot in 1938. Lander's fate is less clear: although an article in the Great Soviet Encyclopaedia[363] claimed he died in 1937 while busy with literary activities during his retirement, other sources say that Lander[364] too was shot in 1937.

The term 'useful idiots', mistakenly attributed

---

[361] Eiduk was arrested in June 1938, accused of espionage, being associated with a counter-revolutionary organisation, and preparing terrorist attacks, convicted on 28 August 1938 by the Military Collegium of the Supreme Soviet of the USSR, and sentenced to death. <https://bit.ly/2sCQB9F>

[362] Karklin was arrested in December 1937, accused of participating in a military terrorist group, and espionage activities, convicted on 23 February 1938 by the Commission of the People's Commissariat for Internal Affairs (the NKVD) of the USSR and the USSR Prosecutor's Office, and sentenced to death. <https://bit.ly/2OESZFl>

[363] <https://biblioclub.ru/index.php?page=dict&termin=710269>

[364] <http://hrono.ru/biograf/bio_l/lander.php>

to Lenin, was coined and widely used in the 20th century: it was applied to those who naively considered themselves to be allies of Soviet Russia and believed they were doing good, but were actually used by the Bolsheviks for their own purposes, like puppets. Can we apply this term to the Quakers? Were Friends being useful idiots when they saved hundreds of thousands of Russian citizens from famine?

We can hardly hold it against the Quakers that they cooperated with the Bolsheviks. You had to get permission from the authorities to travel into the country and help starving people, and you absolutely had to reach agreements if you were to get permission from the authorities. Admittedly, the archive documents show that a few Friends were naive and poorly informed, and often saw the world in black and white. For these foreigners, all Bolsheviks were 'white', largely because Lenin's declared goals seemed justified.

But that was the strength of the Religious Society of Friends: that the erroneous opinions and misconceptions held by certain individuals (often in good faith) could not harm the end result. After all, Quakers were led not by the desire to please the Communists, not to help the Bolshevik authorities towards the victory of worldwide revolution, but by the desire to reduce the suffering of poor, innocent civilians and save hundreds of thousands of people from death.

Quakers' approach and their relationship with

the Soviet authorities are demonstrated by the Rickmans, who registered their own marriage with the local Council of Deputies: indeed, the sentiment 'you commit wrongful acts, but our good will and openness will help you change for the better' has been characteristic of many Quakers. The belief that evil must be met with good and non-violence lives on among Friends today. Misguided evildoers are expected to be discouraged not so much by criticism of their unjust and sometimes violent acts, but by a practical demonstration of good as an alternative to violence. Good conquers evil: as George Fox (the English religious dissident, mystic, and founder of the Religious Society of Friends) said, the nature of the evil manifest in this world is inside, in people's hearts and souls.[365] Back in the 17th century, Fox reminded Quakers that human life is full of evil, sin and despair, but that God's endless love for mankind is victorious: 'I saw also that there was an ocean of darkness and death, but an infinite ocean of light and love, which flowed over the ocean of darkness. And in that also I saw the infinite love of God; and I had great openings'. It was not difficult to see the ocean of evil in Soviet Russia in the 1920s, but the ocean of light and love did not reveal its radiance to everyone. British and American Quakers who saved Russian people in those dreadful years saw glimpses of the ocean of light and tried to bring out the light of goodness themselves.

---

[365] *George Fox Speaks for Himself: Texts that reveal his personality—many hitherto unpublished.* Ed. Hugh McGregor Ross. York: William Sessions Ltd., 1991.

'The Book of Discipline', a fundamental text for British Quakers, was issued by the Society of Friends in London in 1921 and became known as 'Christian Life, Faith and Thought'; more recent versions are known as 'Quaker Faith and Practice'. As stated in its preface, it aimed 'to state truth, not by formulating it, but by expressing it through the vital personal and corporate experience of Friends'. The format of this relatively brief book was unusual: instead of commandments and requirements, Quaker guiding principles were given unobtrusively in the form of recommendations ('advices') and questions ('queries').

Much of this book, which has existed without major changes for the last hundred years, explains the feelings, or, as the Quakers say, leadings, which have guided Friends in their work: 'Be aware of the spirit of God at work in the ordinary activities and experience of your daily life. Spiritual learning continues throughout life, and often in unexpected ways'. And later: 'Are you open to new light, from whatever source it may come? Do you approach new ideas with discernment?'

For the Quakers, the good, noble work of saving people dying of starvation was spirit-led and their beliefs contributed to an awareness of where the spirit of God was leading them. The new life promised by the Bolsheviks, the communist ideals and goals they voiced, would have been perceived by Friends as 'new light'. Each individual Quaker, and the Society of Friends collectively, had the responsibility and insight to distinguish false leadings from sincere strivings.

In the same 'Advices' to Quakers, it says: 'Refrain from making prejudiced judgments about the life journeys of others. Do you foster the spirit of mutual understanding and forgiveness which our discipleship asks of us?'

Ultimately, it does not matter what Soviet officials thought about Friends, since they failed to manipulate them. Every bit of the food supplies, clothing and transport which Quakers brought from abroad was given to people. It did not go through distribution shops, which only served trade union members or members of the All-Union Communist Party (Bolsheviks), but went through schemes in which Quakers were fully involved and where they were able to monitor the process. Quaker principles, combining honesty and openness, friendliness and kindness, played a positive role. Beyond the fact that hundreds of thousands of Russian citizens did not die, but survived, had children and grandchildren, a message was passed on from generation to generation: that the British and American people, who had come to their desperate land from across the sea, had saved them from starvation.

Soon after the famine was over, however, the Kremlin began the ideological indoctrination of the Soviet population. Foreign aid organisations just seemed to dilute the political orthodoxy. At first, official propaganda belittled the importance of foreign aid by distorting statistics, and later the authorities began to lie, claiming that the American Relief Administration – the most effective organisation among those who helped fight hunger – actually sold stale, rotten goods in exchange for church gold and Russian antiquities, and was mainly engaged in espionage by creating a network of agents in Soviet Russia. However, in no Soviet document did I find a single word of criticism of the Quakers. After a while, no one wrote anything at all about how they had helped starving people in the Soviet Union, but at least no one ever vilified them.

The only exception I am aware of was a book by A.T. Sinelnikov, director of the Sorochinskoye Museum of Local History, published in 1996, about the history of the local region. He claimed that 'in Sorochinskoye, as well as in surrounding volosts, there was an American office for food aid. It was run by a certain Jessica Smith. Some old people in the village remember how people who were exhausted from malnutrition at the collection point received certain weights of crushed corn or foreign wheat in exchange for valuables'.[366] The word 'Quaker' is absent here, although the aforementioned Jessica Smith did work in Sorochinskoye as a member of the American ODK group. However, she was never its leader – she was a publicist hired by the AFSC in Philadelphia. The museum director did not mention which valuables were exchanged at the 'collection point'. His allegations are in the realm of fantasy. In addition, paragraph 17 of the 'Agreement of 16 September 1921 between the

---

[366] A.T.Sinelnikov. *This is my city.* Sorochinskoye, 1996, p. 31.

Quakers and the People's Commissariat for Food on food and material assistance to Russia' clearly stated: 'The goods of the Society of Friends are given out to the population free of charge, as gifts from the Society of Friends'.[367]

In 1998, after meeting with me and the historian McFadden, Sinelnikov published an article in the local newspaper in which he wrote: 'I remember a story my mother, former Siberian peasant Anisya Sinelnikova, used to tell me about how she, as a widow of a soldier of the Red Army who was suddenly left alone to look after her young baby, took off her gold cross and swapped it for a few pounds of foreign ersatz flour provided by American or English Quakers'.[368]

Mr Sinelnikov found it conspicuously difficult to explain his story: he was born in 1920 in the Pavlodar region, where his family lived until the 1930s, and where there were no Quakers.[369] I cannot understand what made this man lie. A man who belonged to the Communist Party school of thought, A.T. Sinelnikov cast aspersions on people who saved his compatriots' lives during the years of hunger. This is the only case of vilification of Quakers I have come across.

I have been able to meet many people who remembered Quaker relief work, all of whom spoke of it with great gratitude. I went to Buzuluk for the

[367] State Archive of the Russian Federation (GARF), fonds 1058, series 1, file 5.
[368] *Sorochinskoye* Gazette, issue from 29 June 1998, p.3.
[369] <https://bit.ly/2ZFRAF7>

first time in 1995. At the market there, I went up to old men and women who were selling vegetables from their vegetable patches, since I was looking for people who might have lived in the area when they were children. Everyone whom I talked to about this subject was open and all of them said more or less the same thing: it was a terrible famine. First, the Bolsheviks seized all the grain. Then there was an unusually warm spring, followed by a dry, hot summer. We were dying because there was nothing to eat. But it was foreigners who saved us: Americans and British people. They gave us food: it was their rations which saved us from death.

After my article about the famine and Quakers was published in *Russian Province*, a Buzuluk newspaper, I started getting letters from people who had survived the famine. One of them was N.P. Morozova, who was nine when the Red Army arrived in her village, Torpanovka. She said they were like bandits, robbing peaceful residents: the soldiers confiscated everyone's reserves of food, and took away the horses and carts. That was how the famine began. Sometime later, Morozova recalls, some Quakers arrived in Torpanovka. They opened a children's home in the church school for orphans and for children whose parents could not feed them. She wrote that the Quakers saved her life by giving her quinine when she fell ill with malaria. To that day, the old lady wrote, she remembered the food they gave her: beans, rice, flour, chocolate and egg powder.

Nina Grigorevna Popova, who lived in Sorochinskoye, wrote to tell me that when she was five, an American lady from the Quaker mission had given her a ragdoll. 'It was my very favourite toy: I played with it for a long time and kept it until it fell to pieces, many years later. I have always remembered the name of the American lady. Her name was Miss Pickering'. Hannah Pickering did indeed work at the Sorochinskoye office of the American group of the ODK from October 1922 to July 1923. After she went back to the USA from Samara province, she took an active part in setting up the American Society for Cultural Relations with Russia. Later on, Hannah worked with the Open Road travel agency which had been set up by John Rothschild. From 1927 onwards, it organised study group visits to the Soviet Union, even before the United States had recognised the new state. She went to the USSR several times in the 1930s through a partnership between Open Road and Intourist, the Soviet travel agency.

During my many meetings with people in Buzuluk, Sorochinskoye and Totskoye, I also discovered many local legends and myths. T. A. Konnova from Sorochinskoye, for example, wrote to me that after reading my article in the newspaper, she had remembered a story her grandmother had told her, a story she had never taken seriously before. Her grandmother had said that when she was little, there was a terrible famine and her parents died, but then, according to her grandmother, she was temporarily adopted by an American family and lived with them for a year. American women had saved her life, her grandma would say. Mrs Konnova wrote that she had previously thought that her grandmother had an overactive imagination: 'How could she possibly find American women in our region, in a little village in the steppe?' After my article, though, she realised that there must be a grain of truth in her grandmother's tales after all. There really had been American women in the area, at any rate!

American Quakers Dorothy North and Sydnor Walker wearing Chuvash traditional costumes with Russian peasant ladies

©Courtesy Friends Historical Library of Swarthmore College

During the worst years of hunger, British and American Quakers placed abandoned and lonely children, as well as foundlings, in children's homes, where they were fed, clothed and looked after. However, their actions also led to the creation of local legends. Often the records of the children taken to the orphanage were lost, and so they could not return to their families even if anyone remained alive there. It gave rise to all kinds of speculation: many people living in Buzuluk district assured me that they had a great-uncle or great-aunt who had been taken to America, where he or she probably still lives. Nowhere in the archive documents did I find any information about Quakers taking personal care of one of the local children, though, let alone any cases of them taking a child back to America with them.

The closure of the Quaker office in Moscow in the summer of 1931 marked the exodus of the Society of Friends from Russia and, as such, is the end point of an important period in the history of relations between the Quakers and Russia. It is not hard to explain why the Quakers left Russia in 1931. The Soviet authorities no longer wanted a foreign organisation in the country, but for some reason Friends were not kicked out with fanfare but eased out relatively humanely. No one was arrested, accused of espionage or spreading religious propaganda. Dorice White was even given a Soviet visa for a few weeks in 1931, to put things in order at 15 Borisoglebskii Pereulok and collect anything left behind. Similarly, in the same year, Alice Davis was able to leave for the USA with Nadya Danilevskaya.

The Soviet authorities had created a stalemate situation for Friends by then, not allowing them to do anything. London and Philadelphia had lost interest in the idea of a Quaker centre in the Soviet Union, reducing their financing of the project to zero. The efforts and financial means of Quakers in London and Philadelphia were redirected to other projects: no one expressed a desire to continue the work that had been started in Russia, no one had a vision for further Quaker service there, as Theodore Rigg once had and later Gregory Welch and Arthur Watts. The idea for a Quaker embassy quietly faded away, and the proposals by British and American Quakers for medical programmes which could be implemented by the Bolsheviks were either deflected, put off for another day or rejected. In the end, the Moscow authorities refused to extend the lease of the premises where the Quaker mission was located.

Clarence Pickett, who replaced Wilbur Thomas as Executive Secretary of AFSC in 1930, wanted cooperation between the Society of Friends and Bolshevik Russia to continue. He showed even more sympathy for the USSR than Thomas had, for which he was criticised by Alexandra Lvovna Tolstoy, who had moved to the United States in 1929, and by two former employees of the Quaker office in Moscow, Alice Davis and Nadezhda (Nadya) Danilevskaya.

Alice Davis wrote to Pickett in February 1933: 'It has always seemed to me that many Friends are not very clear in their thinking about Soviet Russia ... [you] will remember the difficulty we had in convincing many Friends (if indeed we have done so), that the antireligious campaign was not simply directed against the Orthodox Church and the evil alliance between church and state, but that communism was fundamentally opposed to Christianity, particularly in such forms as Quakerism'.[370]

Quaker historians (D. McFadden, J. Greenwood and R. Scott) rightly point out that, to a large extent, the Society of Friends was itself responsible for the end of the Quaker project in Russia. According to these researchers, in 1926-1928 there was a good chance of opening a Quaker Medical School, to train nurses under the direction of Anna Haines. However, London and Philadelphia were beginning to calculate what a Quaker project in the Soviet Russia might cost them. In 1926, the London Committee announced that due to the financial crisis that was gripping Great Britain at that time, they could not appeal to the British public to donate money for a project in Moscow. The Committee's decision to issue a symbolic grant to the Moscow centre for the sum of £500 looked derisory, and the Committee in Philadelphia behaved similarly.

When the London Committee discussed the situation regarding the Russian project in May 1930, it noted in the minutes of the meeting that 'it was suggested that only prayer can help to understand the extremely difficult situation in Russia'.[371]

It was therefore the Quakers' loss of interest and the

---

[370] Alice Davis to Pickett, 12 February 1933. Quote from *Bolshevism and Christianity: The American Friends Service Committee in Russia (1919-1933)*. Zachary Oelschlegel. 2012.

[371] John Ormerod Greenwood. *Quaker Encounters: Vol.1, Friends and Relief*, p.251. York: England, 1975.

change in priorities in London and Philadelphia which led to the closure of the Moscow centre. At the same time, we must not forget that by 1931 the Kremlin's attitude towards religious organisations was very different from the mood in Russia ten years earlier.

In October 1921, the People's Commissariat for Agriculture (*Narkomzem*) of the Russian Soviet Republic had published an appeal 'To sectarians and Old Believers living in Russia and abroad'. As famine was threatening the lives of millions of Russian citizens, Narkomzem literally begged believers to come back to Russia: 'Wherever you live on all the earth, welcome! Come and take up work and creative, joyful labour amicably'.[372] Many religious sects were listed: Doukhobors, Molokans of all kinds, *Nachalo veka* (the Chemreki), Jehovah's Witnesses, New Israelites of various branches, Shtundists, Mennonites, Malevans, Yenokhovtsi, Tolstoyans, Dobroliubovtsi, free Christians, teetotallers and Podgornovtsi. The appeal was the initiative of V. D. Bonch-Bruyevich, who claimed, incidentally, that Lenin supported the idea strongly.

However, only four years later, in 1925, militant atheist Fyodor Maksimovich Putintsev[373] sharply

---

[372] <http://molokan.narod.ru/v/v1925_1_5.html>

[373] Fedor Maksimovich Putintsev (1899-1947) was a prominent Soviet atheist propagandist and researcher into the study of religious problems and atheism. He was a member of the Communist Party from 1920 and actively participated in anti-religious propaganda from 1921-1922. He was a member of the Central Council of the Union of Militant Atheists of the USSR from 1925. Over 1932-1934 he was the editor of the *Bezbozhnik*

criticised both the appeal and the very practice of constructive communication with sectarians. In the December issue[374] of *Bezbozhnik* (The Godless Person), an atheist newspaper, he spoke out strongly against sectarians and attacked the afore-mentioned call by the agricultural ministry, Narkomzem. By 1931 relations with religious believers had become even worse. In an anthology published in 1932, Putintsev wrote: 'It is crucial to remember that on the international arena we have, and will have for a long time yet, such experienced enemies of the working class as Catholicism, Protestantism, and all kinds of refined and "scientific clericalism" trying to support and use "our" churches and sectarians with the aim of fighting against the USSR'.[375] The Quakers fitted the above description of enemies perfectly: they were Protestants and did not make any secret of their contacts with Tolstoyans and other 'sectarians'. But the Quakers were certainly not intending to fight against the USSR, even though militant atheists like Putintsev doubted Friends' peaceful intentions. The Tolstoyans, for example, were increasingly harassed: the 'Life and Labour' Tolstoyan community, founded in December 1921, was forced to move to Siberia by 1931. Tolstoyan community leaders began to be arrested by 1936, with arrests of community members continuing in 1937 and 1938. By January 1939 the Tolstoyans were finished: the few Tolstoyans left joined Soviet newspaper.

[374] *Bezbozhnik*, 13 December 1925.

[375] *Militant atheism in the USSR for 15 years. 1917-1932*, p. 50. Moscow: Ogiz (State Publishing House): State Anti-Religious Press, 1932.

collective farms.

While anti-religious propaganda continued into the 1930s in the USSR, for ten years the economic and political situation in the country went from bad to worse. Nadya Danilevskaya, a Russian noblewoman and former employee of the Quaker mission, described this in 1933 in a letter to Clarence Pickett:

The first years after the Revolution I believed that the cruelties of the Soviet government were due to war time, that they were afraid of their enemies from within and without, and that they will cease as soon as they have strong power. Therefore, I firmly believed that the best thing for the country was to see the government become strong and that the duty of each of us was to do its small share in working for the government — as loyally as our conscience permits…

But as time went on, and cruelties continued and became worse, and the Soviet power became stronger and Stalin's policy franker and more evident — I understand that such a regime could not make our people — or anybody — happy and free. Their slogan which we constantly see on posters and in press is: 'Who is not with us, is against us and is our enemy. We should ruthlessly exterminate our enemies for the triumph of Soviet Power'. […] Do you understand what it means to be 'with them' […]? Do you think it is right to strengthen such a government? I think that Friends should only try to help the suffering people in Russia but not become 'Friends of Soviet Russia,' friends of the government.[376]

---

[376] Nadya Danilevskaya to Pickett, 12 February 1933. Quote from *Bolshevism and Christianity: The American Friends Service Committee in*

We can assume that even if, by some miracle, the Quaker centre had not been closed by the Soviet authorities in 1931, its staff would have been arrested soon enough and either shot or sent to the camps. The closure of the centre in Borisoglebskii Pereulok in 1931, something which was happening naturally anyway, seems to explain to some degree the lack of dramatic arrests and sham trials within Russian-Quaker relations.

Looking back today at the history of interaction between Quakers and the Russian authorities, the Society of Friends clearly did extraordinary work. Through incredible effort, hundreds of thousands of people were saved from death. Goodness, honesty, openness and a willingness to help – these characteristics of the British and American Quakers left a warm glow in the heart of each Russian who interacted with them. The Quaker principle of 'there is something of God in everyone', which Quakers follow in their lives, left lasting positive memories for those Russians who crossed paths with the ODK in Moscow, Samara, Buzuluk or in the Russian hinterland. Quakers' traditional friendliness and openness, combined with a desire to help people in distress, found a natural response from the friendly and kind Russian people. The language barrier did not hinder communication between people of different nationalities. In a unique example of folk diplomacy, Russian peasants got to know American and British people, who had come from the other side of the world to save their lives.

These encounters were also an unforgettable experience for the American and British relief workers. One member of the American ODK group in Sorochinskoye described an evening dance at the 'Communist Club', where 'Trotsky or Mr. Karl Marx himself stare down from the wall' at partying Russians and Americans: 'The Communist club isn't much different from other clubs; the dancing is perhaps a little decentre and the "linen" not so good. Pleasant they are socially, like well-fed clubmen anywhere. Whether you dance against the shoulder of a Russian blouse or a black Tuxedo doesn't matter much. I believe that I am beginning to think that neither governments or methods of government matter much – but the soul of man himself'.[377]

---

[377] Guests of the Soviets. June 1923 Friends House London archives. FEWVRC-MISSIONS-8-3-9-3_REPORTS-ACCOUNTS_1923.

Afterword. *Sixty years later, Quakers return to Russia.*

Once the Quaker Centre in Moscow ceased to exist, if Quakers came to the Soviet Union at all, they came as individuals, as tourists. In 1951, when Alexander Evdokimovich Korneichuk, a Soviet playwright, five-time laureate of the Stalin prize and a politician, came to England at the invitation of the Friends' East-West Relations Committee, he extended an invitation to the Quaker delegation – on behalf of the Soviet Peace Committee – to visit the Soviet Union. Soon the British Quaker decision-making body, known as Meeting for Sufferings, received a written invitation confirming what Korneichuk had said. After careful consideration of the proposal, the meeting decided to accept the invitation, and immediately chose seven Quakers for the trip to the USSR. The delegation consisted of Leslie Metcalf, Gerald Bailey, Margaret Backhouse, Paul Cadbury, Mildred Creak, Frank Edmead and Kathleen Lonsdale. They left London in July 1951 and spent two weeks in the Soviet Union being shown a variety of aspects of life and work, as organised by Soviet officials. The foreigners visited schools and hospitals, mines and collective farms, research laboratories and residential buildings, and even prisons in Moscow, Leningrad and Kiev. The Quakers took part in a conference at the Ministry of Education, and met Yakov Malik, the Ambassador to the UN and First Deputy Foreign Minister of the USSR. They had several meetings with trade unions, with teachers, university professors, scientists and doctors. They paid a visit to a Baptist church and attended a service, went to Trinity Monastery in Zagorsk, visited the seminary, and talked to the Patriarch and Metropolitan Nikolai. As a result of the trip, a book called *Quakers Visit Russia* was published, which described the Friends' trip to the Soviet Union in detail, with photos worthy of the cover of Time magazine (or its Soviet equivalent *Ogonyok*).

It is no secret that the KGB treated foreigners very well if they could be useful in influencing public opinion to be more favourable towards Moscow. As Oleg Gordievsky, a former KGB officer, writes in his book[378], foreigners were called 'agents-conduits' and secret 'informers-conduits' of Soviet influence. He explains that these people, 'most likely because of their political beliefs, were sympathetic to some aspects of the Soviet worldview. Many of them were real idealists, and most of them "helped" the Soviet Union unintentionally'. As Gordievsky comments, 'With its inherent cynicism, Moscow used everyone who naively agreed to serve its own interests'. Although Kathleen Lonsdale, a British crystallographer and author of *Quakers Visit Russia*, wrote in the foreword that 'Friends, like most other people, object to being "used". They may be idealistic, but they are not simpletons',[379] there is no doubt that the Communists wanted to use the

[378] O.Gordievsky, *Next Stop Execution: The Autobiography of Oleg Gordievsky*. Macmillan, 1995.

[379] K. Lonsdale, ed. *Quakers Visit Russia*. London: East-West Relations Group of the Friends' Peace Committee. 1952.

British visitors for their propaganda purposes. Realising this, the Friends saw their visit to the USSR as a gesture of goodwill, as an opportunity to show the common people whom they hoped to meet in the Soviet Union that barriers to communication were erected by politicians on both sides, while good relations and direct contacts are important for maintaining peace on earth.

In 1957, a group of young Quakers took part in the International Youth Festival in Moscow. Aside from that event, Quakers made other trips to the USSR, but these were all individual visits without particular consequences.

While Moscow attached the utmost importance to the mass peace movement in the second half of the twentieth century, including the campaign for nuclear disarmament, doing everything in its power to use peacemakers and pacifists to its advantage, the Kremlin did not go so far as to allow the presence of Quakers in the USSR on a permanent basis.

It was only once Mikhail Gorbachev had succeeded the elderly general secretaries of the Communist Party and become head of the Communist Party of the Soviet Union that fundamental changes in the relationship between the Religious Society of Friends and Russia became possible.

In 1991, the Soviet authorities gave permission for Roswitha and Peter Jarman to go to Russia as official representatives of the British Quakers. They lived in Moscow and worked in the country for two years. Almost simultaneously with their arrival, Marjorie Farquharson, a Quaker, arrived in the Soviet Union too and opened an official Amnesty International office in Moscow.

The continuing history of Quaker relationships with Russians is well documented in the memoirs of Peter Jarman and Marjorie Farquharson, and although Jarman and Marjorie eventually left, the connections they had established were maintained. Patricia Cockrell and Chris Hunter came to Moscow to succeed the Jarmans. In the late 1990s, a Quaker Centre was created, a Friends House in Moscow, of which Friends had dreamed at the beginning of the twentieth century.

The story continues today.

Appendix 1

Lists of Quaker mission workers, prepared by
Sergei Nikitin

First Quaker mission to Russia 1916-1919

1. Anderson, Selina K.
2. Baker, Hinman J.
3. Ball, Louisa
4. Ball Richard Reynolds
5. Babb, Nancy J (worked in Russia 1917-1919 and 1921-1927)
6. Barber, Margaret (worked in Russia 1916-1918, returned to live to the USSR in 1925)
7. Barrow, Florence M.
8. Boughton-Leigh, Edith M.
9. Bradbury, Emilie C.
10. Bradley, Dr. Neville
11. Butt, Ellen
12. Catchpool, E. St. John
13. Colles, Charles
14. Cox, Ethel
15. Farbizeski, Amelia
16. Fox, Dora E.
17. Fox, Dr. J Tylor
18. Fox, Elsie L (Mrs)
19. Graveson, Bertha
20. Haines, Anna J. (worked in Russia 1917-1919 and 1920-1926)

21. Heald, Thomas Dann
22. Hoffman, Ruth
23. Jukova (Zhukova), Ksenia
24. Keddie, Frank
25. Kerr, Beatrice
26. Lewis, C. Gordon
27. Lewis, L (Miss)
28. Lindsay, Eleanor T.
29. Little, Wilfrid R.
30. Little, Elizabeth A. (Mrs)
31. Manning, Dr Herbert C
32. Munier, Louise
33. Pattison, Mary B
34. Pearson, Dr George H.
35. Rickman, Dr John
36. Rickman, Lydia C (Mrs)
37. Rigg, Theodore
38. Tatlock, Robert R.
39. Webster, Margaret A.
40. Welch, Gregory
41. Wells, Anne R.
42. White, Dorothy
43. White, Esther
44. Williams, E. Theodora

Second Quaker mission to Russia 1920-1931

1. Albright, William A.
2. Amend, Katharine
3. Asche, Eric

4. Balls, Beatrice
5. Balls, Edward Kent
6. Barrow, Harrison
7. Becker, Meta
8. Blackburn, Willard
9. Bliss, Elma
10. Borders, Karl
11. Branson, Julia
12. Brennah, Wolfe
13. Brocklesby, Harold
14. Brocklesby, John H.
15. Brown, Omar
16. Candler, Irene Muriel
17. Carver, Wilhelmina
18. Catford, Robert O.
19. Christie, Ethel M., Mrs
20. Churcher, Dora G.
21. Clayton, Cuthbert
22. Cleaver, Thomas
23. Coldey, Henry
24. Colville, Elizabeth
25. Copeman, Tom
26. Cotterell, A.P.I.
27. Danilevskaya, Nadya
28. Daunt, Dorothea O'Neil
29. Davis, Alice
30. Dennithorne, John
31. Detzer, Dorothy
32. Dodd, Katherine
33. Dunn, Robert
34. Dunthorne, John
35. Edelman, Louis

36. Elliott, Lucy Dr.
37. Fawcett, Howard
38. Finch, Alfred
39. Fox, Ralph
40. Gamble, Arthur
41. George, Floy
42. Gillham, John H.
43. Goldey, Henry
44. Graff, Elfie Richards, Dr
45. Greene, Ben
46. Gregory, Stanley C.
47. Grundy, Alfreda E.
48. Habegger, Joseph F.
49. Hamilton, Alice
50. Harby, Edward W.
51. Heagney, Miss
52. Herkner, Anne
53. Hildren, Philip
54. Hill, Norah
55. Holmes, Ernest W.
56. Horsnail, Henry
57. Hurley, Beulah
58. Kelsall, Jessie M.
59. Kenworthy, Murray S.
60. Kilbey, Ernest
61. Kilbey, Richard
62. King, Winifred E.
63. Koff, Sidney
64. Krauss, Emma
65. Lampson, Myrle L.
66. Lovejoy, Dr. - visit
67. Lupo, Carl W., Dr.

68. Lupton, Frank G.
69. Macdonell, Archie
70. McConnell, Aida
71. McKay, Edith (Minnie)
72. McKenzie, Melvill (Mackenzie, Melville)
73. McRobie, Carrie
74. Mildern, Philip M.
75. Mitchell, Dr
76. Morris, Edna W.
77. Morris, Harriet
78. Morris, Homer L.
79. Morrish, Grace
80. Neale, Williamza de C.
81. Nicholson, Edgar Samuel, Mr.
82. Nicholson, Elma Rhoda, Mrs.
83. Norment, Caroline G.
84. North, Dorothy
85. Ostler, Gertrude A.
86. Parris, Stanley C
87. Paul, Parry H.
88. Payne, Muriel A.
89. Pennington, Ruth V.
90. Perry, Edgar J.
91. Phillips, Mabelle C., Miss
92. Pickering, Hannah
93. Pyott, Keith
94. Rackstraw, Marjorie
95. Ray, Winifred M.
96. Read, Tom
97. Reed, John
98. Roberts, Betty
99. Robinson, Rosemary

100.	Rogers, Margaret G.
101.	Rowntree, Ernest
102.	Sacker, Margaret
103.	Sampson, Lucy
104.	Schor, Pauline
105.	Shapleigh, Elisabeth R., Dr
106.	Sharp, Evelyn
107.	Shrimpton, Lilian
108.	Sidney, Alex
109.	Simmonds, Emily L.
110.	Smaltz, Alfred G.
111.	Smaltz, Geo (Heine?)
112.	Smith, Jessica G.
113.	Spalding, Kate
114.	Spiekman, Janet
115.	Stevens, Harry
116.	Strong, Anna Louise
117.	Stout, Ruth
118.	Swithinbank, Gertrude
119.	Sydney, Alex
120.	Thompson, Rebecca
121.	Thorp, Margaret Sturge
122.	Tillard, Violet
123.	Timbres, Harry G.
124.	Timbres, Rebecca Janney
125.	Tritton, Fred
126.	Vail, Edwin H.
127.	Wadsworth, Kathleen
128.	Walker, Sydnor H.
129.	Watts, Arthur
130.	Watts, Frank
131.	West, Miriam E.

132.   Wetherald, Samuel
133.   Wetherall, Alfred E.
134.   Wheeldon, William M.
135.   White, Dorice L.
136.   White, Godfrey
137.   Whitson, Esther M.
138.   Wicksteed, Alexander
139.   Wigham, J. C.
140.   Wildman, Walter E.
141.   Wilson, Francesca M.
142.   Wiltshire, Harry
143.   Wood, Laura Leonora
144.   Yates, Florence A.
145.   Yorkston, Wilhelmina
146.   Young, Cornelia

1. Hewson, Cornell (worked in Minsk)
2. Hewson, Estelle (worked in Minsk)

Appendix 2

Chronology of the events described in Friends and Comrades

Sergei Nikitin

[Non-Quaker events are in bold]

Year	Date	Event
1916		
	27 March	Ruth Fry writes to the Russian embassy
	28 March	**First secretary of Imperial Russian Embassy, Sablin, writes to Ruth Fry**
	19 April	Arrival of four Quakers in Petrograd
	7 May	Arrival of four Quakers in Moscow
	16 May	Arrival of three Quakers in Samara
	7 June	Arrival of three Quakers in Buzuluk
	29 Aug	First party of medical workers and aid workers arrive in Buzuluk from England
	15 Oct	Transfer of refugees

and orphans from the
southern part of the
district to the house in
Mogutovo

1917

31 Jan	Opening of the Quaker centre in Efimovka
28 Feb	**February Revolution in Petrograd**
	Tatlock and Fox there at the time
April	Tatlock and Fox meet Olga Tolstaya in Moscow
29 June	Six Americans leave Philadelphia
5 July	The six Americans set sail from Vancouver on board the 'Empress of Asia'
26 Aug	Arrival of the six Americans in Buzuluk
7 Nov	**Bolshevik Revolution in Petrograd**
18 Dec	**Bolshevik forces arrive in Buzuluk**

1918

8 Feb	'The Bolsheviks show their full respect for the Quaker mission'
Feb	Anna Haines meets Raymond Robbins, head of the American Red Cross mission, in Petrograd
March	John Rickman and Lydia Lewis marry in Buzuluk
29 March	The hospital in Mogutovo closes
April	The children's home in Mogutovo closes
21 April	Quakers supply staff and funding for the refugee children's home in Spaco-Preobrazhenskii monastery in Buzuluk
Mid-May	Theodore Rigg goes to Moscow to fetch money
End of May	Quaker mission workers leave the villages of the district and move to Buzuluk
26 June	**Czechoslovaks take Buzuluk**
1 July	Rigg returns and

	reports on trip to Moscow
7 July	The Rickmans leave Buzuluk and travel eastwards
14 July	Rigg and White leave Buzuluk for Samara
4 Oct	Last group of Quakers leaves Buzuluk
26 Oct	**Second brigade of 24th Simbirsk Iron Division led by Commander Sedyakin liberates Buzuluk from the Czechoslovak Legion**
End Nov	Rigg and White on the Zagryazhskie-Stroganovy estate on the outskirts of the village of Znamenka

1919

Jan	Rigg and White leave Znamenka colony for Moscow
10 Feb	Rigg and White leave Moscow for Beloostrov
12 Feb	Crossing the border at Beloostrov
Dec	Gregory Welch accompanies children from Petrograd to

Vladivostok

1920

17 March	Hinman Baker and Frank Shaw arrive in Petrograd with humanitarian aid
April-May	Baker and Shaw meet Semashko, Bonch-Bruevich and Chertkov
June-July	Arthur Watts arrives in Russia with humanitarian aid
23 July	Gregory Welch arrives in Moscow
24 Aug	Gregory Welch leaves Moscow
5 Oct	American Quaker David Robert Yarnall meets Eiduk in Berlin about the Quakers' proposal to send humanitarian aid to Russia
27 Nov	Anna Haines arrives in Petrograd from Reval (Tallinn)
22 Dec	Watts hears Lenin speak at the Eighth Congress of Workers, Peasants, Red Army Soldiers and Cossack

Deputies of Soviet
Russia, held in Moscow

28 Dec   Permission to use a
Tsentrosoyuz warehouse

1921

4 March   **President Harding of
the USA sworn in**

5 March   Watts' article on 'The
Care of Children
in Soviet Russia'
published in *Soviet
Russia* newspaper

14 March   **NEP introduced by
the Tenth Congress
of the Russian
Communist Party
(Bolsheviks)**

16 March   **Anglo-Soviet trade
agreement signed in London**

7 April   Watts writes to
Chicherin, the
Commissar for Foreign
Affairs, requesting
entry visas for four
more Quakers

6 July   **Gorky writes a letter
appealing to the West**

12 July   **Lenin mentions the
Quakers**

18 July	**Central Commission for Famine Relief (TsK Pomgol) set up by decree**
21 July	**All-Russian Committee for Famine Relief (VK Pomgol) offically registered (and nicknamed 'Prokukish')**
20 Aug	**Soviet Russia signs an agreement with the American Relief Administration (ARA)**
27 Aug	**VK Pomgol dissolved**
End Aug	Nancy Babb returns to Soviet Russia
28 Aug	Margaret Thorp and Anna Haines go to Samara
10 Sept	Quakers start work in Samara province (Anna Louise Strong takes humanitarian aid to Samara)
16 Sept	**The Religious Society of Friends (Quakers) in Britain and USA sign an agreement with the People's Commissariat for Food**
Oct	Arthur Watts visits

Minsk

End Oct	Murray Kenworthy, head of the American ODK (Quaker) group, arrives in Moscow
6 Nov	Murray Kenworthy goes to Buzuluk with Arthur Watts
8 Nov	Cornell and Estelle Hewson leave Minsk
12 Nov	J. Wigham: 20 wagons of food left Moscow for Buzuluk
15 Nov	Nancy Babb is treated for typhus in Buzuluk
16 Nov	Murray Kenworthy in Andreevka
25 Nov	Murray Kenworthy returns to Moscow
26 Nov	21 relief workers (Luke Kelly's figures): 14 English workers (Buzuluk) and 7 Americans (Sorochinskoye and Totskoye), including Beulah Hurley and Miriam West
Nov	American ODK obtains a house in Sorochinskoye – the library building at 26

Trotsky Ulitsa

2 Dec	Arthur Watts returns to Moscow from Buzuluk
End Dec	Ruth Fry goes to Russia, to Moscow and Buzuluk
21 Dec-4 Feb	Murray Kenworthy confined to his room in Sorochinskoye with typhus
27 Dec	Death of Mary Pattison in the Haass hospital in Moscow

1922

7 Jan	Ruth Fry arrives in Moscow
10 Jan	Homer and Edna Morris, Robert Dunn, Cornelia Young and Parry Paul leave Berlin for Russia
Jan	Olga Tolstaya receives a certificate of membership of the Society of Friends from Cotterell
Jan	American ODK group gives rations to 28,998 people, mostly children, in one month in Sorochinskoye. They

	cover 18 volosts, and 17 children's homes and hospitals
19 Feb	Death of Violet Tillard in Buzuluk
Feb	English ODK group feeds 70,000 children and 60,000 adults
Feb	American ODK group includes 4 American workers and 20 Russian workers
Feb	American ODK group gives food to 40,601 people at 165 food distribution points in 142 villages. They distribute 3849 items of clothing and bedlinen at children's homes and hospitals
March	American ODK group has 13 workers in Sorochinskoye and takes up two houses
25 March	English nurse Muriel Payne arrives in Moscow
8 April	33 English ODK workers plus 14 American ODK workers = 47 in total (Luke Kelly's figures)

April	Arthur Watts falls ill with typhus
13 May	Doctor McKenzie arrives in Moscow from Poland
14 May	Ernest Rowntree replaces Watts as head of the mission
23 May	Doctor McKenzie arrives in Buzuluk at 7 a.m. and starts work
26 May	Frank Watts writes to Karklin about the Quakers' plans
June	English ODK group feeds 264,184 people in 38 volosts in NW of district and in Buzuluk
June	American ODK group feeds 147,806 people in 18 volosts in SE of district. TOTAL: 411,990 PEOPLE
June	Arthur Watts goes from Buzuluk to Petrograd after illness
27 June	**Lander replaces Eiduk as Soviet Russia's plenipotentiary representative attached to all foreign relief organizations**

11 Aug	McKenzie accompanies sick Watts from Petrograda to Helsingfors (Helsinki)
16 Aug	Grundy, Bliss, Fawcett, Brown and Wetherald arrive in Sorochinskoye
20 Aug	McKenzie returns from Finland. Joint Anglo-American Quaker conference in Buzuluk
27 Aug	Muriel Payne leaves Buzuluk
1 Sept	American ODK group (Quakers) leaves ARA, joins English ODK group
7 Sept	**Soviet post-famine relief (Posledgol) replaces famine relief (Pomgol)**
15 Oct	Ethel Christie arrives in Buzuluk
25 Oct	New agreement between Quakers and Soviet Russia (Lander – Albright and Wildman) for period October 1922 to 30 July 1923
30 Oct	Ethel Christie opens malaria clinic in Buzuluk

1 Nov	Soviet contract with Quakers about tractors for peasants
6 Nov	Moscow Quaker office moves from 43 Bolshoi Nikitskii to 15 Borisoglebskii
1 Dec	Frank Watts returns to England via Moscow
15 Dec	Parry Paul returns to the USA via Moscow
Dec	Walter and Arthur Gamble go to Ukraine (via Moscow) to research situation there
21 Dec	Julia Branson works in Moscow office
21 Dec	Exchange rate: 1 dollar buys 44 million roubles

1923

2 Jan	McKenzie becomes interim head of English mission
Jan	Robert Dunn leaves mission in Russia after 6 months
Jan	Ilya Tolstoy starts work as a translator in the American ODK group in Sorochinskoye

2 Feb	Karklin asks American and English Quakers to supply 40,000 rations to Pugachev district in Saratov province
12 Feb	McKenzie leaves to England for holiday and fundraising
End Feb	Karl Borders leaves Sorochinskoye group
14 April	Walter Wildman requests quinine for Buzuluk
19 April	Ruth Fry arrives in Moscow office
21 April	Ruth Fry meets Lander, who values the Quakers
22 April	Wilbur Thomas, Julia Branson, Walter Wildman and Fry visit the Chertkovs
22 April	Edward Balls arrives from Buzuluk
24 April	Wilbur Thomas, Julia Branson, Walter Wildman, Balls and Fry go to Buzuluk
29 April	Fry returns to Moscow – floods block access to Buzuluk
2 May	Ruth Fry meets Litvinov

4 May	Ruth Fry meets Semashko at Commissariat for Health
5 May	Meeting with Kalinin does not take place
8 May	Wilbur Thomas meets Krasin
May	Ruth Fry leaves Russia
14 May	Wilbur Thomas arrives in Sorochinskoye.
23 May	McKenzie returns to Moscow and meets Elfie Graff at general meeting at Moscow Quaker Centre. They meet Semashko and present their plans
23 May	ODK (Quakers) in Sorochinskoye suggest opening an outpatient clinic for malaria in Gamaleyevka volost
28 May	American ODK group (Quakers) discuss plan for allocating new horses in Sorochinskoye (with Ilya Tolstoy)
4 June	Doctor McKenzie and Elfie Graff arrive in Buzuluk
9 June	Before leaving, Doctor

McKenzie writes
to Ruth Fry about
prospects for medical
work: idea of sending
Russian doctors from
Moscow to Buzuluk

Mid-June

Doctor McKenzie
goes to England.
Falls ill with typhus in
Helsingfors (Helsinki)

16 June

19 tractors are
imported by the
Society of Friends in
Samara province

June-July

Wilbur Thomas and J
Branson disagree about
Arthur Watts' future

27 June

Letter from K. Lander
to Julia Branson about
cooperation after the
closure of Posledgolod

1 July

Alfred Smaltz, head
of the horse section,
reports that American
and English Quakers
have already supplied
over 1700 horses in
Buzuluk district

4 July

Karklin writes to the
Quakers, concerned they're leaving

5 July

Wildman writes to
Wilbur Thomas that

	458 horses were allocated in half a day
7 July	Letter from Quakers to Karklin about plans for medical programme
Summer	William Wheeldon marries Zina Ivanova in Buzuluk
18 July	**ARA stops work in Soviet Russia**
22 July	Arthur Watts returns to Moscow from Australia
9 Aug	McKenzie in hospital in Newcastle with malaria and typhus. Ill for 17 days.
11 Nov	496 horses arrive in Sorochinskoye. Second horse expedition to Petropavlovsk

1924

1 Feb	**Britain officially recognises the state of the USSR**
March	Negotiations about Quaker agricultural school in Oomnovka
17 Nov	Edward Balls marries Natalia Timonova

Oct-Nov	Alice Hamilton (USA) spends time at Moscow Quaker office and goes to Sorochinskoye
Dec	Nancy Babb leaves to go to the USA for Christmas, is replaced by Mabelle Phillips
Dec	Ethel Christie goes to Nalchik with Sablin
21 Dec	Ruth Fry arrives in Moscow
14 Dec	Ruth Fry and Elfie Graff meet Semashko
27 Dec	Ruth Fry goes to Buzuluk with Balls, Wicksteed and Graff
28 Dec	Ruth Fry arrives in Buzuluk, meets Phillips

1925

2 Jan	Doctor Graff, Mabelle Phillips, Edward Balls and Ruth Fry go to Totskoye
7 Jan	Ruth Fry leaves Buzuluk
9 Jan	Ruth Fry meets Litvinov in Moscow

10 Jan	Ruth Fry and Edward Balls meet Semashko, then Kameneva
11 Jan	Ruth Fry and Alex Wicksteed meet Ganshina, lecturer at Moscow State University
15 Jan	Ruth Fry meets Rothstein
20 Jan	Ruth Fry meets Dr Lebedeva
21 Jan	Ruth Fry visits Kameneva, who lives in the Kremlin
23 Jan	Ruth Fry meets Rothstein again, then Lunacharsky
24 Jan	Ruth Fry leaves Russia
30 April	Edward Balls' last day as director
16 May	Commissariat for Health issued 'to whom it may concern' certificate confirming that ODK can help in area of health, signed by Semashko
25 May	Edward Balls hands over to Dorice White
June	Dorice White starts post as director of

Moscow Quaker office

July	Edward Balls leaves Russia

End of year	Two American women, E. Mitchell and Miss Wilson, arrive from the Kuzbass Autonomous Industrial Colony to join Nancy Babb's team in Totskoye

1926

Feb-March	Nancy Babb in Moscow to buy supplies (including seeds for vegetable garden) for the sanatorium. She plans to build hospital in Totskoye

1 April	Chamberlin moves into Borisoglebskii house

9 April	Semashko gives authorisation to Anna Haines

May	Margaret Barber ill in Totskoye sanatorium with husband and son

May-July	Frederick Tritton replaces Dorice White at Moscow office during her holiday,

	then leaves for England
13 July	Commissariat for Health gives Moscow Centre permission to open a nurse training school in Moscow
June or July	Anna Haines interrogated by the OGPU
End Aug	Dr Mitchell and Miss Wilson leave Totskoye for Moscow
3 Sept	Maria Mansurova and her daughter work in Totskoye
30 Sept	Official closure of work in Totskoye. Babb goes back and forth between Totskoye and Moscow
Oct	Anna Haines leaves Russia
20 Oct	Margaret Barber and her family leave Totskoye for Uralsk

1927

9 Jan	Alice Davis and Danilevskaya return to Moscow from Sorochinskoye
12 May	**British police search**

Anglo-Soviet trade body in London

27 May **Britain breaks off trade and diplomatic relations with the USSR**

Sept Nancy Babb leaves Totskoye for Moscow

7 Nov Hospital built by Nancy Babb opens in Totskoye

8 Nov Nancy Babb leaves Moscow for London

11 Nov Nancy Babb sets sail from Leningrad on board the 'Soviet' with Elsa Mehlman, arrives in London on 17 November

1928

Sept Edward Bernstein arrives at Quakers' celebration of Tolstoy

6 Oct Dorice White returns to Moscow from holiday. Doctors Graff and Phillips go to Buzuluk and Andreevka

16 Oct Quakers' plan to work at Tolstoy memorial

Hospital in Yasnaya
Polyana does not work
out – Commissar for
Health Semashko
personally issues
refusal

1 Nov   Danilevskaya and
Davis start work at hospital in Moscow

1929

3 April   Dorice White meets
Semashko about
hospital. Speranskii
now assigned to work
with the Quakers

8 April   Speranskii's draft
proposal sent to Britain and USA

23 May   Dorice White extends
rental contract on Moscow Centre

17-26 Aug   Ethel Christie visits
Buzuluk

1930

25 Jan   Commissar Semashko
leaves his post.
Vladimirskii is new
Commissar for Health;
the Commissariat's
relations with Quakers
die out

| April–May | Clarence Pickett and Gilbert MacMaster pay a short visit to Moscow and see clinic |
| Sept | Dorice White goes to Britain on holiday, refused Soviet visa to return |

1931

20 Jan	Dorice White returns to Borisoglebskii for 2 months
29 March	Dorice White leaves for England. Replaced by Floy George (wife of Paul George, foreign specialist in tractors invited to USSR by the state)
May	Alice Davis and Nadya Danilevskaya leave for USA
	Floy George works in Moscow office
10-19 June	Refusal to extend rental contract on Borisoglebskii
14 Sept	Floy George still in office, plans to close everything by the end of October

Bibliography

List of English-language literature used

Asquith, Michael, Famine. *Quaker Work in Russia, 1921-1923*. Oxford: Oxford University Press, 1943.

Barber, Margaret H., *A British Nurse in Bolshevik Russia*. London: A. C. Fifield, 1920.

Barnes, Gregory A., *A Centennial History of the American Friends Service Committee*. Philadelphia, PA: Friends Press, 2016.

Borders, Karl, *Village Life Under the Soviets*. New York: Vanguard Press, 1927.

Burtt, Joseph, *Relief work in Russia*. London: FWVRC, 1916.

Catchpool, E. St John, *Candles in the Darkness*. London: The Bannisdale Press, 1966.

Conquest, Robert, *The Harvest of Sorrow: Soviet Collectivization and the Terror-Famine*. Oxford: Oxford University Press.

David-Fox, Michael, *Showcasing the Great Experiment: Cultural Diplomacy and Western Visitors to the Soviet Union*, 1921-1941. Oxford: Oxford University Press, 2011.

Fox, Ralph, *People of the Steppes*. London: Constable, 1925.

Friends' War Victims' Relief Committee, *The Unchanging Russia*. London: FWVRC, approximately 1918.

Fry, A. Ruth, *A Quaker Adventure. The Story of Nine Years' Relief and Reconciliation.* London: Nisbet & Co., 1926.

Fry, A. Ruth, *Three Visits to Russia, 1922-25.* London: James Clark, 1942.

Gordievsky, Oleg, *Next Stop Execution: The Autobiography of Oleg Gordievsky.* Macmillan, 1995.

Greenwood, John Ormerod, *Quaker encounters. Volume 1. Friends and Relief.* York: William Sessions, 1975.

Haines, Anna. *Health Work in Soviet Russia.* New York: Vanguard Press, 1928.

Hamilton, Alice, *Exploring the Dangerous Trades - The Autobiography of Alice Hamilton, M.D.* Boston: Little, Brown, 1943.

Kelly, Luke, *British Humanitarian Activity in Russia, 1890-1923.* London: Palgrave Macmillan, 2017.

Kirkby, Joanna, *The Two Oceans. The Dark and the Light, York:* William Sessions, 2001.

Lonsdale, Kathleen, *Quakers Visit Russia.* London: East-West Relations Group of the Friends' Peace Committee, 1952.

Macfadyen, David, *The Genealogy of WHO and UNICEF and the Intersecting Careers of Melville Mackenzie (1889-1972) and Ludwik Rajchman (1881-1965).* Unpublished MD Thesis. University of Glasgow, 2014.

McFadden, David; Gorfinkel, Claire; Nikitin, Sergei (overview). *Constructive Spirit. Quakers in Revolutionary Russia.* Pasadena, CA: Intentional Productions, 2004.

Mickenberg, Julia, L., *American Girls in Red Russia: Chasing the Soviet Dream*. Chicago: University of Chicago Press, 2017.

Oelschlegel, Zachary, *Bolshevism and Christianity: The American Friends Service Committee in Russia (1919-1933)*. Unpublished thesis, 2012.

Patenaude, Bertrand M., *The Big Show in Bololand: The American Relief Expedition to Soviet Russia in the Famine of 1921*. Redwood City, CA: Stanford University Press, 2002.

Payne, Muriel A., *Plague, Pestilence and Famine*. London: Nisbet & Co., 1923.

Pipes, Richard, *Russia Under the Bolshevik Regime*. New York: Alfred A. Knopf, 1993.

Scott, Richenda C., *Quakers in Russia*. London: Michael Joseph, 1964.

Smith, Jessica, *Woman in Soviet Russia*. New York: Vanguard Press, 1928.

Strong, Anna Louise, *I Change Worlds: The Remaking of an American*. New York: Garden City Publishing Co., 1937.

Strong, Tracy B. & Helene Keyssar, *Right in her Soul. The Life of Anna Louise Strong*. New York: Random House. 1983

Tritton, Frederick J., *Carl Heath, apostle of peace*. London: Friends Home Service Committee, 1951.

Weisbord, Marvin R., *Some Form of Peace*. New York: Viking Adult, 1968.

White, L. Dorice, *Ten Years in Soviet Russia*. London: Russian Affairs Committee of the Friends Service Council, 1933.

Wicksteed, Alexander, *Life Under the Soviets*. London: Bodley Head, 1929.

Wicksteed, Alexander, *Ten Years in Soviet Moscow*. London: Bodley Head, 1933.

Wicksteed, Alexander. *My Russian Neighbors; Recollections of Ten Years in Soviet Moscow*. New York: Whittesley House, 1934.

American Friends Service Committee, Papers and Reports relating to the 1921-1925 Relief Unit. Philadelphia: AFSC.

Society of Friends Library archives. London: Friends House.

List of Russian-language literature used

Agrikov, P.A., Bashkirov A.S., Lychev I.A., 'Vojna s golodom v Povolzh'e v 1921-1922 gg.' Istoria SSSR,1. 1963.

Aktsynov, A.V.& Aktsynova, L.M., Po *sterne bosikom*. Cheboksary: Chuvashiia, 1992. p. 17.

Alexeev, V. V., *Zemlia Borskaia. Vekhi istorii*. Samara: Nauchno-tekhnicheskii tsentr, 2016.

Apalikov, V., 'Chernaia godina'. *Niva* (Volgograd). 1990. Issue 2.

Belokopytov, V.I. Likholet'e, *Iz istorii bor'by s golodom v Povolzh'e 1921–1923 gg*. Kazan, 1976, p.329.

Knurova, V.A., 'Deiatel'nost' amerikanskoi administratsii pomoshchi po likvidatsii goloda

1921–1922 gg. v Nizhnem Povolzh'e'. *Vestnik Astrakhanskogo gosudarstvennogo tekhnicheskogo universiteta*, 6:35. 2006.

Knurova, V.A., 'Golod 1921–22 gg. v Nizhnem Povolzh'e glazami ochevidtsev'. *Gumanitarii. Sbornik nauchnykh trudov.* Moscow: Moscow State Pedagogical University (MPGU), 2006. Issue VIII.

Kristkaln, Andris Margerovich. Golod 1921 g. v *Povolzh'e: opyt sovremennogo izucheniia problemy.* Dissertation. Moscow: Moscow State University. 1997.

Kuleshov, S., 'Lukullov pir'. Rodina. 1991. Issues 9-10.

Kurenyshev, A.A., *Krest'ianskie komitety obshchestvennoi vzaimopomoshchi v sisteme sotsial'no-ekonomicheskikh i politicheskikh otnoshenii NEPa*, 1921–1927 gg. (na materialakh Povolzh'ia). Doctoral thesis. Moscow, 1996.

L'vunin, Iu.A., 'Organizatsiia «Mezhdunarodnaia rabochaia pomoshch'» v Sovetskoi Tatarii (1921–1925 gg.)'. Vestnik Moskovskogo universiteta. Series 8. 1975. Issue 4. pp. 35–47.

Latypov, R.A., 'Amerikanskaia pomoshch' Sovetskoi Rossii v period goloda1921-1923 godov'. *Vestnik Instituta Kennana v Rossii.* 2005. Issue 8. pp. 35–42.

Latyshev, A.G., Rassekrechennyi Lenin. *Sobranie* 1-e. Moscow: Mart, 1996.

Lenin, V.I., *Polnoe sobranie sochinenii* [Collected works], vol. 44, pp. 75, 312–313.

Long, D., 'Povolzhskie nemtsy i golod v nachale 20-kh godov'. *Istoriia Rossii*: dialog *rossiiskikh i amerikanskikh istorikov.* Saratov, 1994.

Makarenko, A.A., *Moguchaia sila proletarskoi solidarnosti (podderzhka zarubezhnym proletariatom Sovetskoi strany* v 1921–1925 gg.). Moscow, 1976.

Pavliuchenkov, S.A., *Voennyi kommunizm v Rossii: vlast'* i massy. Moscow: Norma, 1997, p.329.

Poliakov, B.A., Golod v Povolzh'e, 1919–1925 gg.: *proiskhozhdenie, osobennosti, posledstviia.* Moscow: Prosveshchenie, 2007. p. 735.

Poliakov, Iu.A., 1921-i: *pobeda nad golodom.* Moscow, 1975.

Poliakov, V.A., 'Rossiiskaia obshchestvennost' i inostrannaia pomoshch' golodaiushchim v 1921 g.'. Voprosy istorii. 2009. Issue 12. pp. 3–23.

Pomogalova, O.I., 'Masshtaby i prichiny goloda 1921 goda v Povolzh'e v zapadnoi istoriografii'. *Nauchnyi zhurnal,* vol. 11, issue 2 (part 1), 2011.

Red'kina O.Iu, 'Religioznye organizatsii i golod v Tsaritsynskoi gubernii 1921–1922 gg. (po materialam mestnoi periodicheskoi pechati)'. Mir *Pravoslaviia.* Issue.3. 2000.

Rubinshtein, N., 'Sovetskaia Rossiia i kapitalisticheskie gosudarstva v gody perekhoda ot voiny k miru (1921–1922 gg.)'. *Istoricheskie zapiski.* 1947. Issue 22. pp. 140, 143.

Sinel'nikov, A. T., *Eto moi gorod.* Sorochinsk, 1996.

Sinel'nikov, S.P., 'ARA i golod 1922 goda v Tsaritsynskoi gubernii'. Voprosy kraevedeniia. Issue 6. Materialy kraevedcheskikh chtenii, posviashchennykh 75-letiiu oblastnogo obshchestva kraevedov. Volgograd, 2012.

Tsikhelashvili, N.Sh., Engerman D., 'Amerikanskaia

pomoshch' Rossii v 1921–1923 gg.: konflikty i sotrudnichestvo'. *Amerikanskii ezhegodnik*. 1995. Moscow, 1996.

Tskhelashvili, N.Sh., *Amerikanskaia pomoshch' narodam Rossii v nachale* 1920-kh gg. XX veka. Doctoral thesis. Moscow: Russian State University for the Humanities (RGGU), 2008.

Usmanov, N.V., 'K voprosu ob amerikanskoi pomoshchi golodaiushchim Sovetskoi Rossii v 1921–1923 gg'. *Diskussionnye voprosy rossiiskoi istorii*. Moscow: Arzamas, 2000.

Vinogradov, S.V., *Vozrozhdenie mnogoukladnoi ekonomiki Rossiiskoi Federatsii v gody* NEPa. 1921–1927 gg. (*na materialakh Povolzh'ia*). Higher doctoral thesis. Astrakhan: MPGU, 1999.

Joint authorship

'Uzhasy Goloda v Samarskoi gubernii'. (New Year issue of *Izvestii Samarskogo Gubsoiuza*). Samara, 1922.

Sovetsko-Amerikanskie otnosheniia. Gody nepriznaniia 1927–1933. Moscow: Mezhdunarodnyi fond 'Demokratiia', 2002.

Work published in Russian by a non-Russian author

Wehner, Markus, 'Golod 1921-1922 gg. v Samarskoĭ gubernii i reatskiia sovetskogo pravitel'stva' (transl. A. Petrova). Cahiers du Monde Russe, Année 1997. 38-1-2, pp. 223-241.

Index